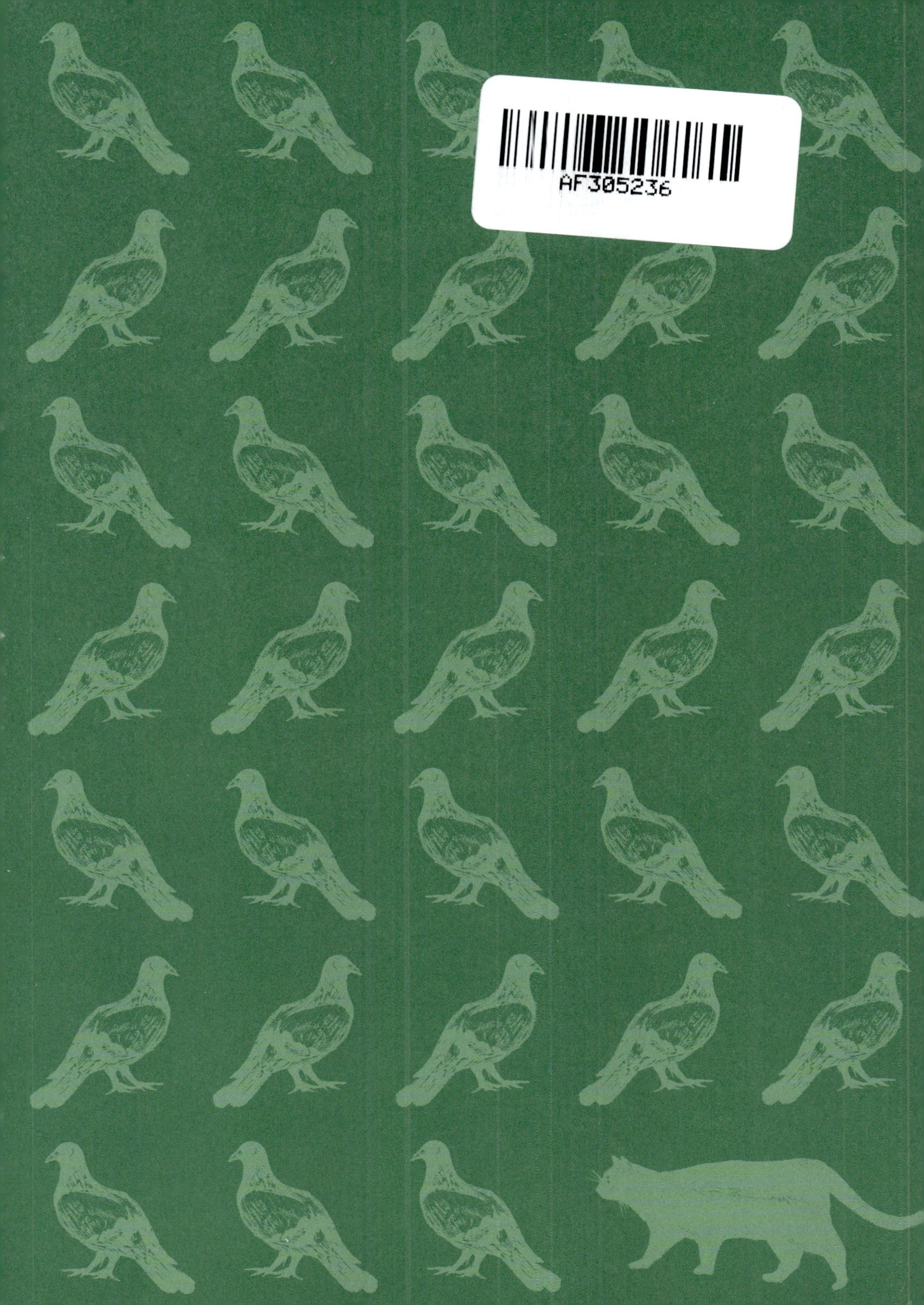
AF305236

Locals

Lydia Wood is a pencil artist who is currently
on a mission to draw every single pub in London.
She shares her drawing process and pub adventures
across her social media channels and the project has
been featured in a number of news outlets including
the BBC, *The Times* and the *New York Times*.

The pub project began in 2021 and, with there
being over 3,500 pubs in London, it could take
a minimum of 10 years to finish.

Lydia was born in Ealing, West London, and
studied Fine Art at Goldsmiths University.
She then went on to teach children art across
schools in South London before focusing on her
own practice. She now lives in South East London.

@lydiawooddrawings
lydiawooddrawings.com/

LOCALS

AN ILLUSTRATED ODE TO LONDON'S PUBS

LYDIA WOOD

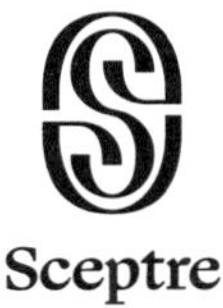

Sceptre

First published in Great Britain in 2026 by Sceptre
An imprint of Hodder & Stoughton Limited
An Hachette UK company

The authorised representative in the EEA is Hachette Ireland, 8 Castlecourt
Centre, Dublin 15, D15 XTP3, Ireland (email: info@hbgi.ie)

1

A CIP catalogue record for this title is available from the British Library

Hardback ISBN 9781399756334
ebook ISBN 9781399756341

Typeset in Sabon and Sofia Pro by Jim Smith Design Ltd

Printed and bound in Great Britain by Clays Ltd, Elcograf S.p.A.

Hodder & Stoughton policy is to use papers that are natural, renewable
and recyclable products and made from wood grown in sustainable forests.
The logging and manufacturing processes are expected to conform to the
environmental regulations of the country of origin.

Hodder & Stoughton Limited
Carmelite House
50 Victoria Embankment
London EC4Y 0DZ

CONTENTS

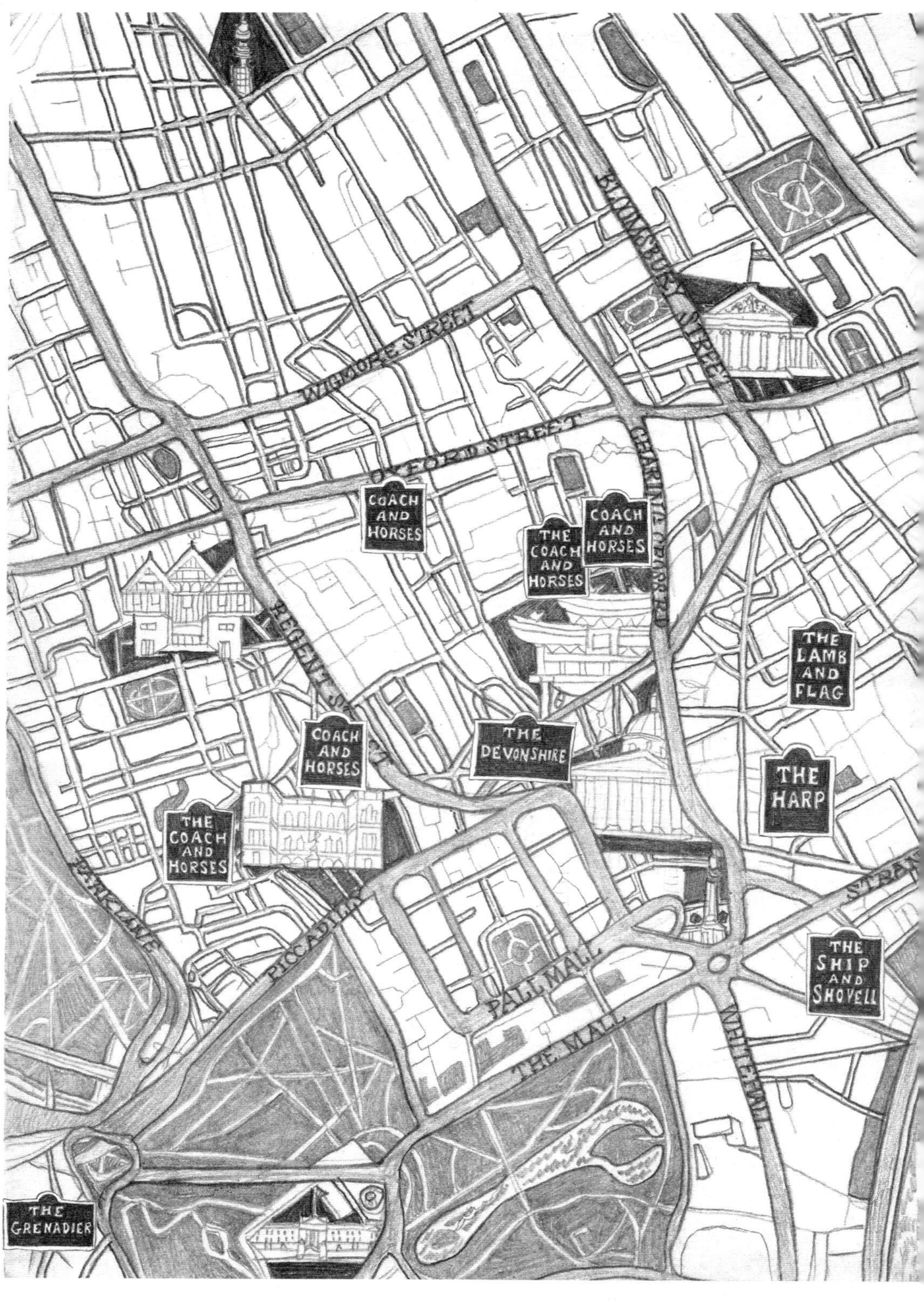

WIGMORE STREET
OXFORD STREET
CHARING CROSS RD
SHAFTESBURY AVENUE
REGENT STREET
PARK LANE
PICCADILLY
PALL MALL
THE MALL
WHITEHALL
STRAND
COACH AND HORSES
THE COACH AND HORSES
COACH AND HORSES
THE LAMB AND FLAG
COACH AND HORSES
THE DEVONSHIRE
THE HARP
THE COACH AND HORSES
THE SHIP AND SHOVELL
THE GRENADIER

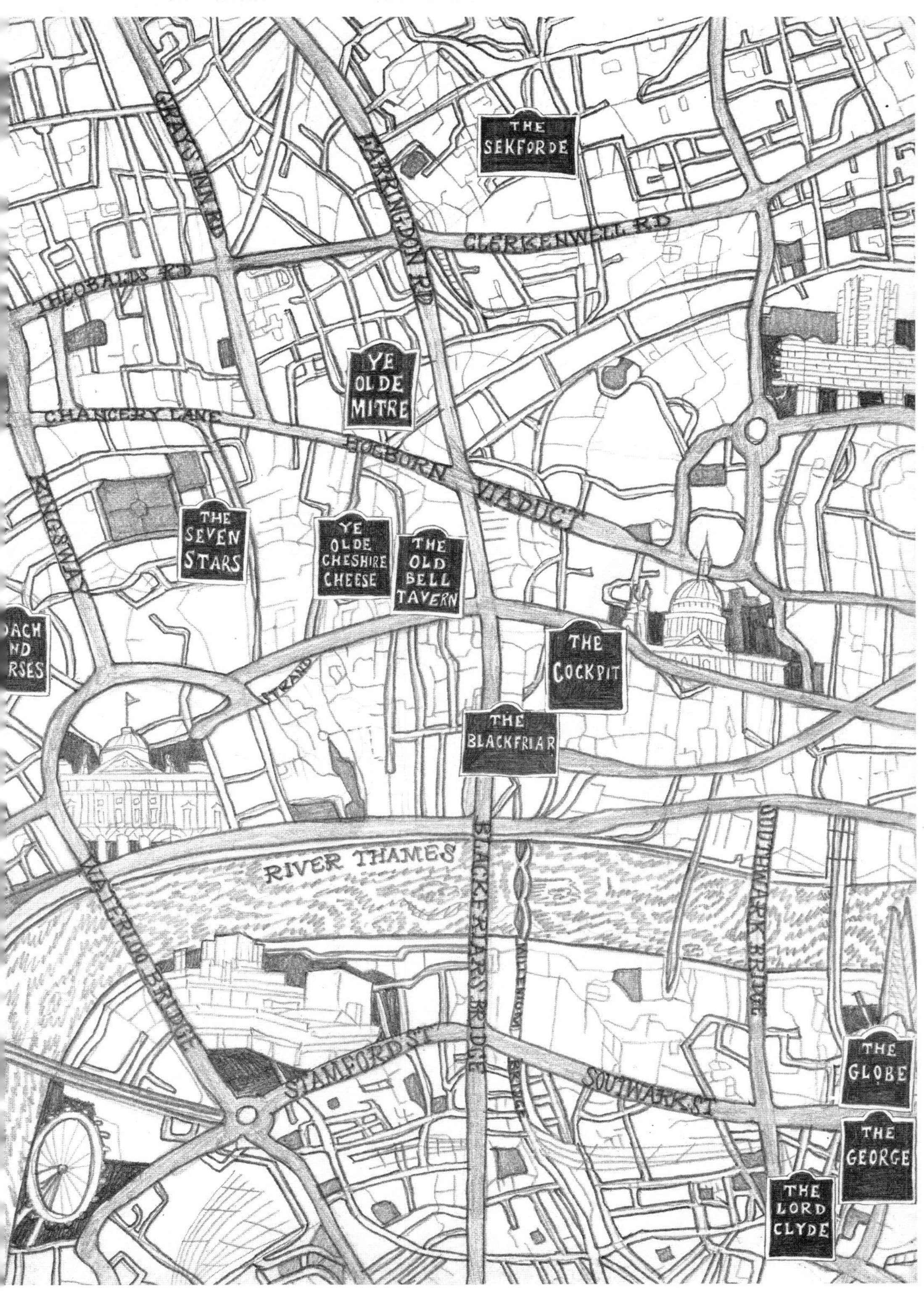

THE SEKFORDE
CLERKENWELL RD
FARRINGDON RD
CHARTERHOUSE
THEOBALDS RD
YE OLDE MITRE
CHANCERY LANE
HOLBORN VIADUCT
KINGSWAY
THE SEVEN STARS
YE OLDE CHESHIRE CHEESE
THE OLD BELL TAVERN
STRAND
COACH AND HORSES
THE COCKPIT
THE BLACKFRIAR
RIVER THAMES
WATERLOO BRIDGE
BLACKFRIARS BRIDGE
MILLENNIUM BRIDGE
SOUTHWARK BRIDGE
STAMFORD ST
SOUTHWARK ST
THE GLOBE
THE GEORGE
THE LORD CLYDE

INTRODUCTION

I remember the big black dog with its shaggy coat and long nose, standing taller than my five-year-old sister. Each time you saw the mutt outside the pub, you knew the landlord was close behind. Like twins, their scruffy hair matched and so did their unsettling silence.

I never once heard him speak, the landlord, as he loomed over the bar in the low-lit local, pouring drinks and taking cash in slow, careful movements. We would always enter via the side door, walking towards the same old men sitting on the same high stools as they smoked their pipes. My mum closed her eyes briefly and inhaled the fumes as she guided my sister and me down the length of the bar. She'd often boast about how she'd never once touched a cigarette, but she smiled in this moment, savouring her favourite scent of pipe tobacco. The dark wooden bar made up most of the room. At one end was a fireplace and a few tables – a crackling hot fire warmed frozen walkers and farmers, who'd been out in the fields all day. Their rosy cheeks and pints of amber ale glistened in the flickering glow. The low black beams and the cold stone floor led you to the other end of the room. This is where the hardened regulars took their place at the bar. I would see them offer a silent nod to their neighbour as a pint was poured and handed to them before their backsides reached their usual seats. We arrived at a table of familiar faces – parents of our classmates, neighbours from the village and even teachers from our school. A bottle of J2O was handed to my sister and me, as my parents joined their friends and we joined ours.

The back room of the pub housed only a pool table and a small sweet machine attached to the wall. With barely any space to squeeze round the chunky centrepiece, it made it difficult to play a proper game, which meant the room was mainly occupied by children. We learnt the rules from the odd parent who swung their head round the door to check on us, and we taught ourselves how to pot the balls effectively enough. The youngest children could barely see over the edge of the table, but we helped them hold the cue and watched as they inevitably scuffed the table's green carpet and hit the lights above our heads. My younger sister was more enamoured with the sweets than the tense games of pool, so she coaxed our parents into handing over twenty pence to release the goods. Kids gathered round, each taking it in turns to slot in their hard-earned pocket money and twist the silver handle until the little door rumbled and the sweets were ready.

Believe it or not, this book about London pubs begins in Yorkshire. I was eleven years old when we moved from our home in London up to North Yorkshire to be closer to my mum's family. My parents exchanged their fast-paced city life for a slowed-down countryside existence. My sister and I swapped our school of four hundred students in Ealing for a village school of only twenty-four. My time spent racing round the block and using the pavement as our playground was suddenly traded in for climbing hay bales and cycling down deserted country lanes. We soon learnt that the local pub, The Black Horse Inn, was the central hub of the village and the place to go to introduce ourselves to this tight-knit community. From being crowned winner of the junior pool championship aged twelve to my first waitressing job at sixteen (at which I was awful), from stealthily purchasing cigarettes from the pub's vending machine with a friend – only to meet our comeuppance on discovering they were boxes of rolling tobacco with no filters (we barely smoked, let alone knew how to roll) – to triumphantly buying my first (legal) pint with my ID at the ready, I saw many iterations of The Black Horse Inn and it, in turn, saw me grow up.

Years later, I returned to London for art school and adopted a new local in an attempt to re-immerse myself in the city I was born in. The Marquis of Granby in New Cross, still run by the same people today, welcomed me and my fellow students to their pub and we quickly became regulars alongside the existing older clientele. I recall how the pub bravely (and involuntarily) hosted hundreds of excitable art students at the degree show opening nights every year – crowds of Goldsmiths students would fill the pub and spill out on to the pavement around it. It was a very different picture to the village life I had become accustomed to but the sense of community here felt the same. The informality and familiarity of the pub suited me, I remember the way we met other students around the pool table, knocking into poor blokes on their way to the loos, as they dodged our pool cues waving around the limited space. On weekends we danced with punters who had travelled from all over London and Essex to The Marquis, before they continued into the nightclub across the road. Of course we went to other pubs in the city, but this was our haven, our stomping ground and our local. The Marquis was the beating heart of my student experience and it was clear to see this warm welcome from the pub helped many students settle into their new home. Here I found my like-minded community that cemented me to London and since then my adoration has only grown for what pubs are, what makes London pubs unique and what they have offered me throughout my time here. The Black Horse Inn is where I first learnt what it meant to be a local, and the pubs of London have further solidified that feeling.

For a long time, a pub project had existed as an improbable concept in my mind. The 2020 lockdowns had lifted, and I was in the midst of rebuilding my business teaching art classes to young children after school across South East London. At the same time I had taken on some commission work in an attempt to replace lost income.

I picked up the pencil to start sketching again, a skill I had almost entirely neglected since school, to draw clients' homes, wedding venues and local pubs. Through these commissions, a portfolio of pub artworks started to grow, as did the seed of an idea – to draw every single pub in London.

While I sketched alone in my bedroom, working mainly from photographs, I dreamt about the possibilities of this undertaking, about using my art as a lens to discover and illustrate all kinds of pubs, from every corner of London, my only limits the geography of the city. I pondered if I would even be able to complete such a project in my lifetime. I already had a clear fondness for pub culture – from those earliest memories at my childhood local, to meeting my friends at university and my weekly ritual as an adult. I looked at pubs how most of my friends or family would; going to the pub wasn't a passion or a special interest at this time, it was just a part of my life.

I questioned whether combining two integral parts of myself through such an undertaking would alter how I enjoy them. Would the artist in me find it hard to commit to this singular idea, become bored, feel limited and change my mind down the line? Would I still cherish my time at the pub in the same way and is it possible that visiting them would start to feel like work? Or perhaps this project could help me look more closely, show me a different side to pubs and my practice. Maybe it would turn me into an explorer and expand my knowledge of the city I live in. And what if this project could lure me into falling deeper in love with my art and the pubs I would get to discover through it? I knew there was only one way to find out.

A year later, after many months of dreaming, I finally decided that I really was going to draw every pub in London.

Sharing photos of my pub drawings with friends, family and strangers online prompted a wave of enthusiasm for the project.

In fact, barely anyone batted an eyelid that I was about to devote many years of my life to this enormous endeavour – most people just really wanted me to draw their local. The stories and personal anecdotes came flooding in; family friends I hadn't heard from in years, old school acquaintances and people from all over the world chimed in suggesting London pubs for me to draw. This type of storytelling struck me in the same way a conversation with a local on the next table at a pub might. People felt comfortable with the subject and were compelled to share their personal connections and memories with me. I was humbled by their trust and determined to see through this project, which I had somewhat haphazardly dived into.

In a bid to escape my bedroom and grasp what this project was going to look like, I grabbed my pencil and went to the pub. Starting with my own familiar locals across South East London, I would eventually travel to far-flung corners of the city, guided by people's suggestions. As I stood on street corners, trying my best not to be in the way, I would huddle close to my easel and keep myself to myself. I soon found out my usual solitary way of sketching was going to look very different going forward. Londoners – the brisk, fast-paced, polite people we generally are – seemed to defrost around my easel. People paused their journey to look at my paper and up at the pub, perhaps noticing the building or inspecting it in detail for the very first time. Passing comments were made and in-depth conversations were started on the subject of their local, and others, even if they didn't go to the pub, were invited into the conversation by the art, too. I began to grow in confidence as I travelled to draw unknown pubs in unfamiliar neighbourhoods, and I realised that not knowing everything about the place beforehand was an enthralling way to start. The legends and historical details were readily shared with me by the ones who knew it best, the locals. Further knowledge was imparted by those who worked in the pubs, as I sipped my pint with my finished artwork in hand – now the customary end to all of my sketching days.

I learnt that my role in this project was not only artist and punter, but observer too. The solitary act of sketching had turned social, but I found quiet moments in between chats to pay attention to my surroundings, studying the building and all its glorious details, mapping on my paper what I saw before me. Watching people around the pub, setting up A-boards, putting out ashtrays and opening the doors, or noticing the first customers of the day, sometimes managing to capture them for my sketch and other times imagining their story and why they were there. I couldn't help but see the streets around me in new ways too. The everyday transformed into romanticised moments, unmissable to my wandering eye. The tree branches hanging over the road, their shapes carved out by the continuous flow of buses hurtling down their usual routes, or the mother pushing her pram, pausing to let her baby inspect a crowd of pigeons besiege a piece of bread. The days I draw in London are a marathon for the senses; they have changed how I perceive the city, and time seems to stand still around me at the very first stroke of my pencil.

As per my fond memories at The Black Horse Inn, I soon found this village pub mentality also existed across the vast London boroughs. Communities of neighbours using their local pub as a second home, greeting each other over a game of pool. The landlords and landladies treating their regulars like family. I discovered that for some regulars, the simple solace of the pub offers them that crucial time for socialising, for others, it's been there since birth and they have grown up around those four walls, and for some of those I spoke to, it's a way to meet people in their new neighbourhood.

From the football pubs, where fierce home fans chant at the TV screen and proudly sport their team's colours, to the old carpeted boozers buried down a backstreet which readily welcome you if you're lucky enough to find them, this book is a record of my drawing days around London. I invite you to join me as I wander around the city, finding myself in some of the most magical boozers imaginable. Follow me down winding alleyways to hidden taverns, duck under doorways to the bar, pet the pub cat who sleeps in the corner and turn the pages of my sketchbook as I arrive outside a new pub. I exercise my particular perspective as both artist and pub lover, illustrating the wide variety of pubs in the city and sharing the stories I've gathered along the way. These written observations accompanied by my hand-drawn artworks share a glimpse into this all-encompassing project, and I hope the stories and artworks compel you to go visit and explore the charm of these pubs for yourself.

A NOTE ON MATERIALS

Pencil is a particularly good match for architecture,
a tool to achieve straight lines with ease that gives you
a second chance if you don't quite nail it the first time.
I enjoy using a fine point that can pick up tiny details
like the crumbly indentations of a brick or the different
textures of plants in hanging baskets. Pencil offers
immediacy, meaning that I can capture the fleeting
moments throughout my day: a discarded pint glass,
the way the shadow falls behind a sign or a dog peering
through a window. The small but mighty pencil is
also accessible – a cheap, ordinary tool. It is, perhaps,
the first thing most of us drew with as children,
not particularly messy or intimidating, the perfect,
lightweight companion for drawing on the go.
I have a pencil on me at all times.

At first, I didn't own the tools to provide comfort and ease on my
drawing days outside. I simply packed a sketchbook and a pencil and
off I went, finding any available step, kerb or bench to perch on while
I bent over my lap to illustrate. I soon realised a proper set-up was
required for both my posture and the quality of my work. So I did
my research and found a lightweight set of drawing tools that soon
became my dependable companions on my trips across London.

Inside my waterproof backpack I pack a sharpener (to keep
the pencil points thin and sharp at all times) and pencil extenders
(small wooden sticks with metal fasteners that twist on to my tiny

one-inch pencils). These extenders elongate the pencil and literally extend its life, allowing me to use it right up to the very end. I'm armed with a rubber (to correct mistakes), which I more frequently use to add light to my drawings. I press the soft curve into the dark surface of freshly shaded graphite, removing layers gradually until a glow appears around a wall light or a dark brick is suddenly washed out by the sun.

I pull apart my travel stool, each piece of plastic clicking into place like a silent accordion. Its bright red parts form a surprisingly sturdy chair for me to perch on to eat a sandwich or take the weight off my feet. I slide a neat sheet of wood, smooth to the touch and covered in grey smudges, on to my tripod. I clip it into place before taking out a roll of tape buried at the bottom of my bag. I have designed a custom masking tape for myself, with miniature versions of my pub drawings, standing in a row, printed along the tape – as if they line their own imaginary (and extraordinary) pub high street. I unpeel the small, neat roll of masking tape and my little hand-drawn pubs disappear as I fold them in on themselves to stick the paper to my board. When I remove the small blobs of double-sided tape off the back of my complete artwork at the end of a long day, the wind has been known to try to steal my paper away in its gusts, so I've found this quick release application, allowing me to stow the sketch in my bag promptly, is my best option.

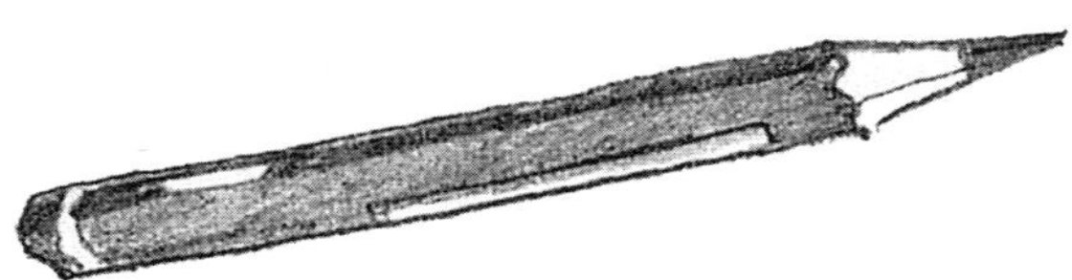

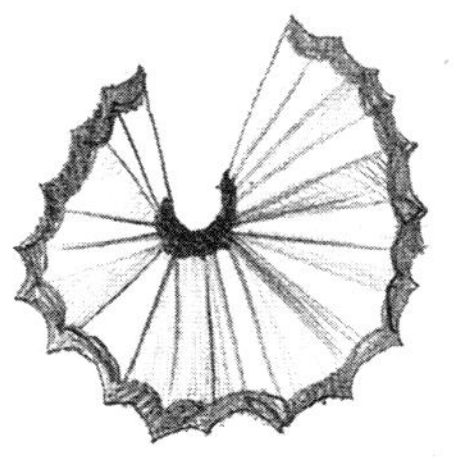

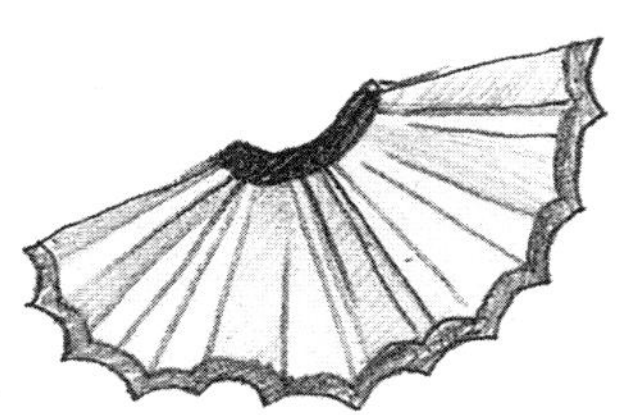

Nowadays, loose sheets of cartridge paper replace my old sketchbook. I carry them in a tatty, torn sleeve, relying on the rigidness of my backpack to keep them straight during my travels. The piece of paper I pull out is crisp and clean. The creamy surface is lightly textured, barely visible to the eye, but I feel its subtle bumps and dips when I brush it flat against the drawing board with the back of my hand. The bright and blank space is my leaping-off point, and from this moment the surface of the paper will continue to transform with each mark of my pencil.

Then there is my right hand. I have a lump on the inside of my index finger because of the way my pencil leans on it and moves against it during every sketch. If you look closely, you can see the curves carved into the paper where my hand has applied pressure to get the very darkest shades of the building.

I don't use colour in my drawings – and some pubs do have brilliant colour – as I've always had a fondness for pencil, it has been the material I've felt most comfortable with and is my favourite tool for sketching architecture. Over the last few years of intense drawing I have learnt not to underestimate graphite and the rich details it can show off. It has become my personal style, the material I naturally grab to illustrate ideas, outlines and notes, and I learn more about the humble pencil every time I draw with it.

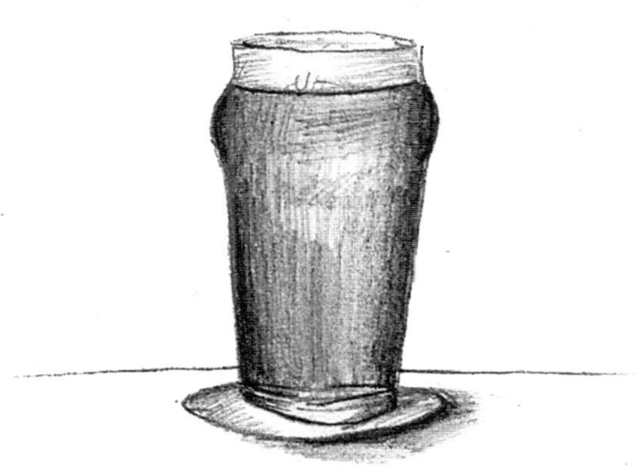

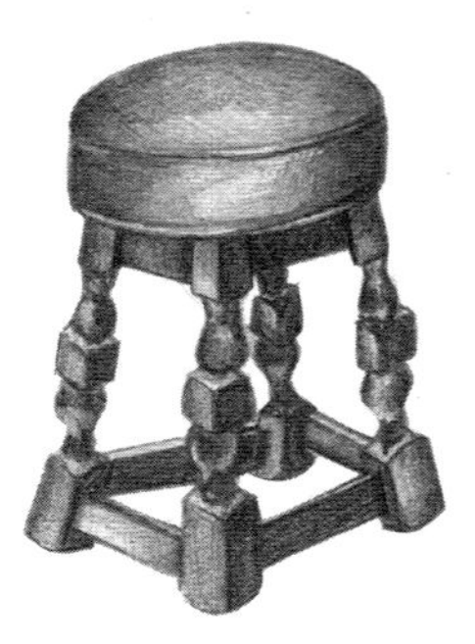

LOCAL

This project started with the best pub
in the world – my local.

It felt important for me to begin this journey close to
home, drawing the places I knew best and sharing those very
first sketches with my neighbours in South East London.
So it feels natural to start the book here, too.

From my art school local in New Cross to the one at the
end of my road in my twenties, this chapter is dedicated
to those places that fostered my affection for pubs, those
early days of the project and my own connection to these
special South East London locals where it all began.

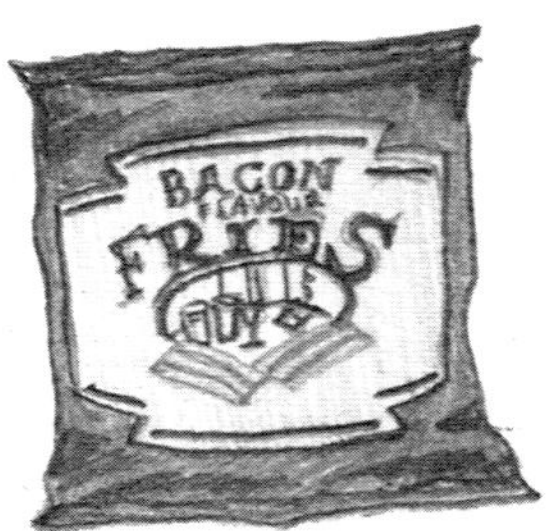

Blythe Hill Tavern, Catford

The Blythe Hill Tavern sits on the busy South Circular, just a couple of minutes from my house. It's exterior boasts a black and cream paint job on the bottom, brickwork on the top. A corner pub that sweeps off the main road up to Blythe Hill Lane, it's adorned with a scattering of colourful Guinness signage, and the recognisable toucan, proudly puffing out its chest, is painted on the curve of the building.

At night, fairy lights give a clue to the warmth inside, and a hum of voices can be heard rising from the beer garden. Out front on Thursdays and Fridays, I often find the pizza guys 'Van Dough' churning out charred sourdough dinners, keeping the drinkers full. Kids play gleefully after school, some happily gaming on their parents' phones or chatting to their siblings, others are seen racing between tables in the beer garden. Unbeknownst to them, they are running on the ruins of what was once an outdoor climbing frame. In the spring, resident fox cubs join the fun by skipping along the PVC roofs above our heads and at night the string lights flash to alert the outside drinkers when it's last orders.

When I head into the pub, always via the side entrance, I see red. Red carpet, red seats and a burning fire in the colder months. The pub is divided into three rooms, the first hosting the long side of the bar where I chat to the manager Terry, a principal character here for nearly three decades, and order my white wine spritzer or half a Guinness and a packet of bacon fries. Two more long-standing barmen make regular appearances. Mark supports his team from behind the bar, sometimes sporting a Liverpool tie, as Eamon carefully ferries settled pints of Guinness around the room. Often, the regulars sit at the far end by the front of the pub, sharing a table at the foot of the bar and ordering drinks from their seats, as they

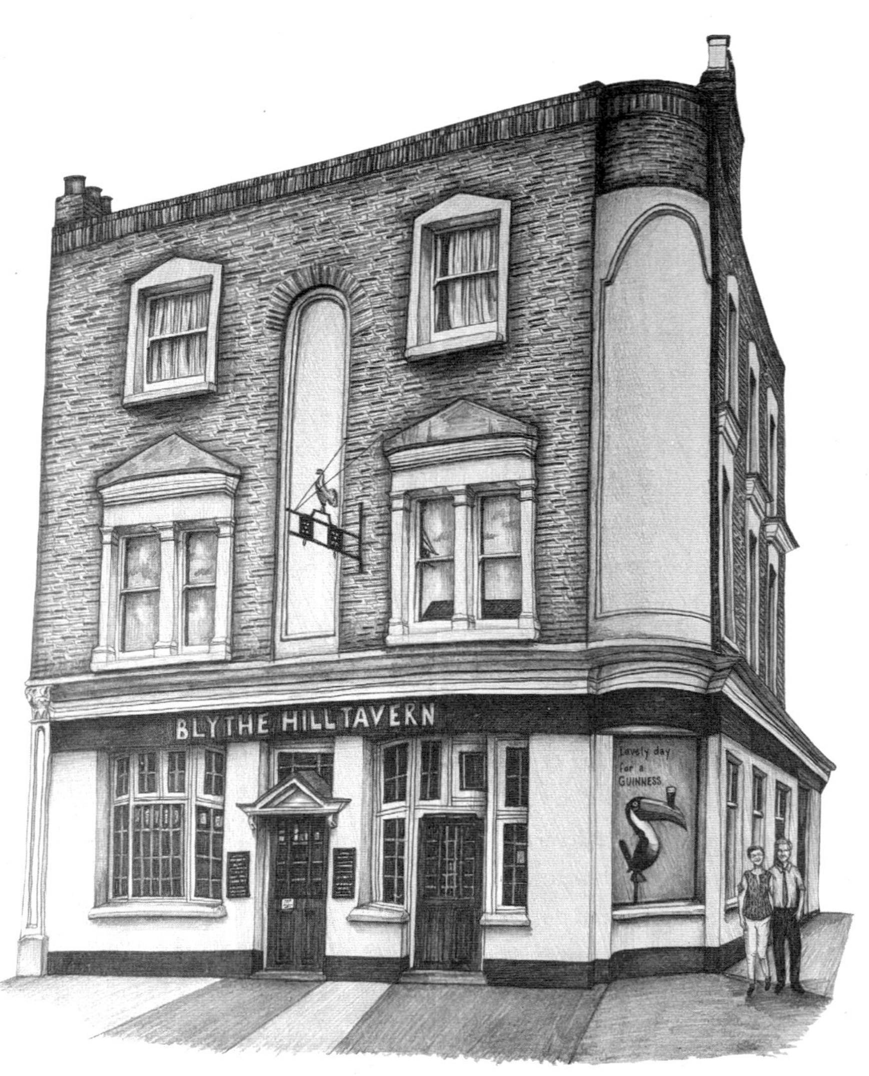
BLYTHE HILL TAVERN
Lovely day for a GUINNESS

have earned the right to do. The TV is nearly always showing some sort of sport but it's not blaring – it serves more as a moving backdrop when I wish to rest my eyes on it.

I walk through the second room to reach the large beer garden at the back. This room often plays host to local sports teams finishing their friendly with a round of drinks. It's where I have to squeeze past people if a big game is on and where I hear the familiar sounds of the Irish trad band that play here once a week. In this room, the wood-panelled walls are mosaicked with racehorse artworks and large gilded mirrors. If I'm lucky I'll see Con, who was the landlord of the Blythe for thirty-seven years, darting about, always on the move, chatting to regulars as friends and newbies as regulars.

I cross the threshold between the two bars and find the smallest room of the tavern. There is another modest TV up in the corner, a couple of tables with scattered stools around them and a small bar which isn't always manned but where I know I'll be served if I hang around long enough.

The Blythe is the place I first come to discuss my pub drawing venture with my partner, Jack, intensely working out the possibilities of the project over a pint. It's where I come to celebrate my exhibition opening with a big group of friends in the freezing beer garden. It's where we wet the head of my baby niece, where Jack and I bring our mortgage statement to be witnessed by Con, where my friend Margo and I come to have a drink instead of going to a boxing class, where we come to decompress almost every weekend after days spent renovating our new flat. It's where I am hit by the smell of must, booze and warmth when I walk past on my way to the post office at lunchtime. It's where I feel a pang of jealousy when I hear the rumbles in the beer garden as I walk up Blythe Hill Lane on my way to somewhere else. It's where I've spent too much money, and it's the first pub I drew as part of this project. It's my local.

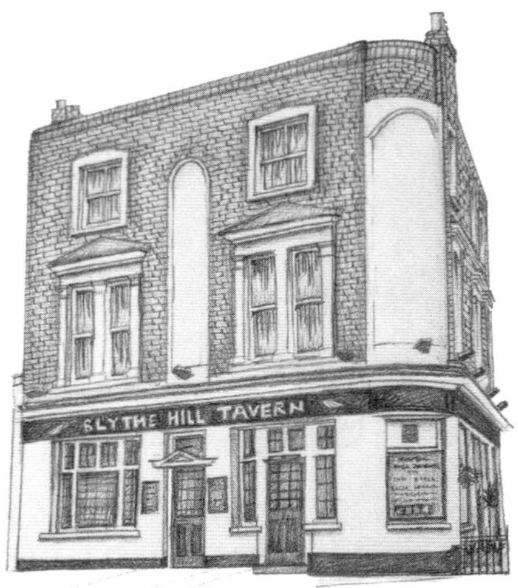

I have drawn the Blythe Hill Tavern at least five times. The first time I draw it, it isn't even my local, it's my sister's.

The second time I draw it, it's a tentative step towards a crazy idea I have about drawing every pub in London.

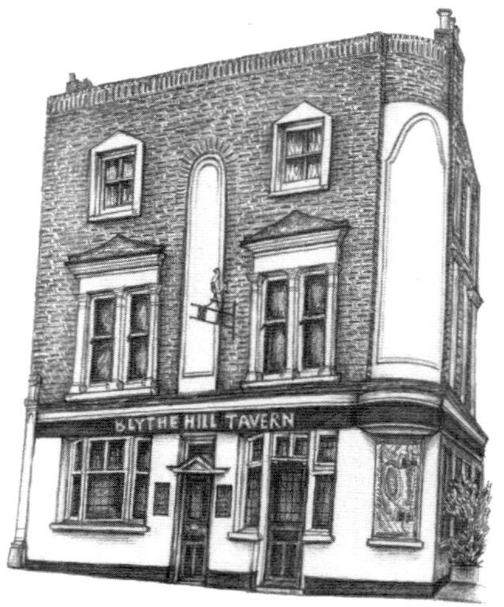

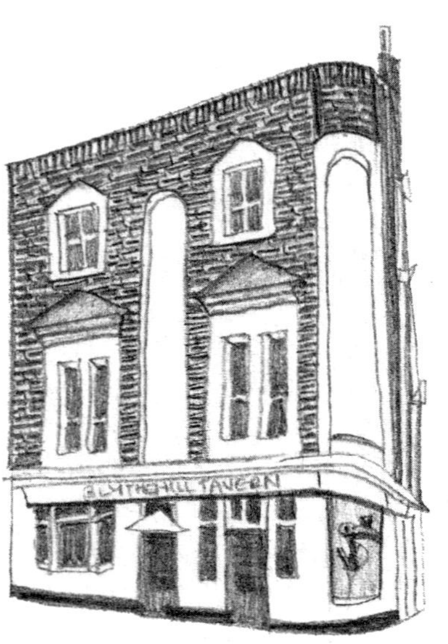

The third time is for a gift.

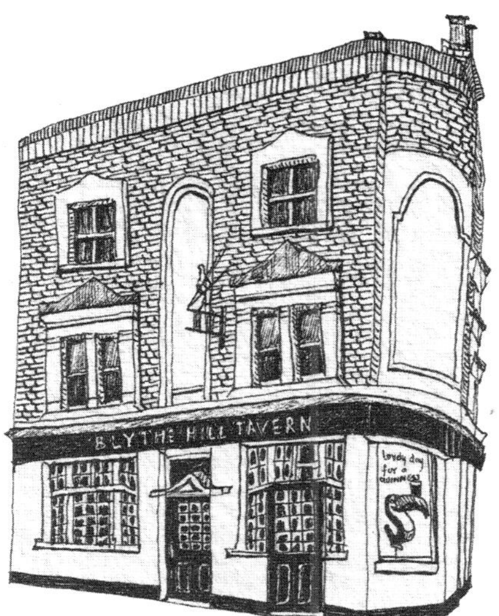

The fourth time, in pen, is for an exhibition.

And the fifth is for Con, the recent landlord. I draw him in front of the pub along with his wife Claire – a special retirement gift from his family.

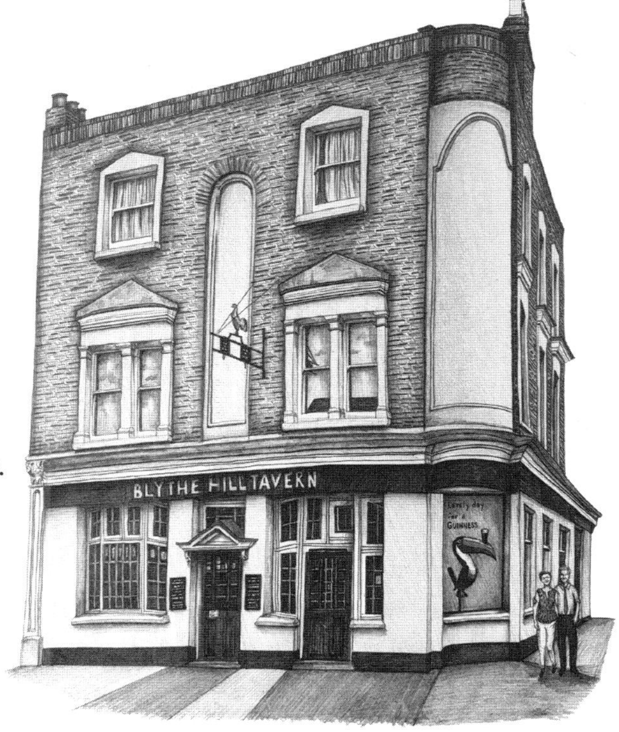

The White Horse, Peckham

As soon as dusk settles on a wintry Friday afternoon, my flatmate Clem and I walk down our dimly lit street to another small alleyway and along the main road until we arrive outside our local at the time – The White Horse. It's believed a pub has existed here since the 1780s. The black-and-white building which sits here today was built around 1936, tucked away from the main road, obscured by trees and signposted by a red telephone box. Its Tudor-style exterior is striped with timber, and a beer garden welcomes us on either side of the pathway at the entrance.

We enter through the pitched-roof doorway and to our right, behind a wood and glass panelled screen, is the pool table, where we put coins down to secure our spot in the queue. I've spent hours around this table, taught friends how to play pool here, brushed up on my own skills (which have somewhat declined since my heyday – at twelve years old), and often come up against other regulars. Right next to the pool table is the dartboard, riskily hanging above our heads, where I once threw a game-winning shot that filled the pub with boisterous celebrations. To the back of the room is more seating space, often cleared on a Friday night to make room for the DJ. This is where we dance.

We walk with purpose, straight to the bar, order our pints of the cheapest-available lager and head back out to the picnic tables to sit in darkness. Loud chatter fills the enclosed beer garden which juts out onto the pavement, and our voices join the excitable chorus. Sitting on opposite sides of the table, facing each other for the evening, we catch up on our week, as friends join us one by one, all of us filled with anticipation for the weekend ahead. Whatever the weather, the same weekly ritual at The White Horse throughout our mid-twenties sees first dates flop, beers poured, cigarettes rolled, birthday parties, shoulders to cry on, games of pool, advice given, big news shared, lost jobs, lost keys and dancing until late – with Clem and me at the centre of every event and always at the centre of the beer garden.

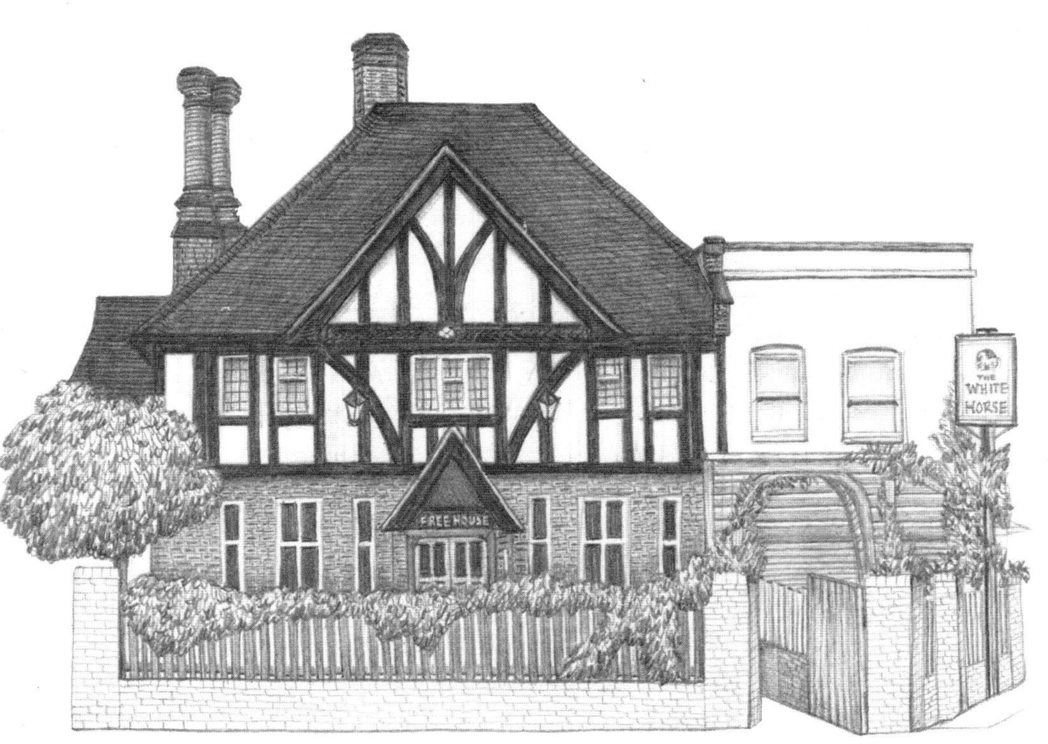

Marquis of Granby, New Cross

I am nineteen and studying Fine Art at Goldsmiths University. As if it's a curricular requirement, the tutors repeatedly recommend that we go to the pub after art talks and tutorials. The pub, the Marquis of Granby, sits at the meeting point of two busy streets, where buses and cars tirelessly travel both ways around the beacon of New Cross Road. The Irish pub's top half is painted in shades of pale blue and deep grassy green to form a mural that covers the exterior, akin to the weather-beaten hills of the Emerald Isle.

I first step inside the pub as a fresher, with friends, following a particularly challenging group tutorial, one where our art was openly critiqued in front of our peers. It sounds hellish, and that's because it was. We cross at the traffic lights and enter the sanctuary away from the busy road. One friend orders a snakebite. It's my first time hearing of the concoction – equal parts lager and cider with a dash of blackcurrant – and it's a no from me. My other friend, who doesn't drink, orders a pint of lemonade. I panic and order a shandy. We sit on a red cushioned bench in the corner and discuss the events of the tutorial we've just left. It's in this moment, as a timid first-year student, that it quickly becomes clear why the tutors suggest we come here.

The Marquis of Granby acts as a place where we students can continue our analysis in a relaxed conversation without the pressure of a classroom. It's a third space. Some of my best concepts are born in these cosy corners with friends, our elbows glued to the beer-sticky table as we excitedly hash out a plan for our next exhibition. A new song is put on the jukebox. We continue to nurture our own education; little do we know we are making lifelong friends over this table, too.

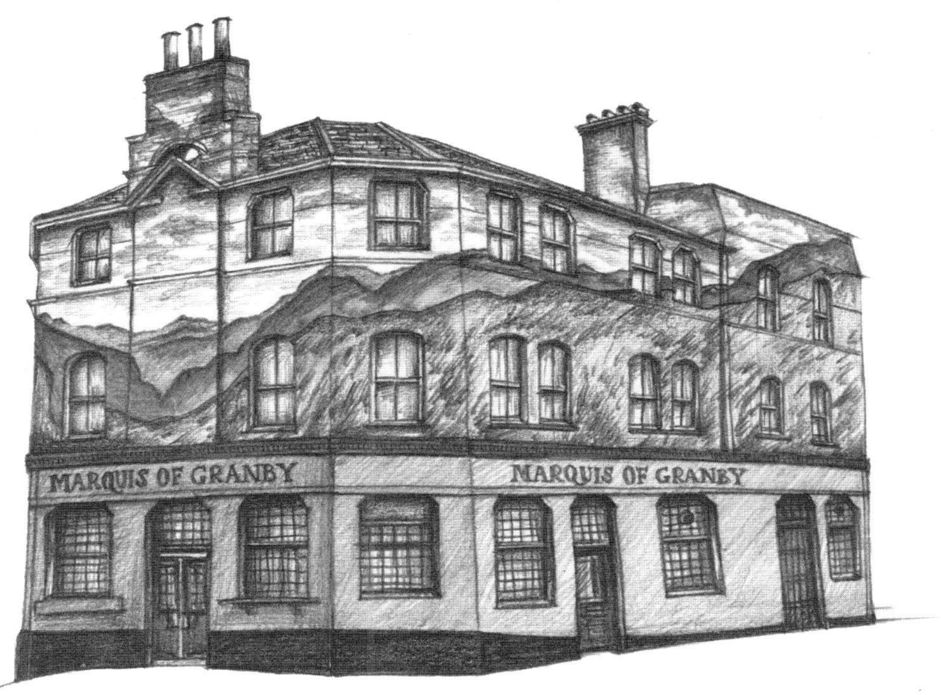

When I come to draw these three pivotal pubs in my life, it's
as if the memories that live within the walls I meticulously draw are
transferred through the soft graphite of my pencil on to the paper.
I draw and reminisce simultaneously, unable to render the building
in front of me without connecting to my own experience of it.
Pubs prompt storytelling, they are places filled with history and
legend, they are a crucial and indispensable part of our culture
and they are personal. That's why, as you turn the pages of *Locals*,
you will find, woven throughout the book, voices from all over
the world sharing their memories of their local.

You never know, your new local could be round the corner,
across the other side of the city, or even in this book …

DETAIL

My hand moves my pencil over the paper in straight
lines – across, up, down, across – repeating the motion,
filling the surface with rectangles, building a pub's walls
brick by brick. I notice the shadow cast by a swinging
sign and I shade in the bricks beneath it. All of a sudden,
a pint glass is left unattended and I must have it for my
sketch – I scribble it in.

The bricks and mortar that hold a pub in place are the foundation
for all my drawings, the architecture itself provides so much detail to
consume me. However, as the light changes, shadows disappear, and
as the pub awakens, doors fling open – even the most unassuming
details found in my drawings have a story behind them.

Come with me to hear how those particular details made it onto
my paper and how even the fleeting moments I capture are just
as much part of the pub as the bricks and mortar that endure
for so much longer.

The Blackfriar, Blackfriars

Each day, over the course of a week, I bring my easel, stool and
extra-large drawing board on the train to come and sit in the middle
of the pavement outside The Blackfriar. The pavement is wide and
busy. There are no corners for me to hide in and no wall for me
to stand by; I have no choice but to stop in the middle of the open
space and stand still amongst the mass of people in constant motion
around me. My drawing board is a wooden rectangle that I use
to hold a single piece of paper; this time the blank page measures
42 x 59.4 cm – four times the size of my usual A4 canvas. This is
the largest drawing I've ever attempted. Generally, my artworks
take me five or six hours to complete. This one takes five days.

Built in around 1875 on the foundations of a former medieval
Dominican friary, the art nouveau structure of The Blackfriar nods
to its medieval ancestry throughout, with its ornate lettering and
carved gargoyles, and the jolly friar sculpture adorning the front,
like the figurehead of a ship. I'm excited that there is extra space
for me to explore every detail meticulously with my pencil. I make
my way down the drawing, looking at the building as separate
layers. One layer is the glass windowpanes which reflect the sky;
gently using my pencil, I add whispers of grey to create clouds, before
boxing them in with the hard lines of the black frame. Another is the
intricate mosaic that divides the top and bottom of the pub's exterior.
I draw hundreds of individual squares, then fill them with a different
tone of grey to mimic the varied hues of green and teal I see before
me. My mind cannot simply relax into the drawing, as I continue
to encounter unexpected elements that need my undivided attention.

During my week outside The Blackfriar, I sit there for so long
I almost become part of the street, like the immovable lamp posts

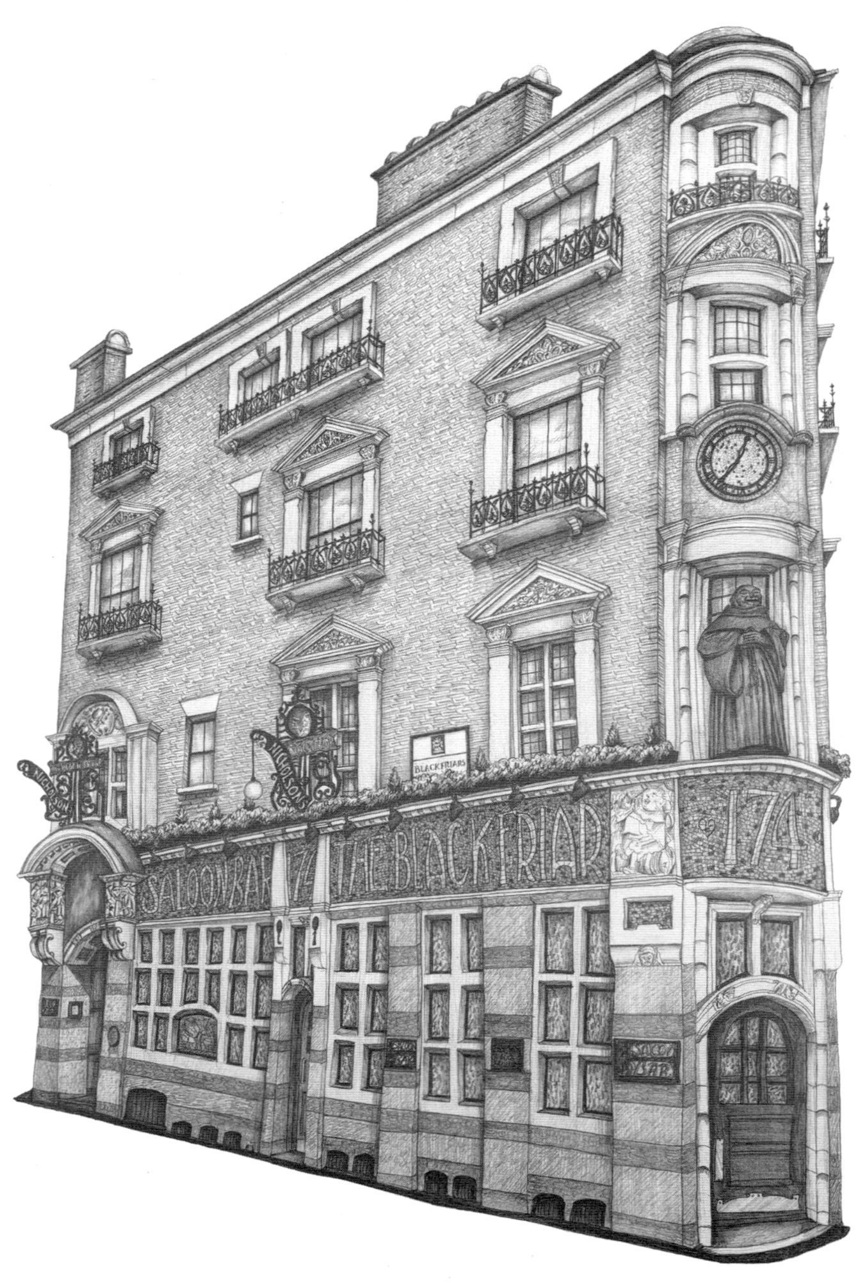

beside me. Each day new textures are added to the drawing and new conversations are had around my easel. A tourist asks me to take a photo of him sitting on my stool in front of my artwork posing with my pencil in his hand – he gifts me a cigarette for my trouble. A week later I laugh as I find the crumpled cigarette at the bottom of my bag, wondering if he has passed the drawing off as his own to his friends back home. Those who work locally wish me good morning as they complete their commute. I meet them again on their way back to Blackfriars station at the end of the day, excited to see what has emerged on my paper. Every day I am surrounded by different groups on historic pub crawls, and I covertly listen to the guides while I sketch and soak up the history they share. I learn that the building was astonishingly saved from demolition in the 1960s as a result of a campaign led by the poet John Betjeman and local politician Lady Dartmouth (Raine Spencer), who were passionate advocates for the preservation of Victorian architecture. To imagine that this Grade II* listed pub could have been flattened as little as sixty-five years ago makes me contemplate the many pubs at risk of closure that don't have the merit of exceptional design on their side.

On the last day, I am met with gale-force winds, the early summer storm rattling my easel and forcing me to hold on to it tightly as I desperately make my final marks. A quick photo of my drawing outside the pub nearly risks the fragile paper, containing so many hours of work, blowing across Blackfriars Bridge. Tragedy averted, I tackle the illustration into my portfolio case and hastily take it inside to the calm solace of the pub. Sitting in a corner after completing my largest pub artwork to date, I relax with my reward (a pint of lager) and rest my weary gaze on the wealth of textures surrounding me. Out of the corner of my eye, I notice some visitors meeting the space for the very first time. Their childlike wonder and genuine interest in the historical significance of a building like

The Blackfriar is compelling. They look around slowly, take photographs, ask the bar staff questions and eventually settle down with their drinks and enjoy the room as intended.

I look up to inspect the same details they see. Wall sculptures made of copper float above the bar, the hammered brown metal depicts friars. One holds out a mosaicked fish which glimmers in the low lighting, a few are huddled together singing prayers from a book, while others dig and water the land – each figure given a distinct expression and personality. The metal friar sculptures mimic the texture of the dappled glass windows. The light from the windows reflects off the gold tables and, whilst the gold mosaicked ceiling draws your eyes up, the creaky floorboards guide them down again. The dark, embellished rooms of the pub are in harmony with the facade I have been looking at for so long, sharing its architectural details: the mosaics, gold reflections and the jolly friar. Each surprising and beautiful.

It's quiet, curious moments like this when I realise how lucky we Londoners are to have these treasures on our doorsteps. And I try to approach each pub, ornately detailed or not, with the same innocent wonder as a visitor discovering The Blackfriar for the very first time.

'The Blackfriar pub holds a special place in my heart,
it's where my boyfriend and I shared our first date
on a warm August evening.'
ELEANOR

The Pride of Spitalfields, Spitalfields

I exit Shoreditch High Street station and turn right towards Brick
Lane. Walking down the narrow pavement, I am startled by the loud
crashes of boxes being thrown into the backs of vans, the whir of bikes
whizzing up and down the one-way road and the sweet smell of cooking
spices that fill the air as the curry houses that line this street ready
themselves for lunch. I turn and walk a few metres down Heneage
Street, leaving the sensory explosion of the busy lane behind me.
I unpack my bag and park my easel opposite The Pride of Spitalfields.
I have no choice but to position myself on the cobbled road, leaving
space for pedestrians to walk behind me. Thankfully this serene
street plays host to less traffic than the neighbouring Brick Lane, but
when a car does rumble slowly past, it is centimetres from my feet.

I attach the board to my easel and press the paper on to it with
masking tape until each of the four corners are stuck down. I pull
apart my travel stool and lock it into place. I put my pencil case and
rubber on it, keeping my tools close by my leg as I stand to face the
empty piece of paper in front of me. I take in the building, and I am
tickled to see the fallen letters of the pub sign. To me, the missing 'F'
and upside down 'L' add some lived-in charm to the exterior. Later,
the lady working behind the bar brings me out a cold glass of coke
and has a look at my progress. She's complimentary and doesn't
mention the sign, but I suddenly feel a pang of remorse, as if I've
made a mockery of their pub by including the lopsided lettering.

A large group of people descend on the street; they are on a tour
of the local area's street art, and they stop further down the road to
look up at a large wall covered in graffiti. I chat to a regular at the
pub while he sips his pint on the pavement. He tells me the alleged
story of a Jack the Ripper suspect that used to drink here back in

the day when it was The Romford Arms. A large white delivery van pulls up directly in front of me, half parked on the pavement and totally covering the pub's facade, a common occurrence when drawing on the streets of London. Naturally, I pause my drawing, and the van driver jumps out and chats to me for a while, before walking down the road to grab some lunch, blissfully unaware. I decide to extend my break and head inside the pub to wait for the van to move.

The traditional carpeted interior, dark wood bar and red comfy stools compel me to get comfy. I grab half a pint of lager and a packet of salted nuts and sit in the corner with my half-finished drawing. There's a piano by my side, a couple of regulars at the bar, photos of the local area hung around me and mugs, jugs and other memorabilia curated modestly around the space. I find out a cat named Lenny was once in residence here, a local legend and famous feline that propped up the bar. I feel sad never to have met him. My glass now drained, and the packet empty, I reluctantly peel myself off the red cushion and head back to the street to finish my sketch.

I am often guilty of omitting a drainpipe or a bin, those permanent features of buildings that show the cycle of everyday life and sometimes distract from the pub's character. But I do want to capture the details that are particular to my visit – to try and catch a moment in time, easily missed features, some we walk past every day, that add a humanness to a rigid block of bricks. I concentrate, then, on the folds in the lopsided parasol that offers shade outside the pub on a warm spring day like today, on the door left ajar that signals the pub is open and behind which I can hear the low rabble of early regulars quietly chatting across the bar.

I decide to keep the wonky lettering of The Pride of Spitalfields and a few months later the pub buys ten of my calendars, of which they are the front cover. They are proud of their brilliant pub, as they should be – 'F' or no 'F'.

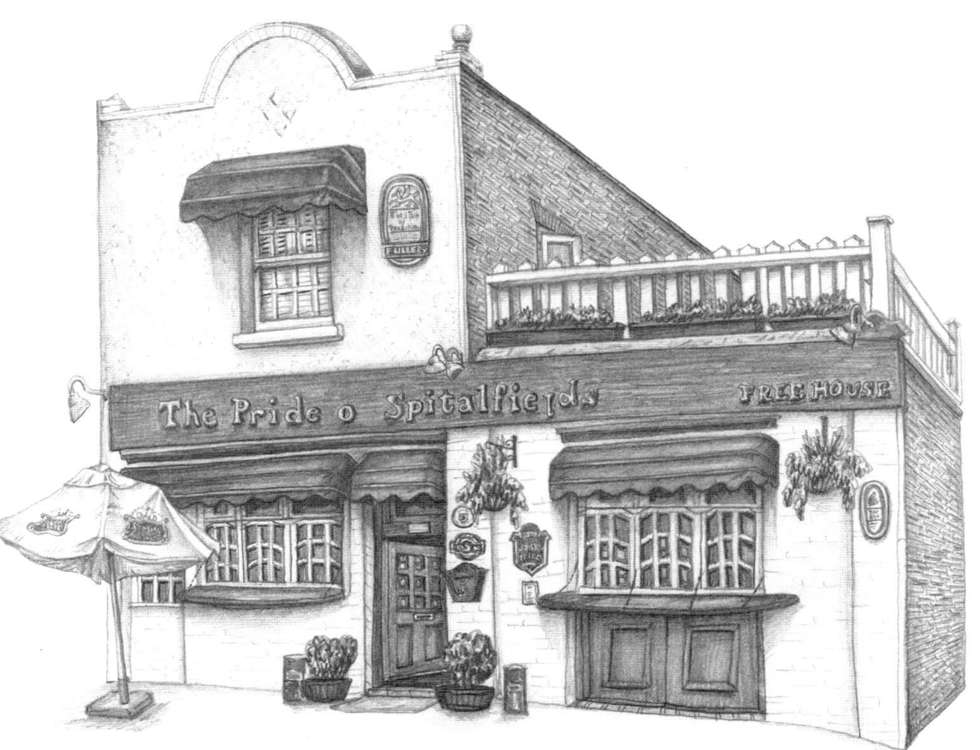
The Pride o Spitalfields
FREE HOUSE
FULLER'S

The Roebuck, Borough

The pigeon is as iconic in London as Big Ben, Beefeaters and red buses. Taking out a sandwich or a packet of crisps on the street almost always means that a bobbing, waddling pigeon, sometimes accompanied by friends, will join you for lunch. As I often have snacks to keep me going during the six-hour drawing days, I've learnt to make peace with the birds and their company.

I sit outside The Roebuck in Borough, the grand Victorian exterior jutting out into the pavement. I take my time rendering the elements that surround the pub – the sea of benches, the telephone box and the yellow smiley face in the building's top window. With its Dutch gable frontage, curved green roof and Jacobean-style pilasters, this pub boasts an eclectic mix of styles for me to sketch. A few people weave through the benches to come see what I'm doing, and bikes travel up and down the cycle lane to my left. The large, imposing windows that span the ground floor offer a glimpse into the warmth of the pub, the low-lit space waiting to welcome its clientele.

Just before I pack up my easel to go sit on the other side of the beckoning windows, I see something from the corner of my eye. It's the particularly persistent pigeon that has not left my field of vision all day, taking off and landing at the highest point of the pub, possibly posing, probably nesting. The plump bird has become a staple of my sketching day, so I decide to sketch it in as the final flourish to my drawing.

Since that day, I've added many persistent pigeons into my pub artworks. In an increasingly cold, reflective city, it makes sense that London's feathered citizens are seeking refuge atop familiar, older, perhaps kinder, structures. These often overlooked city residents, that live alongside us every day, find a home at the pub too.

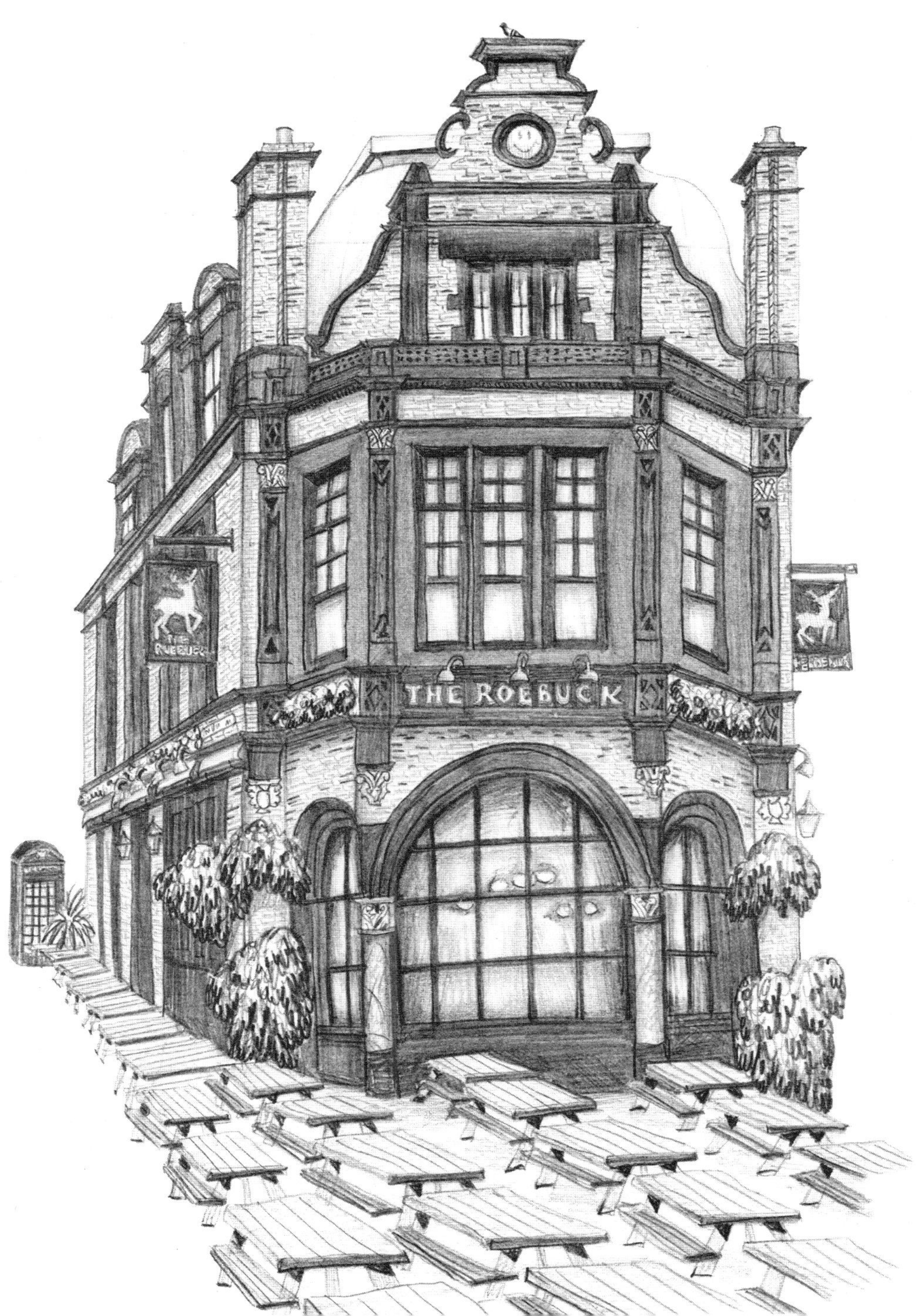
THE ROEBUCK
THE ROEBUCK

The Bricklayer's Arms, Putney

The Bricklayer's Arms sits at the curve of a dead-end street in Putney, symmetrical in shape, more like a picturesque cottage than your typical London pub. Originally named The Waterman's Arms, it was built to cater for local shipbuilders and has continued to welcome Putney residents for nearly two hundred years.

As soon as I set up my equipment, a curious black cat starts to rub up against my easel leg, scratching its cheeks on the buckles, welcoming me to the street and its local. I prepare my paper and begin to outline the architecture before me, making gentle marks with my pencil before committing to the straight lines that create the pub's shape. The sun sits behind the building, and the roof's edge casts a strong shadow, which I shade in heavily. I inspect the unusual angle and cylindrical spout of the chimney; after drawing it, a bloke emerges from nowhere and informs me it was built to eliminate downdraughts from entering the building.

My friends Mariana and Michelle happily keep me company for the afternoon; they perch on the low brick wall that runs alongside the pavement next to me. The quiet dead end begins to show signs of life as large trucks reverse down the road, delivering to different flats at the end of the street – we giggle as each one takes it in turns to block my view. The pub doors eventually open, and I run inside to order us refreshments while my friends guard my easel. I see other beautiful renditions of the pub framed on the wall. The ceiling is saturated in pump clips – an array of beer badges that have decorated the taps on the bar across the years – each one a different shape, colour and size, and Chris the landlord welcomes me in, insisting our drinks are on the house.

We enjoy our beers together on the street while I continue my sketch and observe the activity around the oldest pub in Putney. Chris is relieved to discover that I've omitted the bright red wheely bins out front. The pile of kegs awaiting collection are lifted, rearranged, removed and added to throughout the day, and my pencil attempts to keep up, until I finally settle on a composition. To me, they reflect the ever-changing craft ales of this particular local and the state of flux of any working pub.

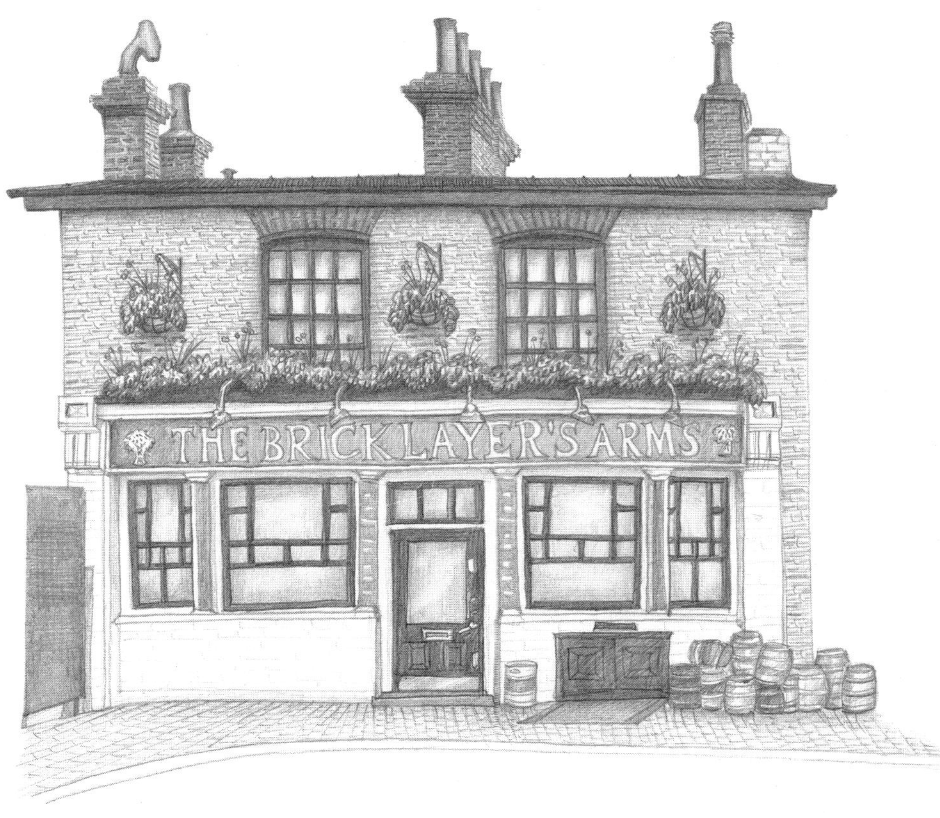

The Devonshire, Soho

It's a cold February day at Piccadilly Circus. The huge glitzy red letters that spell out 'MOULIN ROUGE' act as my backdrop, and the infamous Devonshire pub is my muse. I have barely set up my easel before I am greeted by Oisín, the landlord. We have never met, and he shakes my hand after learning about my ambitious project. It's 11 a.m. on a Tuesday and I am shocked to see a security guard lining up a long rope to cordon off the drinking area outside, already anticipating large crowds on a freezing weekday morning.

On the first day, my friend Gemma joins me for a while. Both huddled in our big coats, we chat around my easel as my hand stiffly moves across the paper. She brings me a cup of English breakfast tea with a dash of milk; the kind of scalding tea that's just about drinkable after an hour. I use the hot paper cup to warm my frigid fingers periodically between sketching. An inquisitive construction worker in a hard hat and hi-vis vest comes over to chat at different points in the day – he is working on a site across the street. He admits he has little knowledge of pubs and doesn't tend to use them, nevertheless he is very interested in my project. He compliments my work with enthusiasm and shows me photos of his daughter's colourful paintings on his phone. The combination of the tea and his warmth in conversation provides the much-needed antidote to the outdoor chill.

The cold weather and lack of light mean this particular drawing takes two days to complete. As I battle through the finishing touches on day two, I exhale a cloud of frozen breath, vigorously stomp my boots and try to ignore the lack of feeling in my feet. To distract myself from the bitter cold, I fixate on the glow coming from within the glossy green pub. Little lamps, one in each window, illuminate the faces of happy lunchtime drinkers. Pints of Guinness, silky and

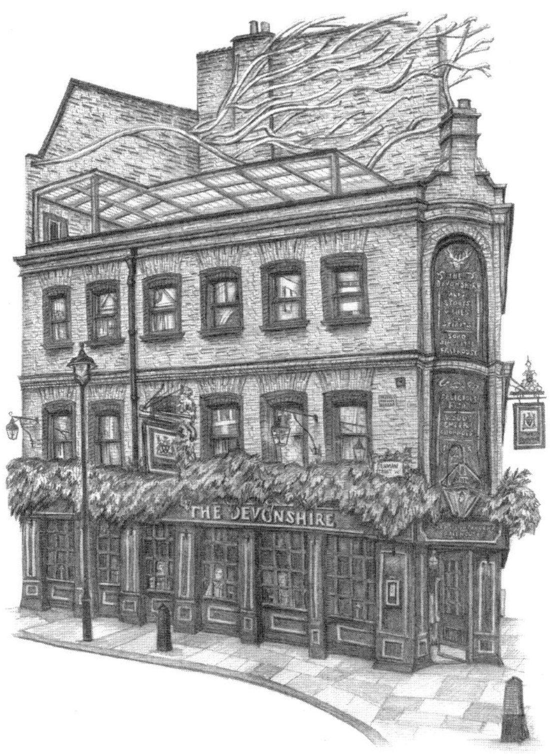

inviting, peer over the window ledge. Sketching the punters' faces
and imagining their comfort turns out to be the perfect incentive
to continue my work.

Eventually, I step inside to thaw. It is busy, but surprisingly not
crowded; there are groups of co-workers, friends and tourists all
dispersed around the bar. The traditional pub furniture, textured
ceiling and wood-panelled walls collectively hold the jovial atmosphere.
A long row of pint glasses full of settling Guinness sit on the bar
and one of them is for me. I talk at length to the friendly bar staff
and show them my drawing. The next time I visit The Devonshire
I bring the pub a print of my artwork to hang on their walls, and
Oisín welcomes me back inside the warm pub like an old friend.

The Barley Mow, Shoreditch

I typically arrive to draw a pub at around 10 a.m. on a weekday
morning. Most pubs aren't open yet. In the quiet I am able to start
my drawings with a rough outline on the blank paper, no rulers
or perspective techniques; everything is done freehand and by eye.
Throughout my day I see the pub evolve, the upstairs windows close,
the front door opens and – most importantly – the punters arrive.
The pub and, in turn, my drawing begin to show signs of life. I am
there sketching as the first customers of the day arrive and am gone
before you can't see the pub for the people. It's a chance for me to
dissect the architecture of the building and to highlight particular
moments and details from the still parts of the day.

As I stand across the road from The Barley Mow, a Shoreditch staple
that opens at 4 p.m. on a weekday, the heat of the summer sun edges
round the corner of the building. I drink my ice coffee from the
trendy cafe behind me, the ice melting faster than I can sip, and I
set it down on my stool. The traffic proves difficult to sketch around.
I peer over the tops of cars, sometimes waiting for buses to move
slowly past. Luckily for me, the architecture is compact, repeated
and neat, meaning I can momentarily work from memory behind
any stubbornly stationary vehicles.

    I am nearing the end of my drawing, and I can see I'll be finished
before the pub opens, when, suddenly, a van pulls up, and a bloke
hops out and knocks on the window of the pub. Kegs are piled on
to a metal frame with wheels, each plonk of the cylindrical barrels
echoing across the street. It's a repetitive beat, as the kegs are dragged
across the floor of the van and stacked on to another keg beneath it.
All of a sudden, the cellar doors, hidden amongst the pavement slabs,
are flung open from within. One by one, the delivery driver drops kegs,

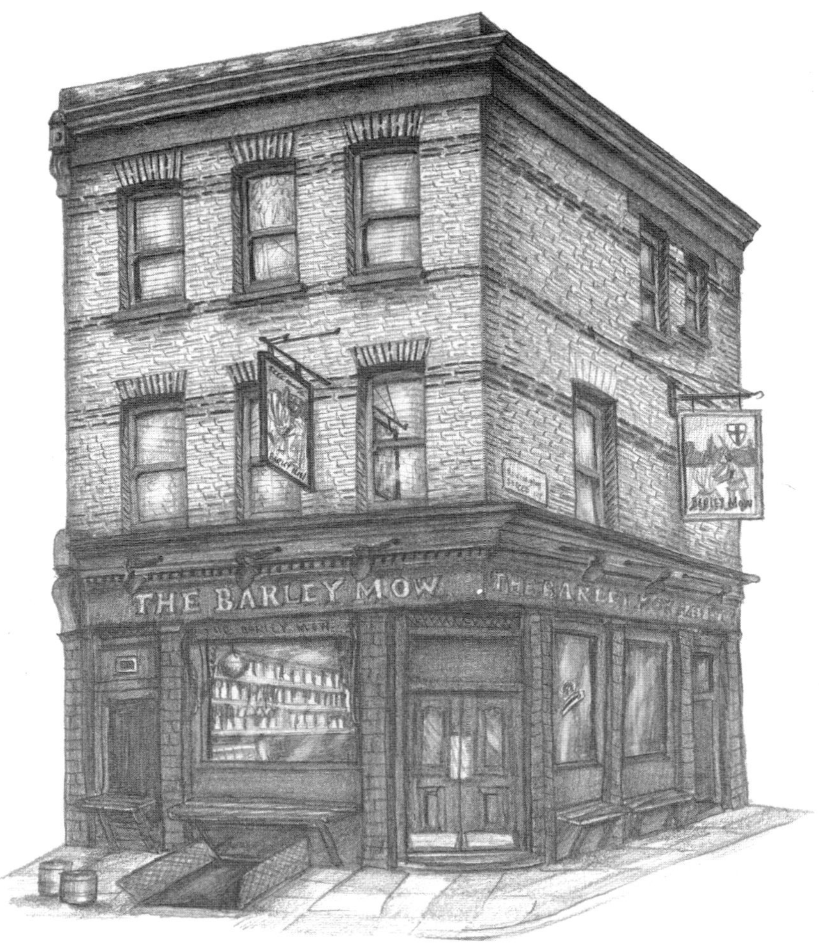

and they disappear into the dark pit. A muffled slap is heard as
the hard metal is caught by the cushioned layer on the cellar floor.
I grab my rubber and erase the closed cellar doors on my page,
redrawing them as I see them now – flung open with two barrels
patiently waiting their turn to be dropped below. The rhythmic
process is one of my favourite scenes to witness at any pub on
the brink of opening time.

The Rose and Crown, Ealing

I am racing through an alleyway to reach my destination, The Rose and Crown in South Ealing. After deciding to take the scenic route along back roads and pedestrian walkways, a sharp shower erupts. My phone screen is saturated with raindrops, and my fingers no longer control the maps that guide me beneath the slippery screen. Although just a postcode away from where I was born, this is a pub that is brand new to me, and I am lost trying to find it.

With my plans to draw the pub today dashed by the weather, I decide to continue my search anyway. Eventually I find the pub, tucked away on a quiet street, opposite the Grade II listed St Mary's Church.

I stand outside the friendly-looking local, rain drips off my nose, and my inadequate waterproof is failing me. I see the pub's pitched roof and white shutters, and I head forwards to run inside for cover.

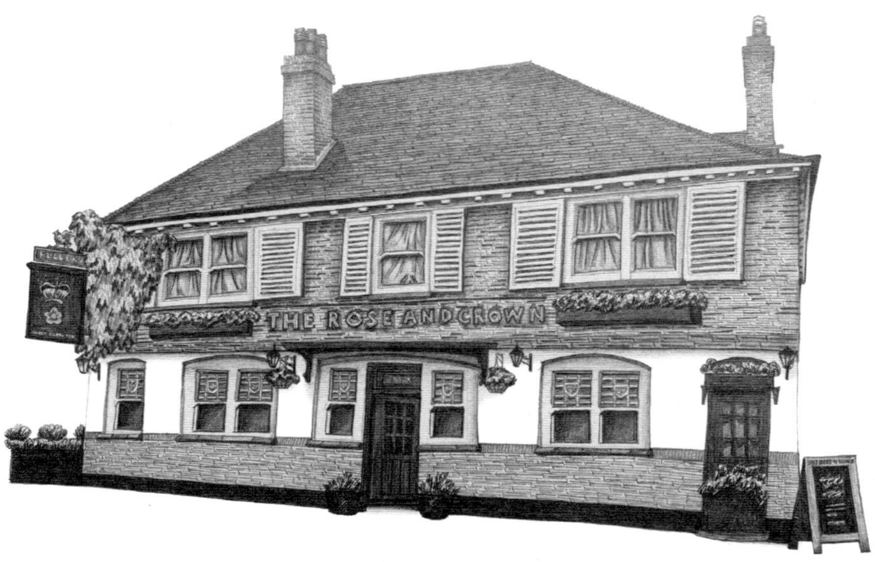

Luckily this is a pub that opens early. It is a haven, an inviting shelter from the storm. Looking up for a moment, I notice a face in the window. A snout and two heavy eyes peek through the droplet-covered glass. A dog.

It's a moment that compels me to stand in the rain a little longer. I take a picture of the handsome building and run for cover. I eagerly enter the large interior, careful not to slip on the varnished floors. The warm paint, wallpaper patterns and gentle background music lure me and my beer to a corner by the window. I look out through the stained glass pattern, at the soaked pavement I was meant to draw from. My journey is not wasted, though, because I've met Finn, the resident pooch, a detail I would have missed for my drawing if I hadn't found myself outside The Rose and Crown today.

The Lord Clyde, Southwark

I first visit The Lord Clyde one St Patrick's day, having stumbled across it on a backstreet in Southwark. The loud, excitable chatter, along with the warm yellow glow that colours the windows, invites my family and me inside. Pints of Guinness secured, we perch on three low stools, sharing a table with strangers, feeling at home and like we're part of the furniture and have been here all along.

Years later I come to draw the pub, and I stand outside on the narrow road, facing the front door. I sketch the original Truman Brewery signage, outlining the extra-large lettering against the pale tiles and paying close attention to the font style and words so I don't make a spelling mistake. The recognisable green tiling, often seen on old Truman-owned establishments, is still intact and above the door you can see the name 'E.J. BAYLING', the landlord when the original

Victorian pub was rebuilt in 1913. The triumphant eagle that
adorns the front of the building is an emblem that can be seen on
a number of London pubs. The bird is the signifier of the East End
Truman Brewery, originally called Black Eagle Brewery and situated
near Brick Lane. The ceramic adornments and vintage signage
mean The Lord Clyde is unlike any pub I've drawn before. I use
the sharpness of my pencil to outline the crisp lettering and deep
shading to ensure each unique detail pops off the brickwork.

People stop to look at my work, and I chat to those passing by
on their mid-morning coffee run as I piece together my drawing
with my pencil. One of those to stop is Daniel, a local resident, who
recognises my work and tells me he has suggested I draw the pub
before. I thank him for the brilliant suggestion and later he emails
me to enquire about the original drawing.

I stop for lunch, a cheese baguette, some chips and half an Amstel.
Eventually, the lunchtime drinkers head back to work, and so do I,
returning to my easel to add the final details: the inside of the bar,
which can just be seen through the open door, and the lone punter
outside, listening to music with a lager as they wait for a friend.

I head inside to order another beer after six hours of drawing.
Upon entering the traditional interior, I am greeted by the same
warmth I felt all those years ago. Red benches line the red-carpeted
room. I look through the etched glass windows engraved with the
pub name to see the outside space fill up with cheerful visitors.
Heavy velvet curtains are pulled to the side of each door, like a stage,
ready to be drawn at closing time. But there's nothing showy about
this boozer. Understated beauty is found in each functional detail.
Without any need for extra interior embellishment or intricate
gilding, The Lord Clyde is unpretentious, yet, to me, it is dazzling.

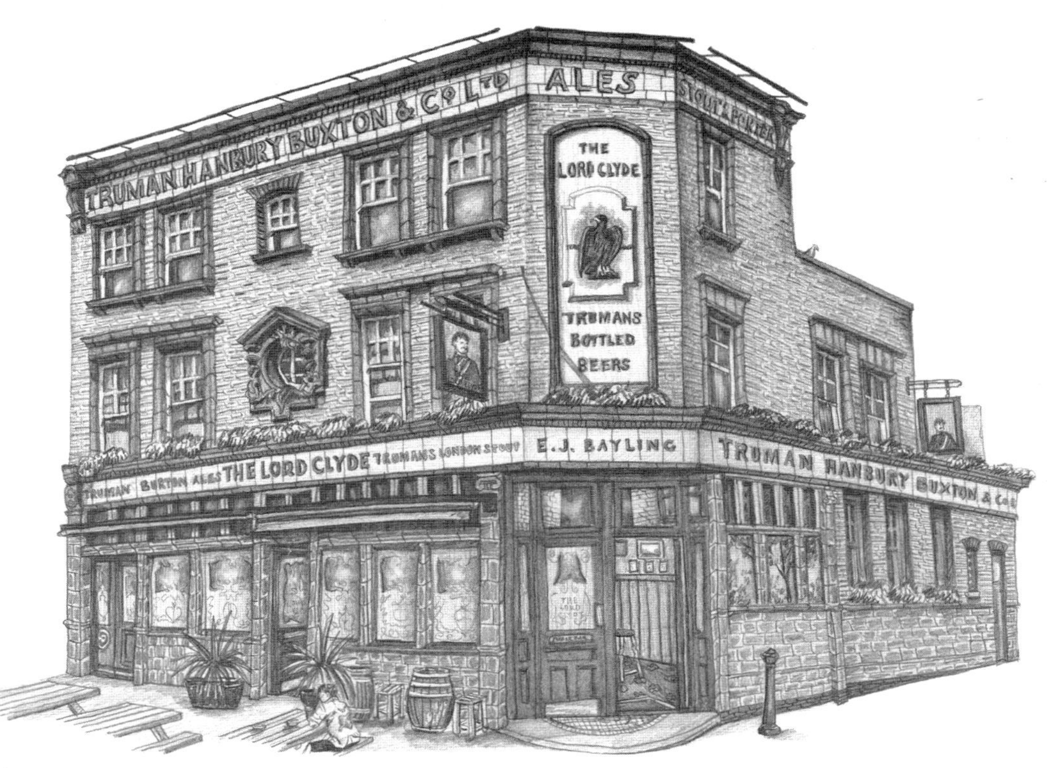

'The Lord Clyde … a real "proper" pub with a dartboard,
local regulars and a warm welcome. I have spent many a
happy evening there missing doubles and sipping pints
with great friends old and new.'

JASON

SMALL

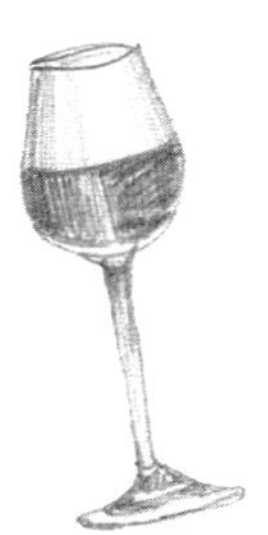

The competition for London's smallest pub might be fraught but the city is full of pint-sized gems. To sketch their modest facades is often a shorter process, but it still comes with challenges. I must decide where to place them on the empty page, squinting as I sketch the details on minuscule pub signs. More importantly, will I be able to fit inside afterwards for a pint?

In a big city where space is shrinking and towers are growing, these clever little locals utilise their architecture both inside and out, creating some of the most iconic pubs in the city and providing that crucial third space, however small it may be.

Upon entering a tiny tavern, you might expect to squeeze between chairs, shuffle to the front and wait shoulder to shoulder for your pint. From sharing tables with strangers to the relief of being only a few steps away from the bar, these small establishments might cleverly fit into repurposed buildings, hide on high streets and remain big in character – if not in size.

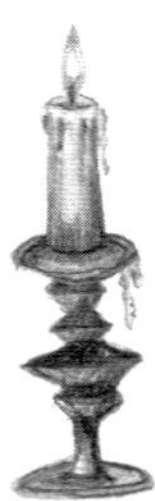

The Harp, Covent Garden

I leave Charing Cross station via the side entrance and head down the steep steps to walk in the direction of The Ship and Shovell. Upon entering its alleyway, though, I see one half of the pub is patterned with a grid of cold metal poles. The beautiful red pub is covered in scaffolding. I decide I'd rather draw a pub without the builders' climbing frame, so I quickly scramble together my knowledge of the area and think of an alternative place to draw. After a few seconds, it hits me. A brilliant pub resides just round the corner, and I am yet to draw it. I waste no time rerouting my steps towards it. I give The Ship and Shovell a nod, knowing I'll be back to see it another day.

The Harp is sandwiched between two buildings and stands tall and narrow, as if the force from both sides has squashed its original shape. Its plain white frontage is accented with colourful stained-glass windows and a single swinging pub sign. On my sketch of the tiny sign, I painstakingly draw the folds in the musician's dress as she strums the curved harp beside her.

I look up from my paper and see police on horses slowly patrolling the street. As they plod past, the barman walks by with the tallest tower of pint glasses I've ever seen. His face is seemingly unperturbed by the delicate structure of stacked glass that sways above his head. I am joined by my dad who has come to explore the pub for the day. He emerges from the door, hands me half an ale and leans against the wall to watch the world go by. He watches people pass me on the busy corner opposite the pub. Some stop momentarily to peer over my shoulder, a few stay to chat and others offer compliments in my artwork's direction as they rush by. 'Looks sketchy!' a bloke blurts, delivering his drive-by dad joke with a grin – my own dad belly laughs at the gag (of course).

It can be a fascinating experience for my friends and family to watch me work, seeing so many people come up and chat to me so openly is a novelty to them. But to me these moments at my easel, when strangers connect over art and pubs, have become a common occurrence and a fundamental part of my drawing day. The conversations I fall into with curious passersby not only serve as a welcome interruption to the consuming act of drawing but also offer a rare bonding experience I wouldn't have sketching alone in my studio.

I draw the final element of the scene, a small segment of the bar that can be seen through the open door, which eventually beckons us inside. I squeeze past the regulars by the entrance; the closeness of the room is accentuated by the hundreds of different coloured pump clips collected across the top of the bar. I walk through the pub and find a sliver of space to order our pints over a customer's bald head. As the barman pours our beer, I observe how the molten amber neatly falls into the tilted glass, the steady pour of lapping liquid reaching the top of the rim as the hand that holds it gradually straightens. The room is full but not rowdy, busy but not loud. I cheers my dad with our elbows in tight, our glasses clink and we look around at the people who have also chosen to crowd into this small space. We soon settle into the close atmosphere, a result of this comforting congregation of people.

'The place you went with your Dad – first for a "bottle of pop and a packet of crisps", then for your first pint, then when you were home from college to catch up with "your old man" (and get a free pint), then there was the first pint you bought for your Dad, and then it became a ritual, right until you remember that last pint and the pub culture he taught you before he passed.'

STEVE

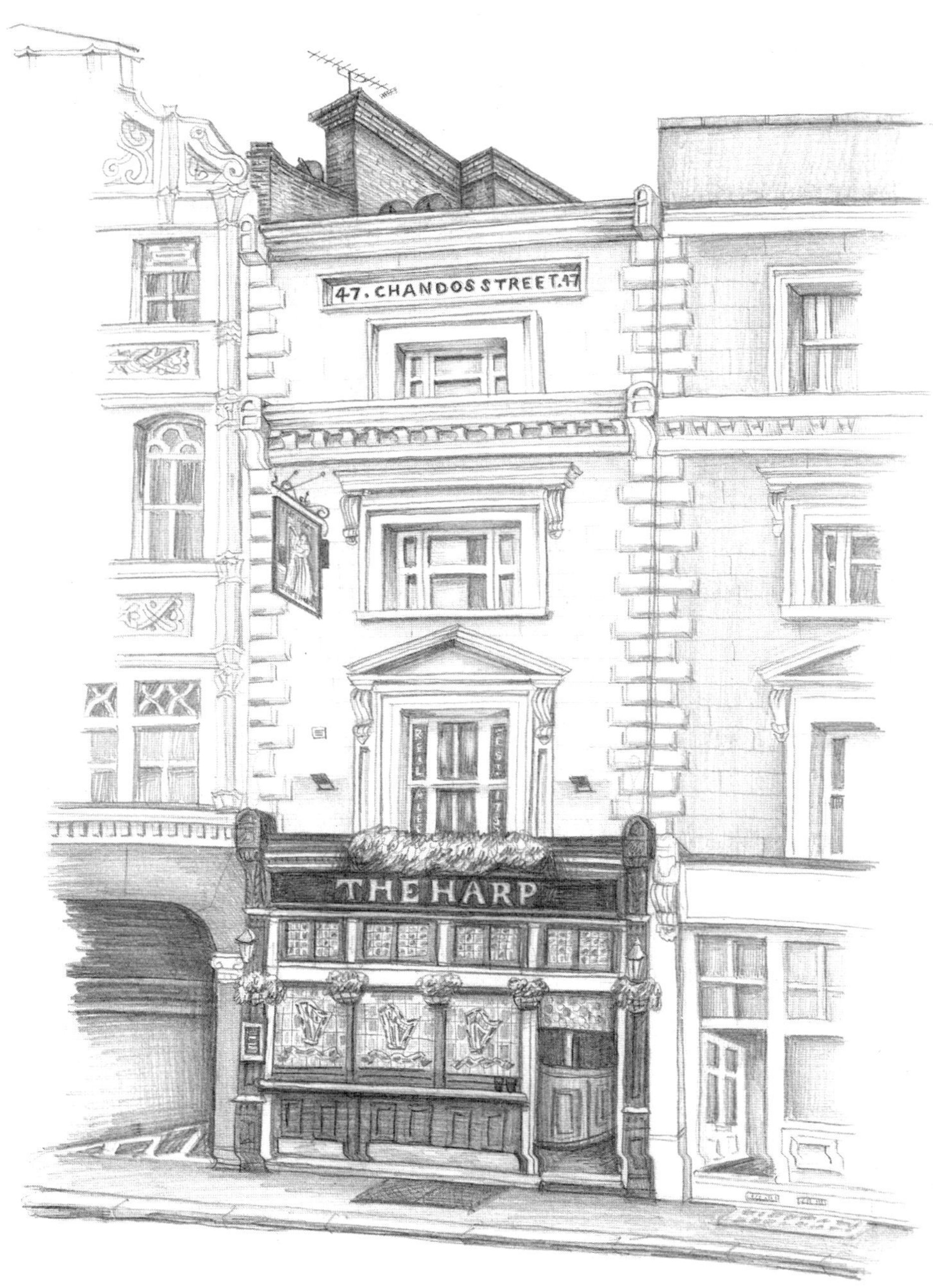

4·7. CHANDOS STREET .47
THE HARP

The Grapes, Limehouse

I cycle across the river to The Grapes, charmed by the warehouses and cobbled streets of East London that line my journey. I travel down Narrow Street, a fitting name, as the pub I'm planning to sketch is exactly that. I find my spot across the road and balance my sketchbook on a bollard for the afternoon. I decide to sketch the pub standing alone, the edges of the building disappearing into the paper. Only suggestions of its neighbours exist either side: a shared street sign to the left and a blue plaque to the right that reads 'The Grapes 1583'. A delivery driver abruptly pulls up along the pavement and jumps out of his van holding a parcel. He pauses to look at my page as I fill in the brickwork. He excitedly asks if I know who owns the pub. I say no, and he simply replies, 'Gandalf', before disappearing into the block of flats behind me.

I continue to sketch the lanky local, which has sat here for almost five hundred years. It is remarkably straight and upstanding for such a small, old building. I press my pencil into my sketchbook; the painted surface of the black glossy bollard beneath is too hot to touch in the heat of the sun, but it makes an adequate drawing table for today. I scribble the tangle of vines on the pub sign, the tiny letters on the side of the building and the pattern of the etched glass window. Each line requires me to sharpen my pencil to illustrate the fine details of the tiny building in the centre of my page.

I finally head inside for a drink. A few punters are scattered around the slim, serene space on this quiet afternoon. I wait while my half pint is poured and study the artefacts behind the barman. One I recognise as Gandalf's staff from *The Lord of the Rings* films, a tall gnarly stick bolted to the back wall, and there's a tiny figurine of the character sat on a shelf next to it, wielding the same staff.

I take my beer and head to the back room of the pub; I peer out of the window to see a modest balcony which looks out over the River Thames. There is a figure in the water – I recognise the work of the artist Antony Gormley – a bronze sculpture standing in the river, appearing and disappearing with the tide. There is a sign on the wall that outlines how many people can stand on the balcony – only fifteen at one time. Suddenly my legs wobble at the thought of the rickety wood separating me from the drop below. I hastily sit down in the cool dark room and enjoy the view from the comfort of the window seat instead.

After packing my drawing away safely, I put on my helmet and unlock my bike. I notice a door open next to the pub, and standing in the doorway is 'Gandalf', aka Sir Ian McKellen, the famous actor and co-owner of The Grapes, accepting a parcel on the doorstep. For a fleeting moment I want to show him my drawing, but he's gone before I make up my mind. A few weeks later, when I'm back at this little pub, I hand over a gift: a print of my drawing and an extra one for Ian.

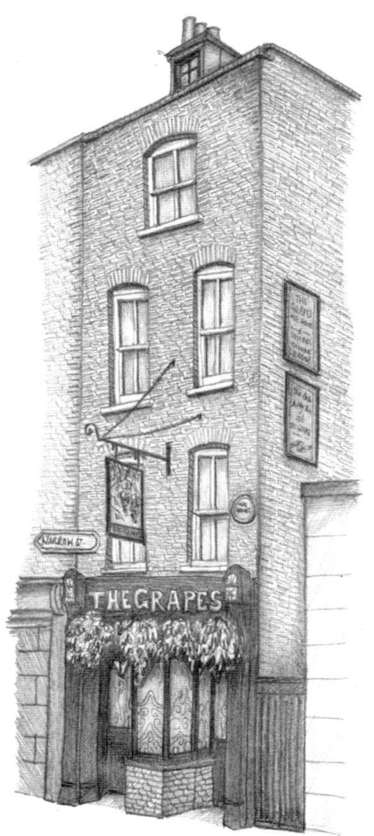

The Shirker's Rest, New Cross

I stand outside my old university local, The Marquis of Granby, and head a few doors down towards a less familiar frontage. What was once a solicitor's office is now a brand-new micropub. The modest facade retains its wonky roof, big enough for only one window amongst the brickwork. This is the shortest shop on the street. And now there's a solitary rocking chair out front and a sign that reads 'The Shirker's Rest'.

Aptly named and situated across from the university library, this is a pub that beckons tired students away from their books. I am greeted by Andy who has invited me to put on an exhibition upstairs, just a few weeks after The Shirker's Rest has opened. We look around the space together, appreciating the handmade bar and the lovingly sourced furniture, as he animatedly explains the vision for their new pub. I stick my drawings to the yellow walls upstairs until they cover the old office space. I head down for a drink; Andy suggests a local ale I might like and pours it himself. We chat about their new venture, and he introduces me to the other co-founders of the pub. The warmth of the newly renovated space is cemented by the collective enthusiasm and ambition for the future of this new little local.

I visit the pub again to deliver a print of my drawing. The small squat building modestly takes space on the page, textured bricks and uniform tiles surround the black windows, and the rocking chair takes pride of place outside. The print I gift them immediately goes on the wall next to the varied selection of crisps, hung alongside photographs, scribbles and cards – an array of personal dedications to the new pub on the block. I take my seat on the rocking chair outside, enjoying another recommended ale. In front of me is the chaos of New Cross Road and behind me the peace of The Shirker's Rest.

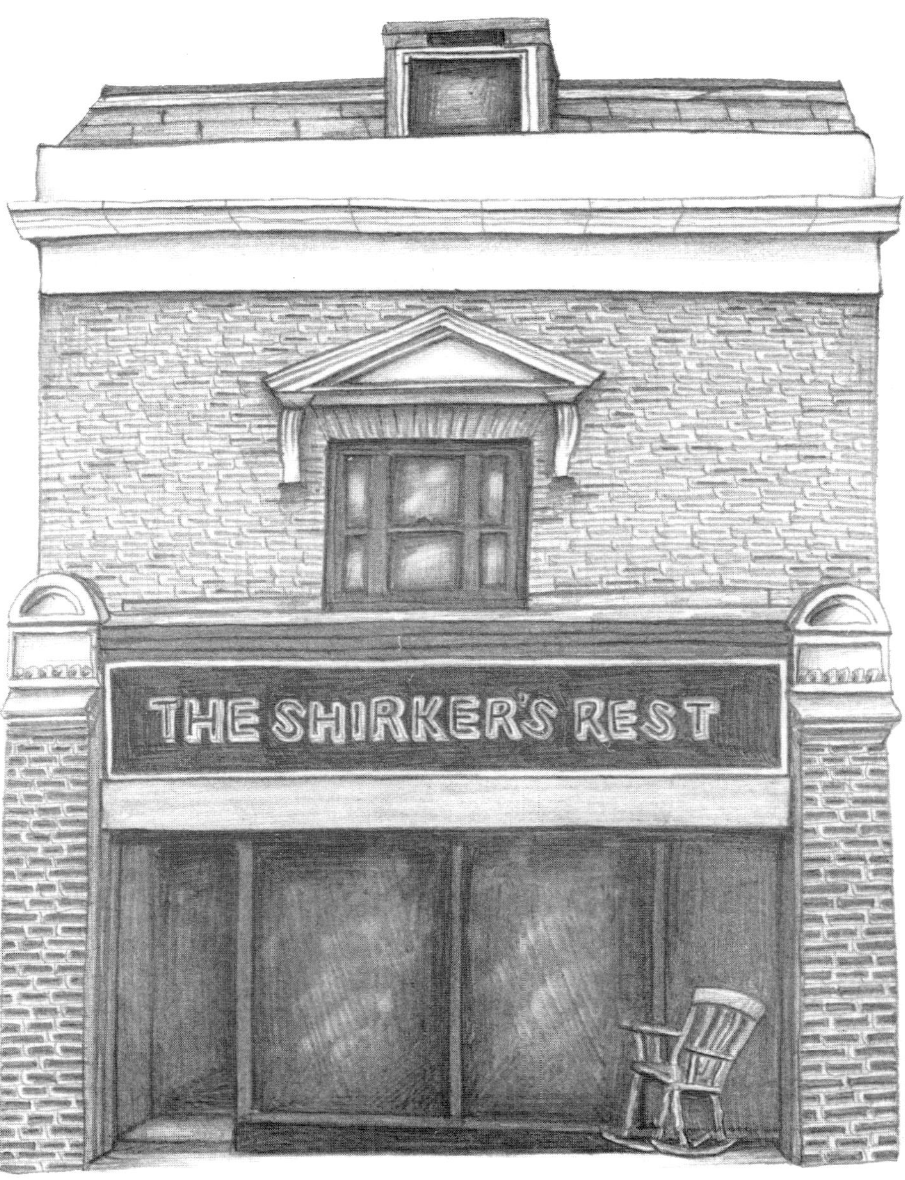
THE SHIRKER'S REST

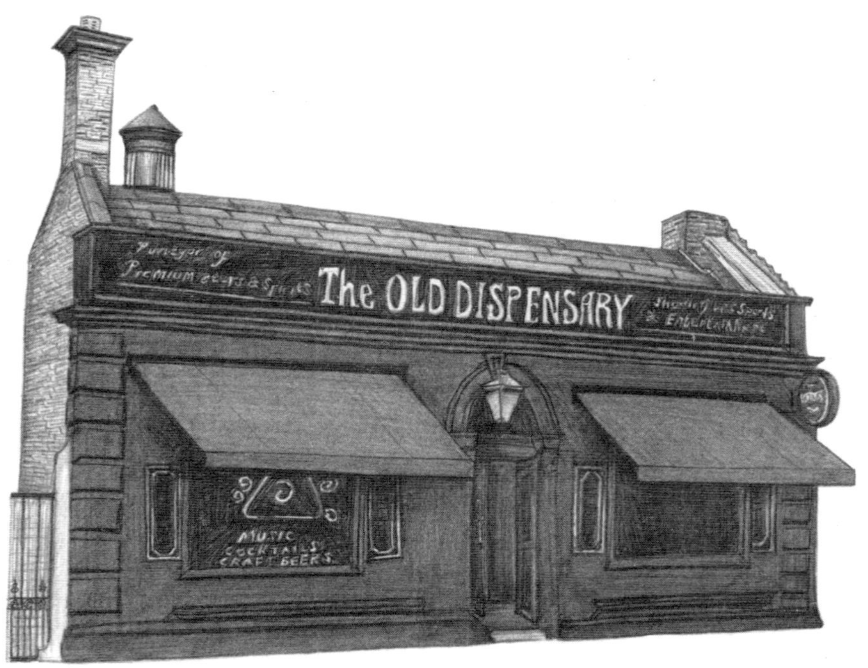

The Old Dispensary, Camberwell

The bright flashes of red buses whizzing past distract me as I try
to catch glimpses of the single-storey building behind them. The
unyielding traffic of Camberwell hides the pub I'm trying to draw,
which retains its name from when the building was Camberwell
Provident Dispensary, which was established in 1862 to assist people
in need in the local community. During this time, it was a place
where members – of which there were more than six thousand in
the 1870s – could receive medical assistance and medicine.

Finally, there's a lull in the traffic, and The Old Dispensary comes
into view. The short facade is painted black and the pub name in gold

pops off its dark background. I leave the letters unshaded, so they are the brightest part of my drawing.

I stand in the summer heat, the polluted air hanging heavy around me and the sun sinking into the matte paint of the pub's front. The fumes cloud my senses, and I start to question my sketching location for the day. I carve out the Irish pub's outline with my pencil, shading the paper's surface to mimic the distinctive, dark paint job and the strong, straight lines of its architecture. The brutal surroundings of the road and the foot traffic rushing past encourage me to colour in the outline with haste. My hand moves back and forth across the paper, scribbling lines together until they meet to make a dark grey wall. I take out my softer pencil and push it over the grey to form the darkest shadows under the awnings.

Soon I dart across the road with my finished drawing under my arm and through the arched doorway. I enter the pub expecting a bungalow-type interior, but I am surprised by high ceilings and a light-filled room, thanks to a bright skylight. Each window lets in the sun, which surrounds and reflects off the hanging chandelier in the centre of the ceiling. I head to the bar, and the landlord welcomes me, offering me a drink. I sit in the corner by the door, looking out on the chaotic road I've just left behind. Soon, a few of my friends join me, and we move to occupy a bench outside in the shade of the awning.

We hear a loud tapping, the strum of an instrument and the boom of a drum. We peer through the window to see a group of people head to the base of the stage at the back of the pub, and they huddle at the band's feet. We head inside following the heavy bass, filling the available space alongside the other punters. The bandmates flick their long hair as they energise the crowd in front of them. We drink our pints and vigorously nod our heads to the beat before heading back outside and into the refreshing chill of the evening air.

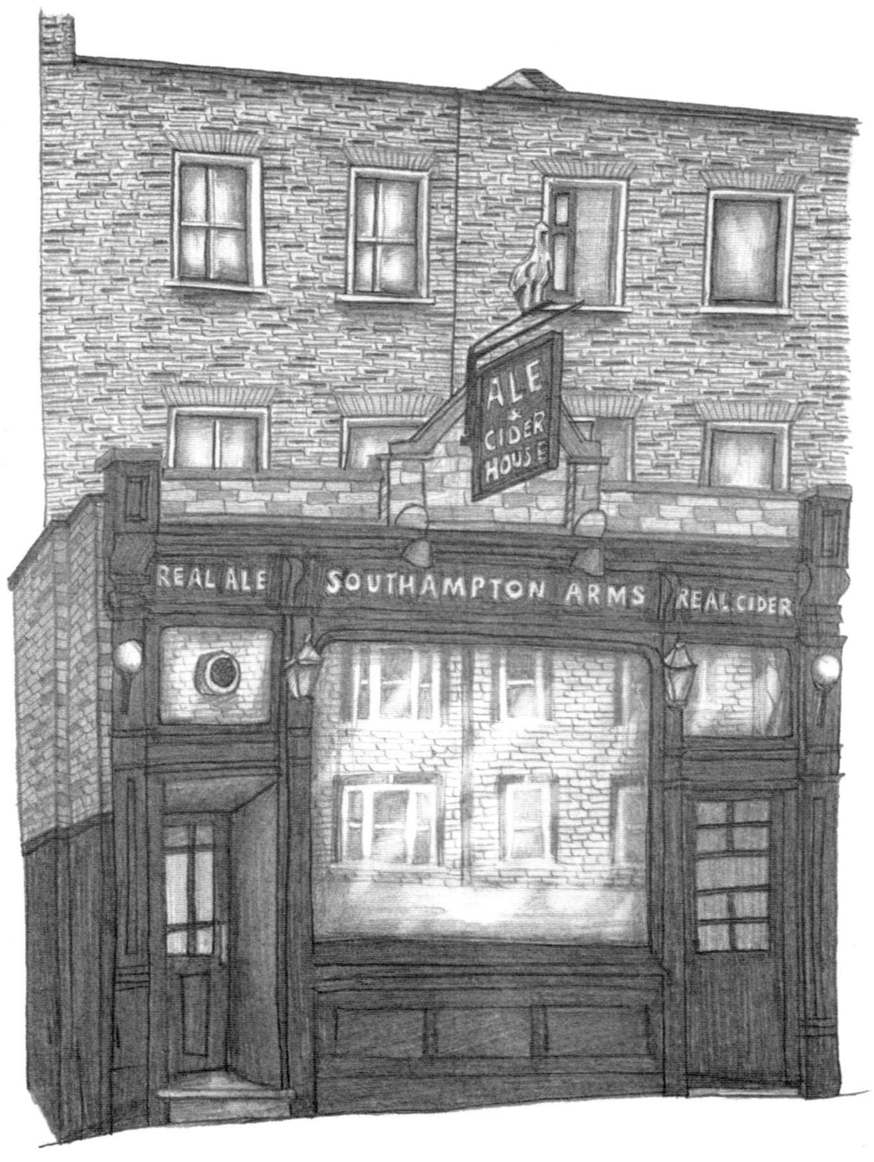
ALE
&
CIDER
HOUSE
REAL ALE   SOUTHAMPTON ARMS   REAL CIDER

The Southampton Arms, Kentish Town

When I sketch the dark painted frontage of The Southampton Arms, I try to capture its small and wobbly shape, sloping into the incline of Highgate Road. I make the lines in my drawing slightly wiggly to illustrate the age of the building, but straight enough to show it's still plausibly standing. The large white text painted on the side of the building, only visible if you stand next to the pub, reads 'ALE CIDER MEAT'. The independent pub is clearly proud of its straightforward fare, keeping it simple and serving the same three quality components. So secure in its offering, they claim to be the only dedicated ale and cider house in London to serve beers and cider from wholly independent breweries.

I use my rubber to glide across the graphite, removing its colour, leaving behind bold reflections in the large glass window. I try my best to see behind the glinting glass, into the dark inside, but the reflections of the buildings opposite are all I can draw. Next, I sketch the brickwork of the flat above the pub, and finally the golden bird balancing on top of the pub sign.

Later, after finishing my sketch, I walk past the window and into the pub. The sunlight shining through the large glass frontage meets the light coming from the back door, which leads me out to a hidden oasis, a modest beer garden under the fire escape, surrounded by green trees and bushes pushing over the fence. It's too chilly to brave the garden today so I head back inside. At the bar, I don't recognise a single pump clip, all the beer names and logos are unfamiliar; it's a CAMRA member's dream. I opt for a pale ale called 'Stairway to Simcoe', and its hazy liquid is handed to me in a small dimpled tankard glass. I grab the handle and take it back to my corner opposite the piano.

The dark red ceiling absorbs the light, creating a close feel in the room. Conversations had at the front of the pub can be heard word for word at the back. I sit silently on the creaky wooden bench, flitting between my ale, my phone and my book. I look up to see someone writing on the wall. As they move away, I squint at the scribbled list of independent beers and breweries, and, underneath, a note from the pub asking its customers for suggestions. All of a sudden, the dark room is drenched in a bright red glow as the number 88 stops in front of the pub. The floor-to-ceiling window is covered by the side of the bus, and every corner of the pub is saturated in its colour.

I hold the pleasing handle of my tankard, take my last sip and reach for my coat. A rich cooking smell fills the room. The barman briskly walks through the space carrying a large roast joint on a tray. Fresh out of the oven, the scent and crackle travel around the space, alerting each punter that the pub's famous 'MEAT' has arrived. The roast is taken to the far end of the bar and placed inside a heated glass box; it is then shredded and made ready for the popular pork baps. Everything that happens inside The Southampton Arms is a humble ritual: the everyday workings – from the cooking, the pouring of ales and the arrival of new guests – are close by for all to observe inside the one small room of the pub.

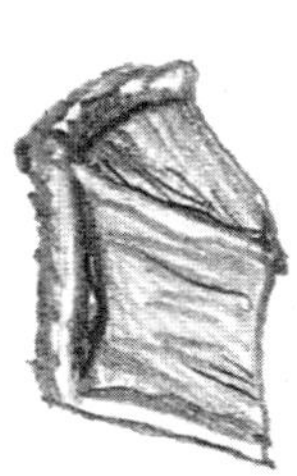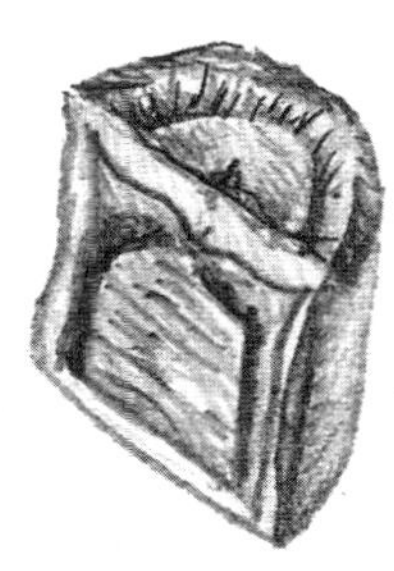

'One of my favourite memories of the Dog and Bell
in Deptford is stumbling across it whilst walking
to Greenwich for a Greenwich pub crawl with my
then new boyfriend, going in for "one" and not
leaving for the whole day.'
REBECCA

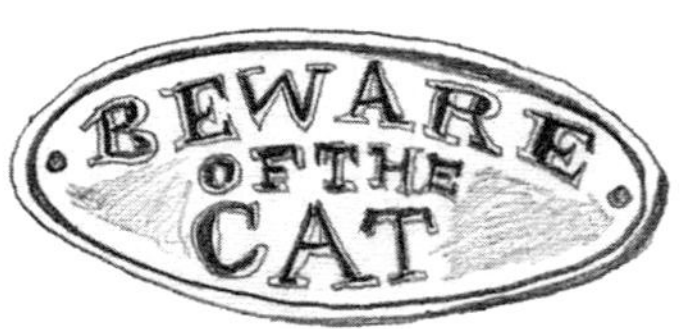

CATS

You will see the signs of a resident pub cat if you look for them, be it the food bowls hidden in a quiet corner, a round fluffy bed, feline-themed artwork or – in the rarest of cases – the cats themselves.

Their quiet command of the space is palpable and demands respect. You are entering their home, after all. A resident cat can be as integral to a pub's character as the furniture they lie upon. They add a homely charm, their distinct characters are well known by the regulars and, undoubtedly, they are part of a pub's community.

When I come across a pub with a resident feline, my excitement to sketch them is clear to see as I follow them round the bar, keeping a respectful distance and scribbling their cute faces with my pencil. I try my best to catch the tiniest detail, whether that's a fluffy white chest, a diamanté collar or a grumpy demeanour. I'll often place the cat next to the pub, sitting up proudly as if guarding their domain. They are always the perfect addition to my sketch, the pub and my day.

The Lord Tredegar, Mile End

Beyoncé

I turn down College Terrace in Mile End and am confronted by a
wide building at the other end of the street: a pub with striking black
paint and brickwork, sandwiched between two terraced houses.
The Lord Tredegar draws me to it like a beacon. There is a small
island opposite the pub that holds space for a parking bollard –
it's the perfect piece of pavement for my easel and me, so I decide
to claim it and face the pub for the day.

The pub is emerging on the paper from my steady lines and continuous
shading when I notice a small figure in the doorway. Her eyes pop
brightly against the darkness of the closed pub. I quickly scribble her
shape, her alert ears and beady stare, next to the iron railing before
she saunters across the street to greet me. She knows something
unusual is happening outside her pub and she's come to inspect it.

She beckons me to someone's front doorstep, and I oblige.
She flops down on her side, and I offer a hand. She bats it away.
There's a loud bang from an engine two streets over, and she darts
back across the road to oversee the keg deliveries instead. I know
I've just met the pub cat, Beyoncé, and this is her gaff.

The day continues to cement itself in my memory. I witness a
couple transport a king-size mattress on their heads, I meet a nine-
year-old aspiring artist and have countless encounters with lovely
locals. I've nearly finished the drawing – a couple of free drinks later
– by the time the pub opens at 4 p.m. I order a pint of local ale at
the bar and relax for a while, knowing my work is not done yet.

Across from me I see a black paw poking out from a large red
leather armchair. This is my chance to finish Beyoncé's portrait,

the final piece of my artwork. The resident cat sits comfortably on her red leather throne; I continue to draw her likeness as she poses for me and accepts chin scratches in return.

The Lord Tredegar is both home and public house. I meet the proprietors along with their baby daughter, who claps and giggles as I show them my drawing – the sweetest round of applause I've ever received for a finished piece. They welcome me to their family establishment just as they welcome neighbours to Beyoncé's tenth birthday party a year later. With themed games, drawing competitions and even a Beyoncé birthday cake, the party and the people who attend it show how Beyoncé and pub cats everywhere are loved by their locals and how much of a celebrity they can be.

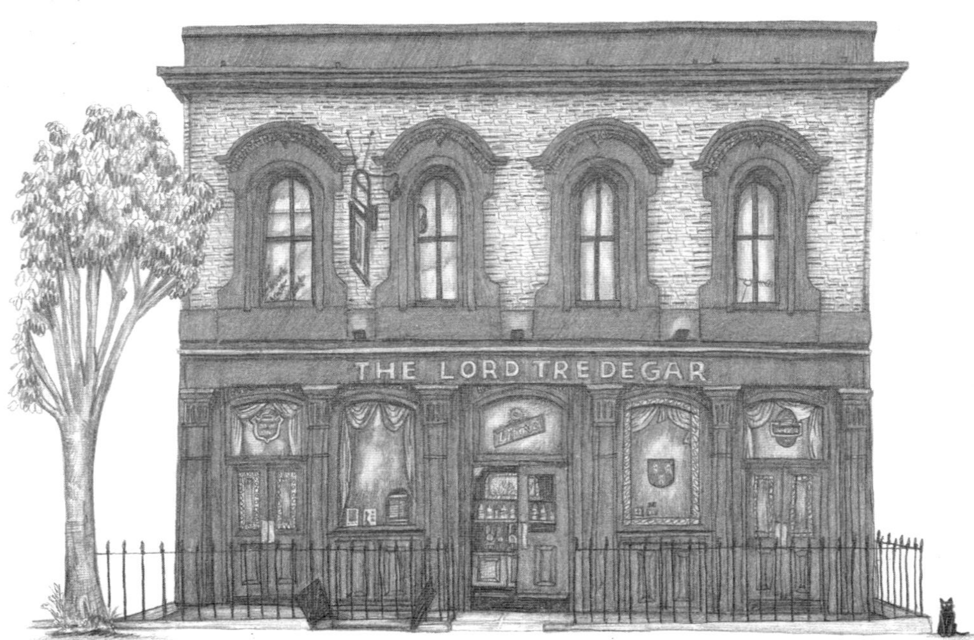

The Seven Stars, Holborn

The General

The General is probably London's most recognisable pub cat, mainly for the fact he sometimes wears a ruff for a collar. The Elizabethan accessory is fitting given that The Seven Stars, thought to be one of London's oldest drinking establishments, dates back to 1602.

As I sketch in the white fabric curtains and the warm light glowing from inside the Grade II listed alehouse, I imagine William Shakespeare strolling in for a tankard after working at the nearby Blackfriars Theatre. I think of Dutch sailors merrily piling out of the door after settling nearby and visiting this local over four hundred years ago. In my mind, I see time passing: the medieval streets that surround the pub transform and the Royal Courts of Justice are built opposite, changing the face of Carey Street forever. I imagine the judges and barristers celebrating closed court cases, relaxing in the cosy tavern, as they still do today.

Inside, I look around to see The Seven Stars' charming wonky red ceiling, the bright chequered tablecloths and the snug, which is aptly nicknamed the 'Wig Box' and was originally a legal wig shop later obtained and renovated by the pub. I hand a calendar, which contains my drawing of the Seven Stars, over to the infamous landlady, Roxy Beaujolais, who briskly asks me to leave it on the bar as she hurries away. I oblige, slightly embarrassed, and head upstairs by squeezing up the extremely narrow staircase, careful not to knock any of the frames off the wall. Out of the corner of my eye, I spy an open door next to the toilets, The General lounges on the carpet of the small private office space, his ruff sits on the desk above his head – he's evidently off-duty today.

Heading back outside with my beer, I join the other punters spilling on to the tranquil street, some perching on the opposite wall, others sitting on the pavement in front of the quirky little boozer. I too sit on the wall and behold the pub that's seen it all, surviving both the Great Fire of London and two world wars. I come back to visit a few months later, surprised to find my calendar hanging at the back of the bar for all to see, the greatest compliment, if ever there was one. The Seven Stars is an institution, one with a rich history and filled with extraordinary character. The magic of the pub today owes much to Roxy and to the five generations of ruff-wearing pub cats who've called it home in recent years.

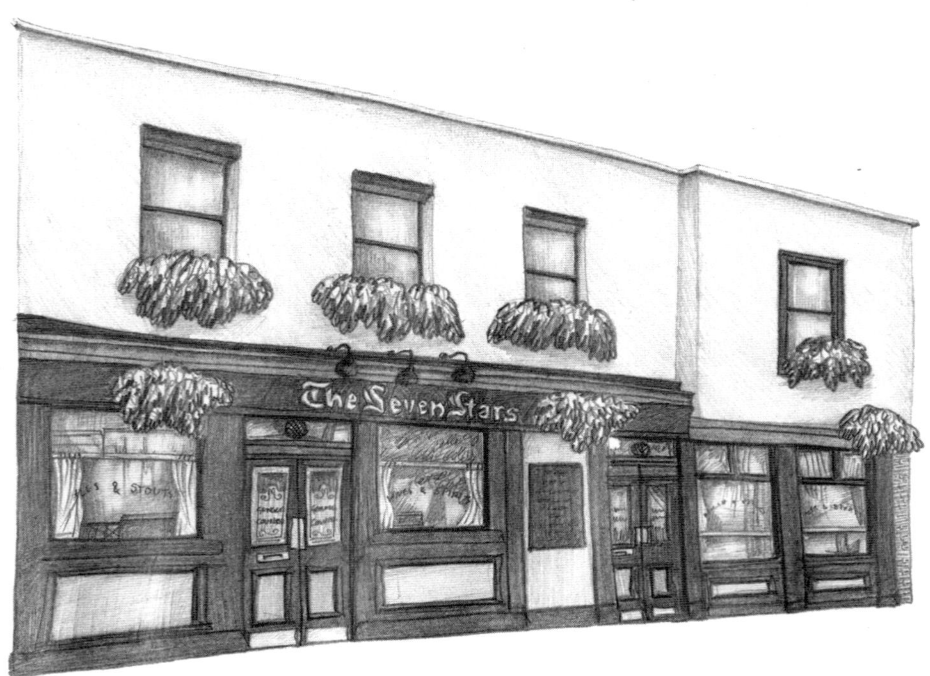

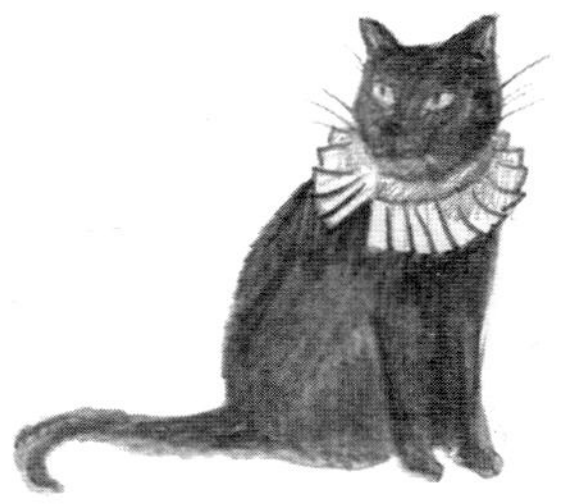

Tom Paine, 2002–2012

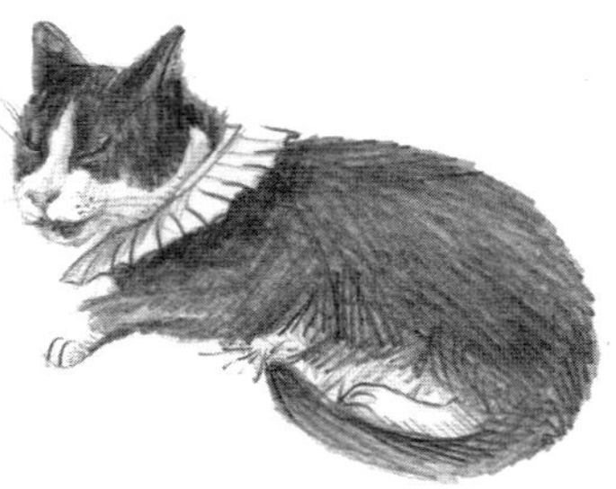

Ray Brown, 2012–2014

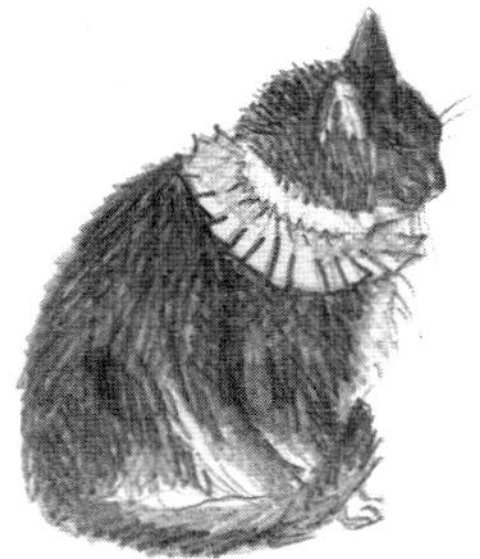

Peabody, 2016–2019

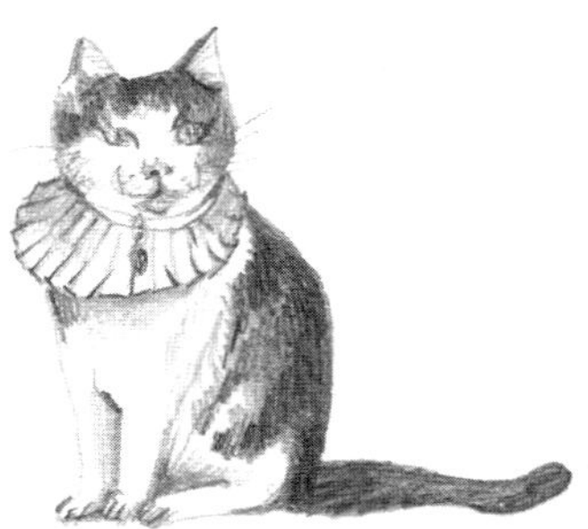

Clement Atlee, 2018
– enjoying retirement

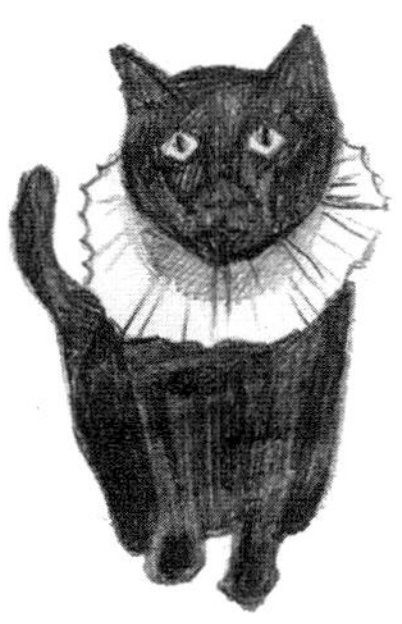

The General, 2021
– present purveyor

The Rosemary Branch Theatre, Islington

Mariah

Every week eagerly await for 'Mariah Monday' on The Rosemary Branch's Instagram page. The pub account shares photos of their resident feline playing cards, climbing on boxes of deliveries and draped in tinsel – her namesake, the Christmas icon Mariah Carey, would be proud!

I come to visit The Rosemary Branch early on in my project, with no choice but to plonk myself down on the traffic island in the middle of a very busy road to get the best angle. No easel yet so it's just me, my pencil case, sketchbook and a rickety travel stool. I lean my sketchbook on my lap, crouch over the page and begin the outline of the pub. My pencil copies its curved corner shape, and I sketch in each individual brick attentively. The pub/theatre sits directly next to another pub-looking building, now converted flats. The Southgate Arms faces its neighbour, green tiles and signage standing strong, though sadly no longer a running pub.

I take my sketchbook inside, relieved to find serenity away from the rushing cars. There's a small theatre upstairs which hosts an exciting variety of performances and I notice a very impressive collection of board games in the corner. Some friends who live nearby join me as we relax over a pint and one informs me that I've forgotten to draw the striking wings that crown the top of the pub. Instead of heading back outside to draw them, I stay late into the evening, playing games and dancing beside a life size cardboard cut-out of Dolly Parton. Since then, I've realised that they're not the only thing missing from my drawing. When the pub adopts Mariah, a new permanent fixture, I decide she's a detail my drawing can't be without.

This diva's origin story is one of rags to riches: a sudden appearance outside the pub, followed by regular visits, prompted the manager who lives there into action. Attempts to locate Mariah's owner were fruitless, so the kind team at The Rosemary Branch welcomed their new feline friend in with open arms. Fittingly, today I find the legend donning a glitzy diamanté collar. She wears a new design every week.

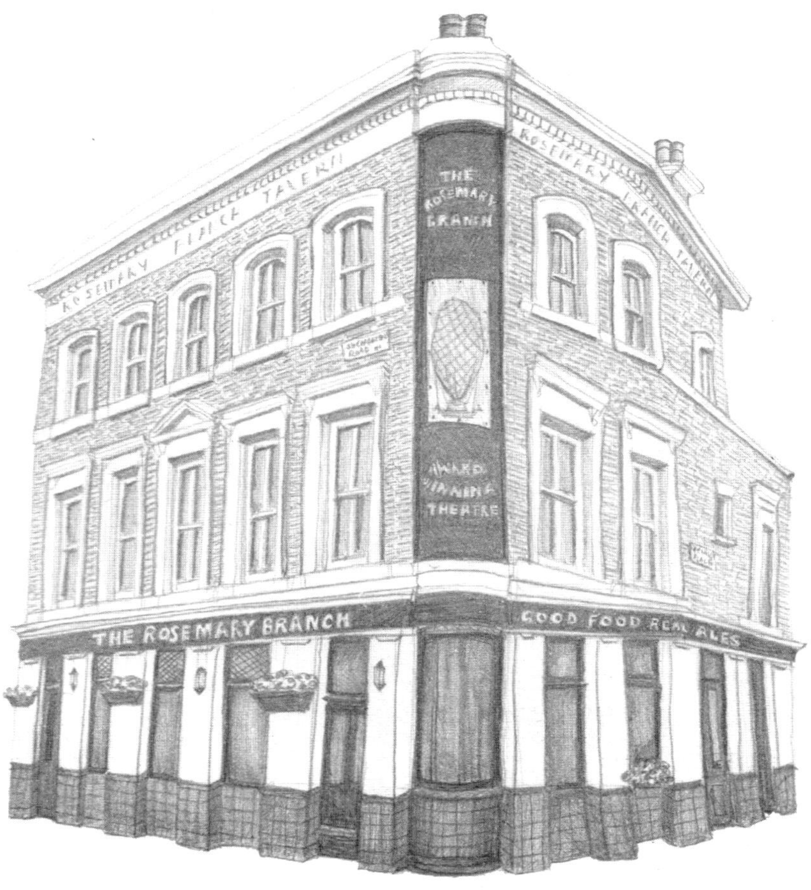

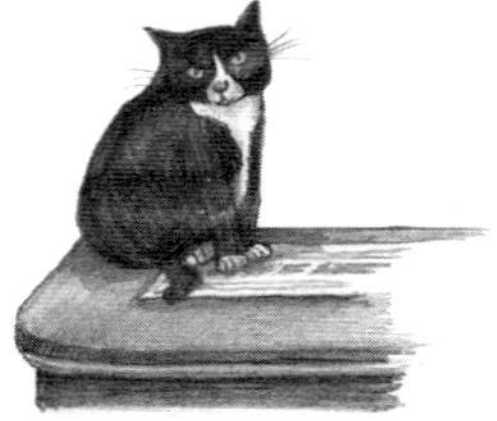

The Plume of Feathers, Greenwich

Matey

I have never met Matey, the pub cat at The Plume of Feathers. The oldest pub in Greenwich, dating back to 1691, it's now a family-run pub, licensed by the Rose family since the 1980s. I have been to the Plume a handful of times and seen the plaque that greets you at the front door: 'Beware of the cat'. I've also read the small blackboard sign on the bar: 'Beware! Grumpy cat has been extra grumpy recently, so stay clear and approach at your own peril!' But I have never seen the grouchy feline himself.

Today is the day I am set on drawing The Plume of Feathers. Located next to Greenwich Park, it's one of the most serene sketching locations I've come across. Originally, the inn was on the busy Dover Road, the main route out of Greenwich towards Kent. Horse-drawn carts would pass by the ideally located tavern, where travellers could break their journey. Today, barely a car or passerby travels along the quiet backstreet. The weather is chilly, and the trees are bare as I draw their reflections in the windows. Two friends who come to sit out front are the first people I see all day; I draw their relaxed posture and the different shades of the tiles that form their backdrop. I meet Sue, the landlady, who says she's flattered I'm drawing the pub and welcomes me inside after I've finished my work.

I add the final touches to my artwork just in time to escape the looming April drizzle. I run inside looking for a cup of tea to warm up and the missing piece for my drawing: Matey. Again, he is nowhere to be seen. I ask after him, wondering if I may have missed him snoozing in the back. Sue checks upstairs, he is there, asleep, taking a well deserved break. As I can see from the pub's interiors,

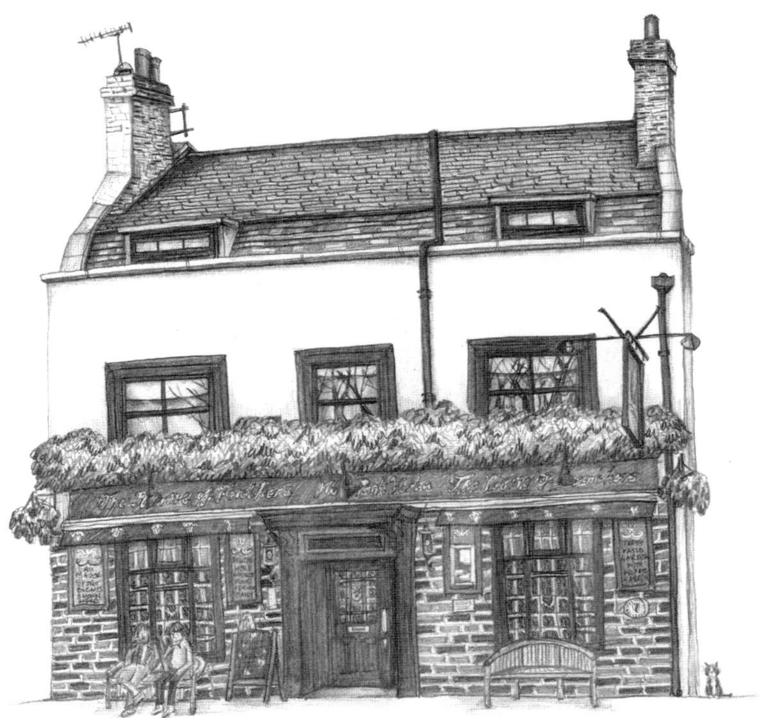

this is a feline who runs a tight ship. There is an open fire that pleasantly warms the room, and a group of old friends eat lunch while I warm up my fingers and check out the curated collection decorating the walls: plates, clocks, framed portraits and royal photographs. The Plume of Feathers, a gold emblem of three ostrich feathers and the heraldic badge of the Prince of Wales, can be seen adorning the bar.

So as not to disturb Matey sleeping, I work from a photograph shown to me by the barstaff, who chuckle at his cantankerous ways. Since that day I still haven't ever caught a glimpse of Matey in the flesh, but one day I hope to meet him and show him his portrait – from a distance.

Tapping the Admiral, Kentish Town

Nelson

Tapping the Admiral takes its name from an unpleasant and possibly apocryphal sort of drink. After the death of the British naval officer Horatio Nelson, his body was said to have been placed and preserved in a barrel of rum or brandy for the long journey home from the Battle of Trafalgar. Legend has it that the sailors would often 'tap' into the barrel, drinking the alcohol to toast the late admiral. It's also said that Nelson's uncle lived near the original pub and often brought his nephew with him to drink there. It makes sense then, that with this history, the resident cat is called Nelson.

Often seen sitting at the bar as if ordering a pint, napping in his fluffy bed or swiping a seat from the regulars, Nelson is a well-regarded personality of the pub. As I sit across the road sketching the building's exterior, I catch glimpses of him throughout my drawing day as he ambles around his domain. These sporadic sightings mean I can piece together his portrait – his wiry whiskers, white socks and big beady eyes. I decide to place him beside the pile of kegs, beneath the leafy tree in my sketch.

I take a trip inside to find that there are multiple artworks devoted to Nelson and the pub itself. The interior is spacious, and the familiar combination of deep red furniture and wooden surrounds keep the room comfortable. There are a few locals dotted around the space, each one known by name. There's a long line-up of cask ales and ciders on the bar, and as I wait for my drink, I notice a small golden plaque dedicated to a treasured regular who has recently passed. I find Nelson asleep on a chair; I take a quick photo before running back outside to sketch his fluffy white bib.

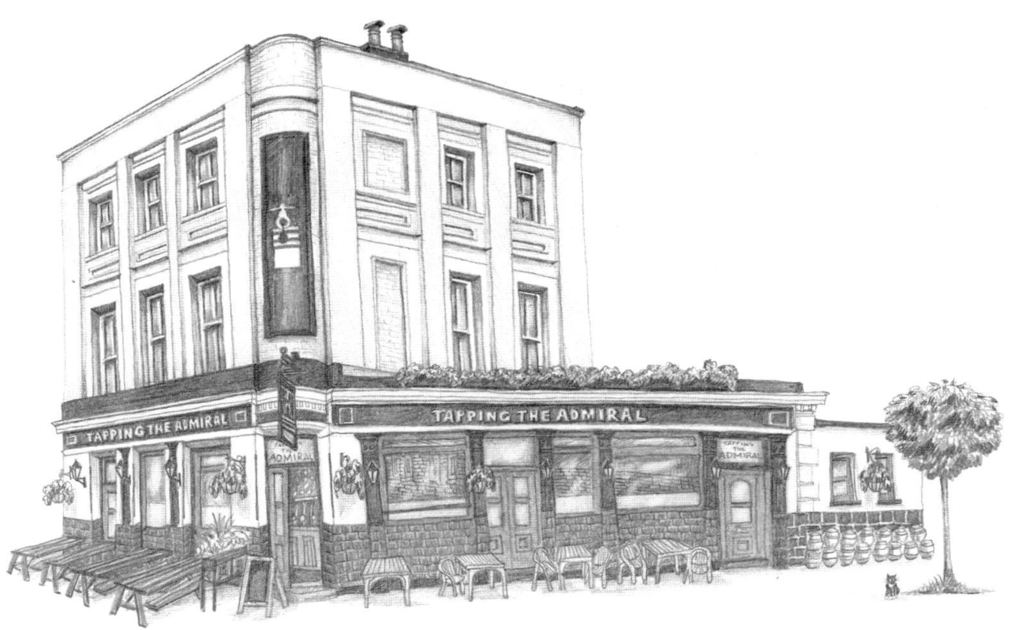

He's not the only regular I meet. A local named Jeff is a familiar face at Tapping the Admiral. He introduces me to the other usual punters and carries my finished drawing around for the whole pub to admire. He pops in and out to see my artwork develop throughout the afternoon, looking out for me and wholeheartedly welcoming me to his local. Nelson the pub cat, just like the seasoned regulars, is a treasured part of this community. They run alongside each other harmoniously, they are part of the furniture, and the pub would no doubt be very different without them.

ALLEYWAY

There is something extra special about happening
upon a backstreet boozer, and it's even better when
that place is found amongst a web of alleyways.
As you intuitively wind your way down crooked city
streets that have wound like this for hundreds of years,
it's as if you're walking through history or a stage set
– as long as you ignore the shiny silver skyscrapers
towering above your head.

When I first started this project, I was daunted by the pubs that
lived along alleyways, thinking of the perspective lines my pencil
would have to carefully replicate, the specific shadows the narrow
walls would cast and the physical process of finding the best spot to
draw from. Now, I seek out these city corridors, emphasising the
alleyway's characteristics and enjoying the unusual space in
which I find myself sketching.

There are pubs that curve round alleyways, some that sit at
the very dead end of them and others that are split in two by
the narrow pathways. It's easy to love an old London pub
hidden down an alleyway, like precious treasure, but it's
not always easy to draw them.

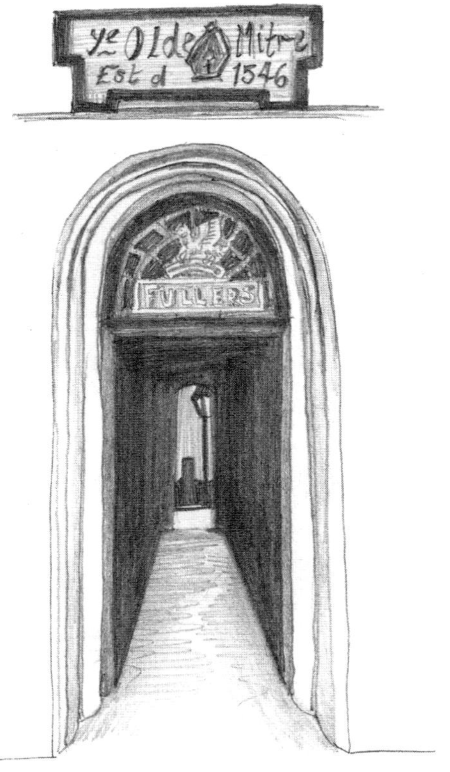
Ye Olde Mitre
Est d 1546
FULLERS

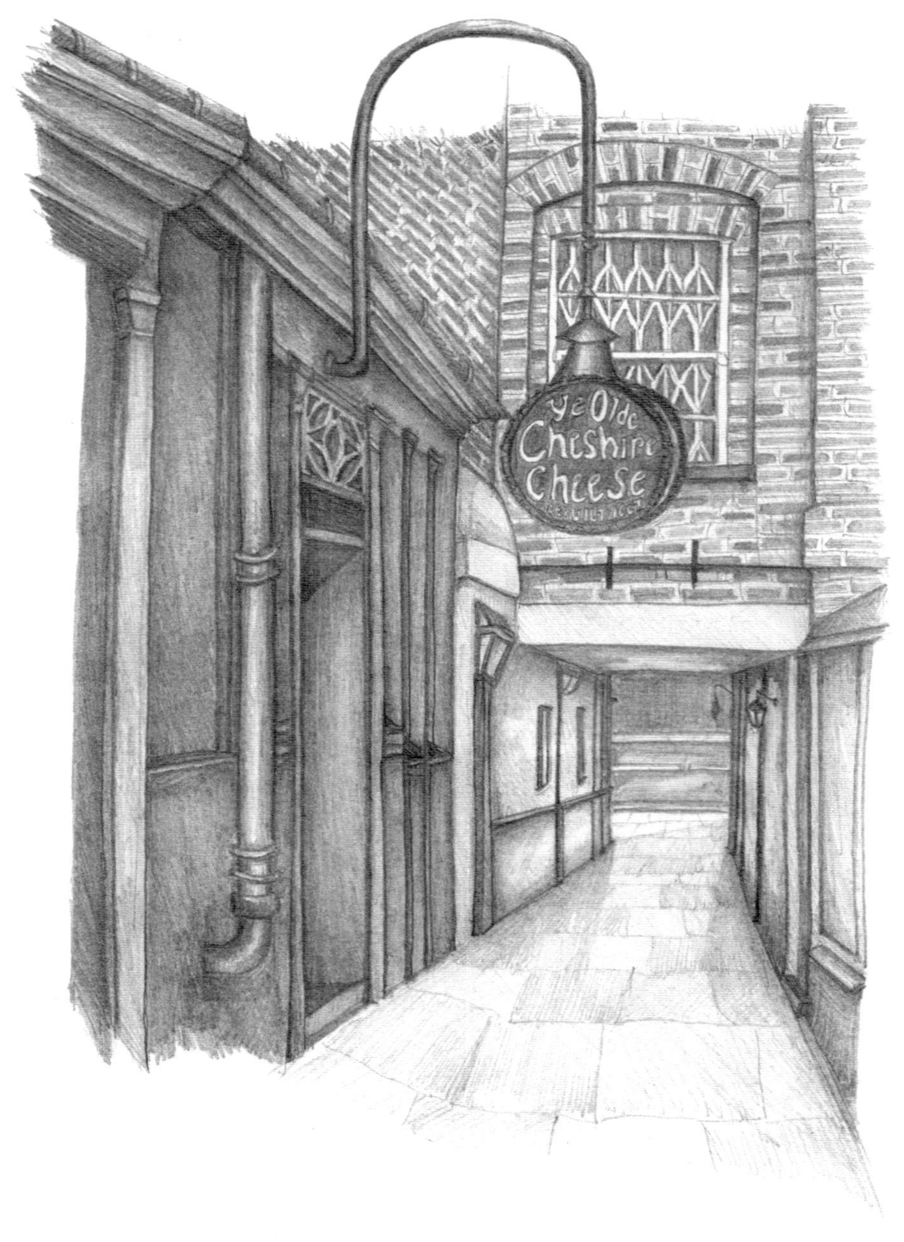
Ye Olde
Cheshire
Cheese

Ye Olde Cheshire Cheese, Fleet Street

I stroll down busy Fleet Street, a road scattered with a healthy number of historic pubs. It's mid-morning and a wave of suits head out for coffee breaks and business meetings across town. On the other side of the street, a large tour group fills the walkway and stern Londoners huff as they drop off the pavement into the road to swerve the crowd, narrowly missing the passing buses as they do. I instead fixate on the large lantern that illuminates the archway to my right – I know this is my cue to turn off the bustling city street and down the alleyway that is Wine Office Court. Another circular black sign juts out above my head, and this is where I find the pub I want to draw today: one wall with windows, a door and a sign.

Before I tackle the outline of Ye Olde Cheshire Cheese, I tackle the alleyway. Predictably, this alleyway is thin and narrow. Houses, stoops and a falafel shop line the street opposite the pub. The pavement is too slim for me to stand and draw, where I would anyway be too close to see the pub head-on. After being denied access to sit in a couple's doorway for the day, I opt for the small wall where the footpath begins to widen. I place my sketchbook on the wall and stand as far out of the way as possible. I am challenged by perspective lines and gloomy shadows and ultimately, I succumb to the fact that my drawing will be all alleyway. I walk down the narrow path and imagine doing so 350 years ago, each step contributing to the uneven paving stones, and eventually I enter Ye Olde Cheshire Cheese through its large sloping door.

The feeling of discovery and time travel doesn't end at the alleyway. Stepping over the threshold, the corridor ahead of me is shrouded in darkness. Dimly lit chandeliers, an open fire and quiet conversation transport me to the seventeenth century.

It's almost museum-like in its 'oldness', with more 'mind your head' signs than choices of beer: this is a pub so well maintained that it's hard to believe its authenticity. I duck under a beam and down the steep steps to the basement, thought to be the oldest part of the building, dating back to the thirteenth century and belonging to the Carmelite monastery that once occupied this site. The vaulted cellars are eerie, only the low mutterings of lunchtime punters can be heard amidst the gloomy brick corners. Re-emerging up the stairs, I hear a gentle clanging of cutlery ringing across from the Chop Room, where traditional meat pies are being served beside an open fire.

The portraits and photographs that hang on the walls tell me a story of past punters and proprietors. One famous resident of Ye Olde Cheshire Cheese is Polly the parrot, now stuffed and sitting above the bar, once an African grey renowned for mimicking punters and regurgitating their bad language around the pub. On her death in 1926, the announcement was reported across hundreds of newspapers and on the radio. I glance up at the feathered celebrity as I continue to revel in the corner of history I find myself in. I exit the pub looking back at the warm light glimmering through the stippled glass, which harks to the days of candlelight. I consider that this passage might be part of the charm of the place, and I decide it's the perfect angle for my drawing after all.

The Ship and Shovell, Charing Cross

Every time I visit The Ship and Shovell, I find myself in the alleyway
that divides it. In the bitter cold months, the pub's interior is full
to the brim. I wrap up and opt for a space outside in the cold,
heading inside only to warm my toes and order a round at the bar.
On a scorching hot day, when the passageway fills with people
enjoying the longer days and the loud voices bounce off the walls,
I will always stand beside the barrel that holds my drink alongside
huddles of other visitors.

I arrive to a deserted alleyway, the scaffolding now removed, the
windows dark. I head towards the tall black lamp post at the far
end of the lane and take my tripod out of my bag. I place my travel
stool beside the lamp post and sit down at my easel using the post
as my backrest. I look up at the pub, which is comprised of two
buildings, originally two separate terraced houses that were turned
into two distinct pubs: The Ship on one side and The Shovell on the
other. Despite the remaining physical division, today it is a single
pub. One Ship and Shovell, owned by one brewery and connected
by one underground tunnel. While the exterior buildings are a close
match, harmonious with their red paint, matching lettering and
brickwork tops, their interiors are a different story.

I like that you can opt for either interior on any given visit and
therefore conjure a different experience from within the same pub.
The larger interior of The Ship and Shovell is an open space with
gilded mirrors that glisten from the light of the chandeliers, a model
ship that lives in the fireplace and the curved wooden bar that is the
focal point of the large room. I walk over to the south side of the
pub, the smaller of the two halves, where the character is different.
The red patterned ceiling overhead brings warmth to the room.

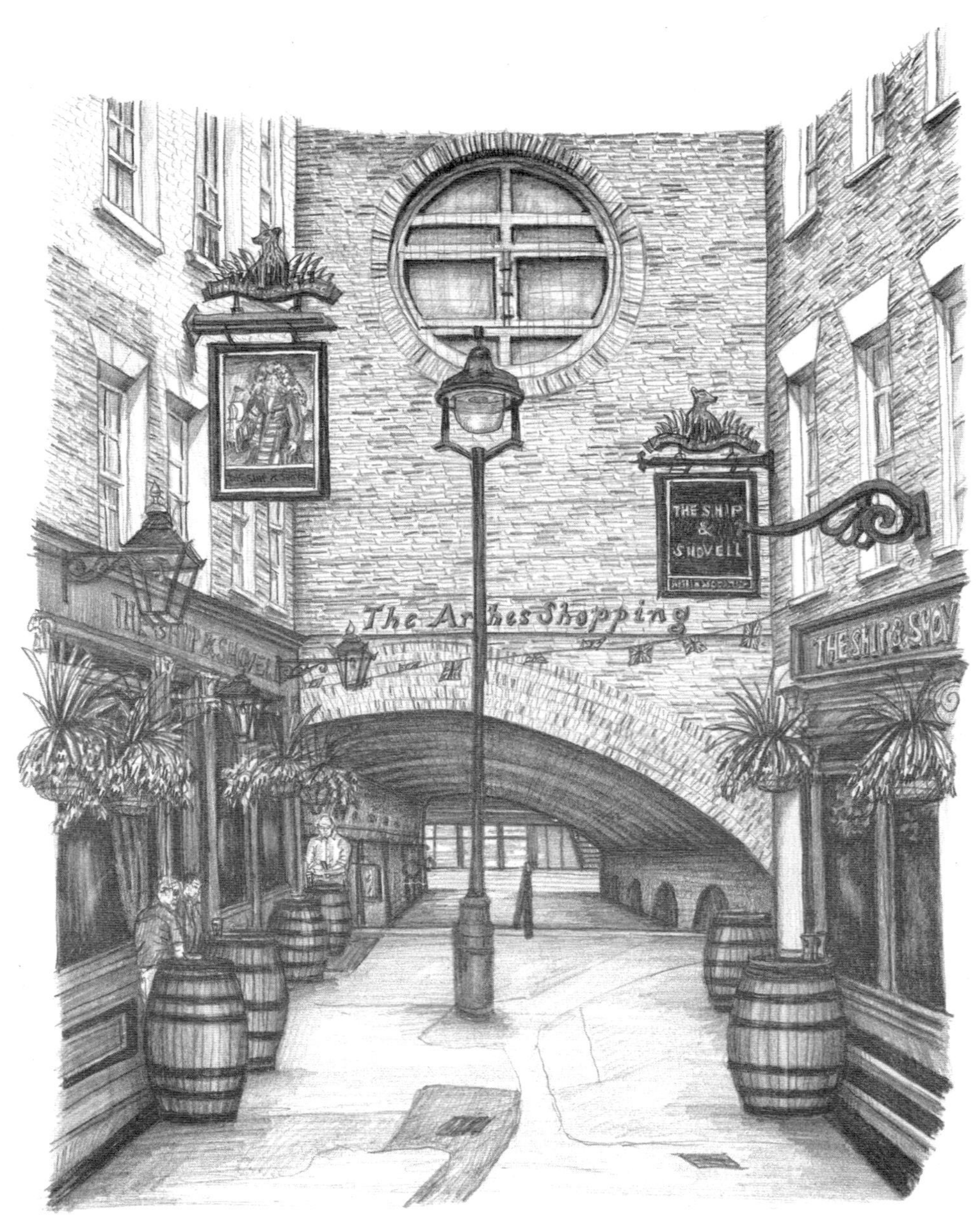
THE SHIP & SHOVELL
THE SHIP & SHOVELL
THE SHIP & SHOVELL
The Arches Shopping

There are snugs and booths, wooden screens that separate tables and a small bar as you walk in. Both sections of the divided pub have distinct characters and vibes.

Outside, I choose to draw the alleyway, and pub, head-on. I sketch in the different details that protrude from the pub and over the empty space: the swinging signs, the lanterns and the hanging baskets. From this angle, it is necessary to include the brick wall, shopping passage and the distant street that form a backdrop to the scene. The drawing is ninety per cent alleyway and only about ten per cent pub. The inevitability of this leads me to think that the alleyway – like the pavement to many Soho boozers – is an extension of the space and really a part of the pub. Craven Passage doesn't divide these buildings after all, it connects them. That is why it feels natural to stand in the alleyway every time I visit; it beats as the very heart of The Ship and Shovell.

Ye Olde Mitre, Hatton Garden

Whenever I come to Ye Olde Mitre, I walk down Hatton Garden, mesmerised by the diamond shops, sickeningly curious to see who goes in and out of them, so much so that I miss the turn-off for the pub – every single time!

In my defence, it is one of many rounded archways that are repeated down the street, the others leading you to diamond merchants and more concealed passageways. The alleyway I want, which will lead me to the pub, is Ely Court. Outdoor tables and chairs line one wall, leaving just enough space for a short, single-file stroll to the small courtyard in front of Ye Olde Mitre. A smaller passageway leads me round to a choice of two entrances and, even further round the building, at the back, a beer garden is hidden.

Early on in my project and without an easel, I choose to sit at one of the tables that line the main alleyway and use it as my drawing board for the afternoon. I wrap my scarf tightly round my neck, burrowing into the warmth of the fabric, trying to shelter from the draught whistling along the narrow passage behind me. I order a cup of tea and concentrate on drawing the crown glass. Each circular puddle punctuates random panes of the large windows, rippling like water to its outer edge, with a bullseye in the centre. One side of the pub hides behind a brick wall, so I fixate on the barrels that hide the front of the building and the mass of plants that hang over it.

I suddenly notice my tea start to dance, the milky surface broken by the same ripples I have just drawn on the glass windows in my sketchbook. The rain gets harder, my page gets soggier, I decide it's time to shelter inside. I enter the small and relaxed interior, the patterned carpet and beer-bottle-lined room compelling me to hide in a warm corner. Near the bar, there's an unusual sight.

Stretching from floor to ceiling, a tree trunk stands encased in glass: a cherry tree once said to have occupied this alleyway. Queen Elizabeth I and Sir Christopher Hatton, politician, commoner and the queen's favourite, apparently danced around this tree that now holds up the front of the pub.

I order a cheese and pickle sandwich, and the bright yellow mustard is so hot my eyes start to water. I finish my lunch, try to count the mugs on the ceiling and succumb to the cosiness of the pub, opting to come back and finish my drawing another time.

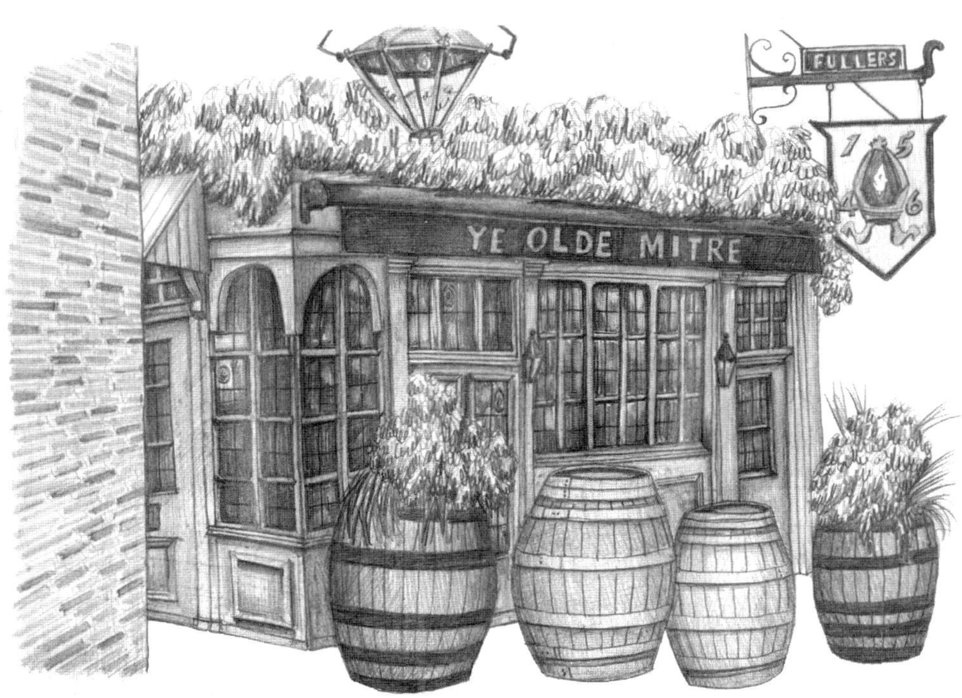

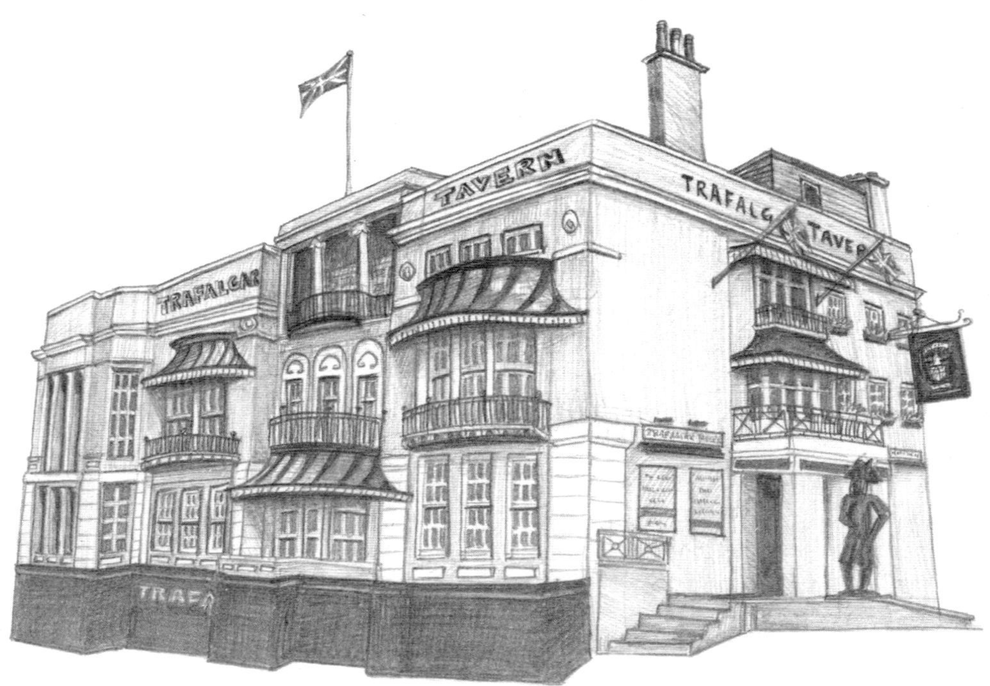

Trafalgar Tavern, Greenwich

I stroll along the narrow Thames Path, with Greenwich behind me and the grand white museum buildings at my side. I watch the water slap against the wall beneath me, raising a cold spray that hits my ankle, and I speed up to escape the next sway of the river. Soon, I am greeted by the Trafalgar Tavern; the cobbles in front of the pub are lined with benches looking out at the choppy water. Glancing up at the grand frontage, I am struck by its powerful presence and the way it commands the water beneath it and everything else around it.

People fill up the benches, grabbing the best seats outside the pub even on a blustery day. Some elegantly drink glasses of wine and eat little battered whitebait, others hunch in big groups chatting over each other rowdily. The solid pub dominates the space, and visitors take photos with the building and all its accoutrements, like the interconnecting and never-ending fairy lights that create a warm yellow glow around the pub, and the bronze statue of Admiral Nelson, made by local artist Lesley Pover, much photographed and posed with. Nelson, popping his hip, looks unamused.

I draw the elegant structures around the curved bay windows, the fine white lines framing the glass. The satisfying bowed awnings cast shadows over the balconies, and I finely etch the small white trim on their edges. The bottom of the pub disappears into the river, and that's where my drawing ends.

Inside the impressive tavern I stumble into an array of magnificently decorated rooms. The gallery walls display an unending collection of paintings, depicting nautical scenes, historic portraits and local landmarks, each one ornately framed in gold. Glass chandeliers dominate the ceiling space and sparkle as they catch the lights behind them. Natural light also floods the rooms, seeping through the wide curved windows, which look out over the water. The large space from the seats by the bar to the tables in the window bay is full to the brim with people and noise, and the lively atmosphere beckons me to stay a while, so I take a seat with my drawing and a small white wine. The opulent interior continues to fill as the evening draws in, so eventually I take my leave and head outside for some quiet.

While the Trafalgar Tavern is an unlikely addition to this chapter, the grand pub also known as the 'Jewel of the Thames' is included here because it boasts one of my favourite external aspects – and I'm not referring to its popular river view. As I peer round the back of the pub, I find the quiet passageway that leads you further down the Thames, away from Greenwich. It's an unexpected corridor nestled behind the grand building; little cobbles make a small line down the middle of the larger paving slabs, each stone a different size that makes for an uneven walking surface. Looking up at the pub's back wall, I see mounds of beautiful flowers in different hues of red, purple and green. As I continue down the path, away from the crowds, I find I am sheltered from the wind blowing across the river and cocooned by the walls either side of me. I look up in awe at the hundreds of flags, from all over the world, dangling across the space and moving in unison, so many that it appears like one block of fabric. Their tangled strings and vibrant colour create a softly swaying ceiling right above my head, guiding me further down the alleyway.

The Cockpit, Blackfriars

The Cockpit sweeps round the alleyway that is Ireland Yard. My easel stands between me and the pub, and I am sandwiched between my easel and the bike racks behind me. I look up and notice the small rectangular plaque on the building opposite, which tells me William Shakespeare purchased lodgings in this area in 1613. The curvy corner pub is a joy to stumble across amongst the interconnected backstreets of Blackfriars, and it stops tourists in their tracks to pose for photos.

I am keen to draw the alleyway to the pub's right. Because of the tricky angle, my drawing takes me twice as long as normal to complete. During my two-day venture, I witness the ebb and flow of the city through the scenes outside the pub. As soon as it hits midday, smartly dressed groups of co-workers stroll up the hill to queue outside a little Vietnamese restaurant to the right of the pub for their bánh mì. After this lunch rush, the space outside The Cockpit begins to fill with more city workers, choosing to follow their sandwich with a lunchtime pint. From 2 p.m., the alleyway begins to clear and only a couple of blokes stay behind. They stand in the shadow of the pub, down the narrowing road to the right; they chat and smoke. I intensely jot down details of their poses before their cigarettes burn out. One looks down at his phone, the other stares straight ahead, almost directly at me, as if noticing he is having his portrait scribbled.

I turn my attention to the pub's swinging sign. I attentively sketch the two cockerels in the midst of battle, drawing their fanned wings and sharp claws, a powerful painting representing the pub's dark past. The blood sport was prohibited in England from 1835 so perhaps this is what prompted the pub to change its name to The Three Castles and distance itself from the violence, before reverting to its historic namesake again in 1970. Now, feeling tired but triumphant, I proudly take a photo of the finished piece and head inside with my drawing. I enter the modest carpeted room and look up at the balcony that lines the space. This is where punters would stand and watch the cruel cockfights, placing their bets and shouting down to the pit in which I currently stand. Today, the calmness of the pub seems antithetical to its namesake. The different seats around the room host everyone from regulars and after-work drinkers to tour groups. Behind the bar is Candice, who has worked at The Cockpit for fifteen years. I show her the two scribbly figures I've included at the side of the pub; she immediately knows their names, how long they've been drinking here and their professions. She kindly offers me a pale ale on the house and introduces me to the group of regulars around the bar. We strike up a conversation about where my next adventure will take me, and they suggest new watering holes all over the city. From Candice's personal knowledge of the clientele to the friendly locals and fascinated visitors from all over the world, The Cockpit is a melting pot in the centre of London, hidden down an alleyway, waiting to be found.

'My favourite pub in the world. I used to travel to London for work a few times each year, and I stayed in a hotel near St Paul's. Every time I went to The Cockpit I was greeted as though I was a regular, which I clearly wasn't. Still, it felt like a home away from home – the carpet, the smell, the history, the people, it was heaven. I don't get to London as often as I used to, but I never miss a chance to go to The Cockpit…'

JASON

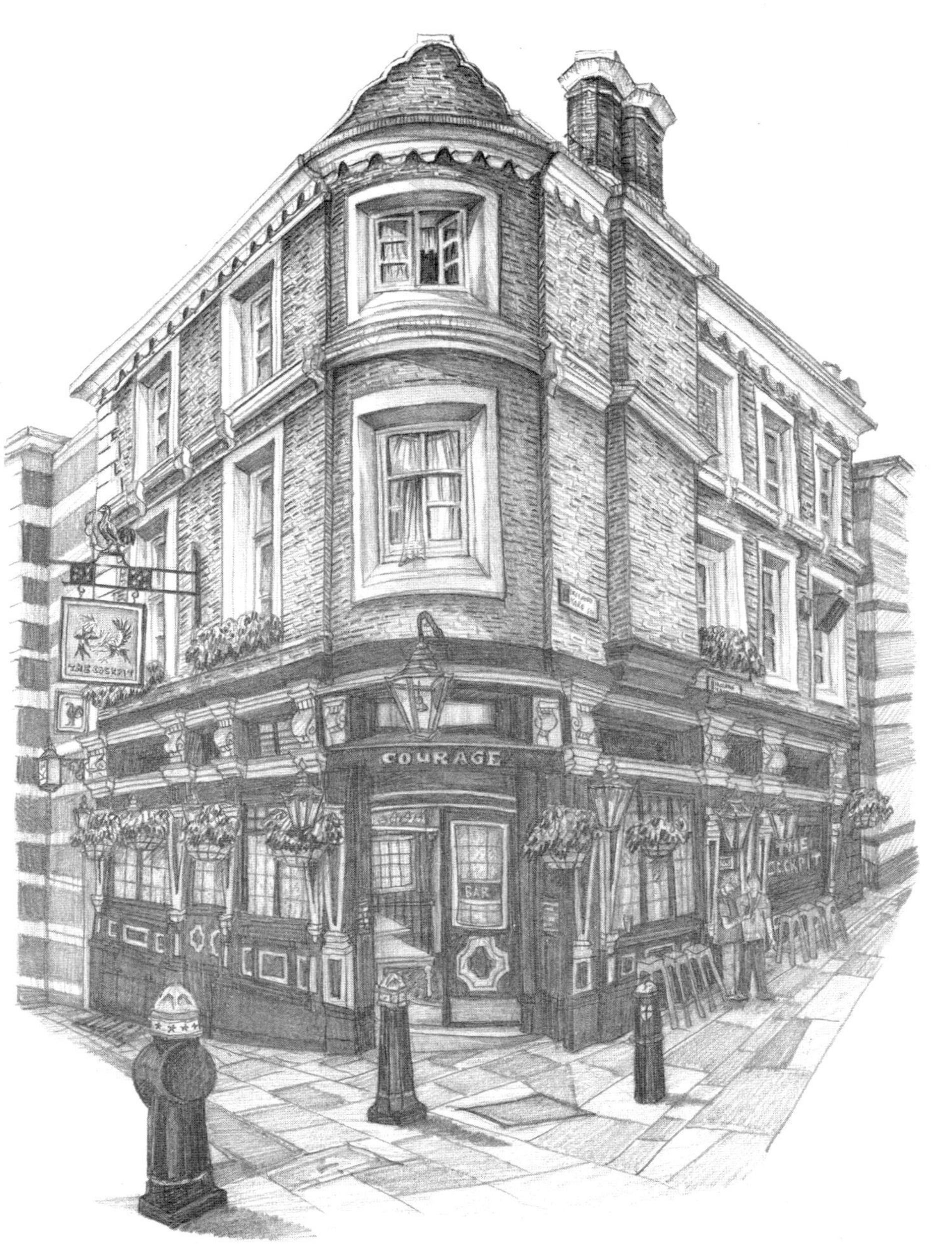
THE COCKPIT
COURAGE
BAR
THE COCKPIT

NAMES

The pub name 'Coach and Horses' typically derives
from the era when horse-drawn carriages were
transporting people across the city. The taverns that
lined the main travel routes were often referred to as
'coaching inns' during the eighteenth century. It's hard
to imagine that before the brightly lit rickshaw bikes
that blare music and transport giddy tourists on short
journeys around Soho today, there were once slower-
paced equine alternatives bumping over dirt tracks.

As I travel further through my project, I continue to build a portfolio
of drawings and it's interesting to find the similarities amongst
the hundreds of pubs I've already drawn. I soon discover a close
collection of pubs with the same name, and a project within a project
begins to emerge. I grab my pencil and head into Mayfair, Covent
Garden and Soho to visit these six central London pubs all called
The Coach and Horses.

In this chapter I find that although they are close in proximity,
they each have a unique architecture, backstory and character –
even if they do share a name.

The Coach and Horses, Greek Street, Soho

I tuck myself and my stool in a corner next to a boarded-up bay window, burrowing against the white wall and trying to disappear out of view. The Coach and Horses (aka Norman's Coach and Horses) sits opposite me, and a blank sketchbook page stares up at me from my lap, its well-travelled corners curling up at the edges. Attempting to ignore the jolting bangs and cracks of passing supercars, the sea of foot traffic centimetres from my crouching body and the incessant rumble of background noise, I zone in on the red and white building ahead of me.

I place the tip of my pencil at the centre of my page and draw the straight lines that make up either side of the pub. Then, I approach the curves, looking up to see which direction they travel down the street. The little rounded rectangle sits in the middle of the blank cream space, and it's difficult at this stage to imagine how it will transform into a detailed rendition of what might be Soho's most famous pub.

The cobbled space outside hosts a rabble of different groups: friends, family and co-workers, standing in circles, sipping their cold frothy pints. They don't notice me, in fact barely anyone does. Passersby move too quickly to pause and find me in the unsuspecting corner in which I'm perched. I squint at the details ahead of me, starting with the sun-washed windows which call for my rubber to dab away the light grey I've just shaded in. I sketch the columns that line the front of the building, and they pop against the windows that hide the pub's interior. I leave the signage to last. Hardly pressing the paper with my pencil, the small marks begin to resemble little horses. I carefully write each word, colouring around it and outlining it again. The letters are so small my pencil can barely fit them in.

Once I'm finished, I scramble up from my corner, gallop across the road and make my way through the people and into the pub. The Coach and Horses has one room and a long, straight bar curves around it at both ends. Two divider walls create archways and give the feeling of three different spaces. The floor is laid with cream, black and maroon tiles that criss-cross in a repeated pattern. They are worn away down to the floorboards near the bar. Here are the traces of footsteps left by regulars, as they shuffle in and out of their usual spot.

Each 'room' holds a few tables at different heights, stools with cushions and bar chairs with backs. Newspaper cuttings, paintings and posters are curated across the wood-panelled surroundings. One of my favourite artworks here is a very narrow painting depicting the gent's toilet by Mark Wade. 'NORMAN', painted in big, gold lettering on a metal sign, is tucked around the corner, a nod to the old landlord Norman Balon. An infamous character once known as London's rudest landlord amongst seasoned Soho regulars, he can sometimes be spotted playing cards in the pub today.

I often go back to The Coach and Horses where I order a perfectly smooth Guinness, am greeted by Ali the landlady and walk to the very end of the bar. I always stop just by the lifting gateway that staff use. I smile as I see my little drawing, hanging in a wooden frame, taking pride of place alongside the collection of other artworks that fill the space.

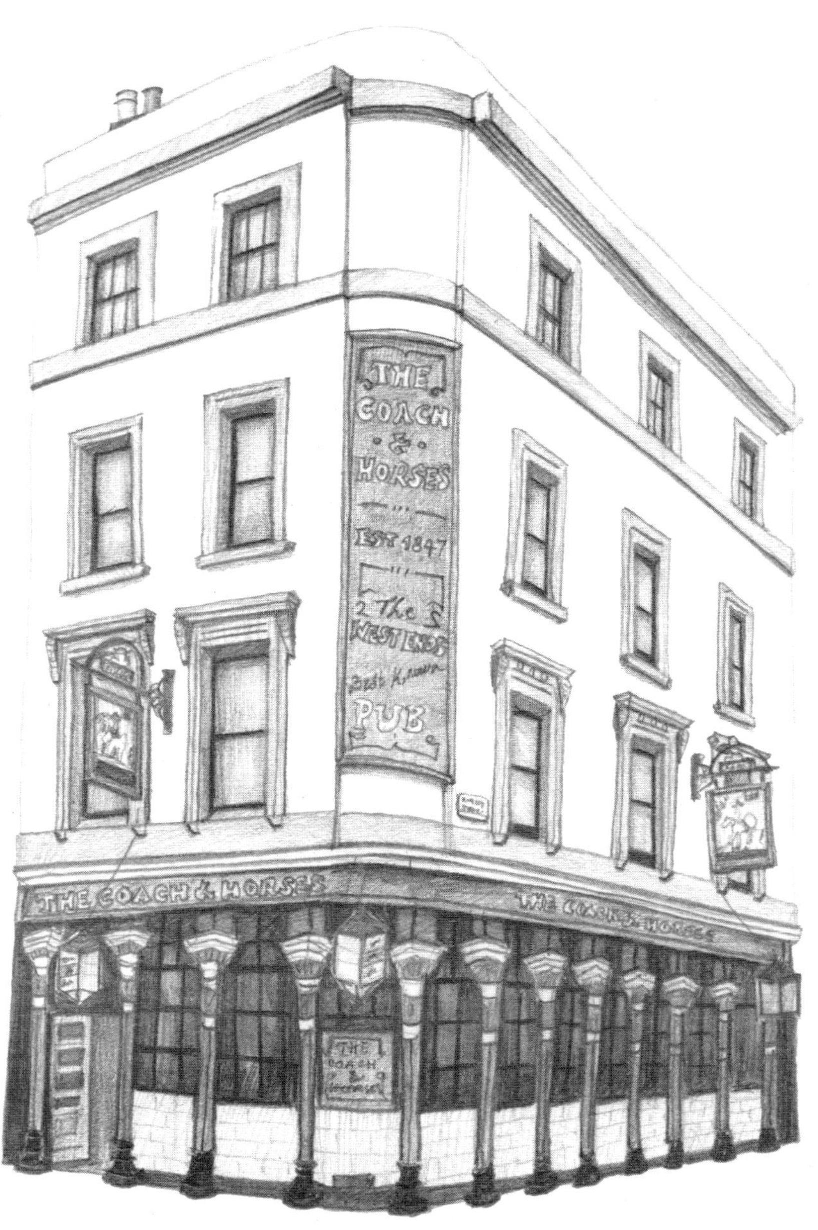
THE
COACH
&
HORSES
EST 1847
2 The
WEST ENDS
Best Known
PUB
THE COACH & HORSES
THE COACH & HORSES
THE
COACH
&
HORSES

Coach and Horses, Old Compton Street, Soho

Just around the corner, the chaos of Soho envelops me once more. This time I'm sitting on the busy Charing Cross Road, right on the brink of Shaftesbury Avenue. Londoners boldly stride past, weaving between the slower-paced pedestrians, and tourists take their time drinking in the atmosphere of central London, their shopping bags swaying by their sides. I squeeze myself beside a black fence and a few bollards. Behind me is a closed restaurant surrounded by metal gates, ready for refurbishment. I take out my easel, keeping the drawing board as close to me as possible; my pencils rattle in my pocket and I look up to find a parked double-decker bus where the pub should be.

Eventually the Grade II listed corner pub comes into view. I outline the gold letters that spell the name on the curve of the building; its white rendered top is greying from pollution and age, so I gently shade in its weathered frontage. I can see its street number above the door; number two is befitting given this is the second Coach and Horses I've drawn in Soho. The open door leads my eye to the bottles that line up above the bar. This pub has had a variety of different names in recent years, changing to Molly Mogs in 1996, then to The Compton Cross in 2017, before reverting to its original namesake in 2019 – The Coach and Horses that I draw today.

The chaos of the day is punctuated by moments of calm. A friendly bloke peeks at my drawing board, then unpacks prints and paintings from his shopping trolley, asking me to differentiate the watercolours from the inks for him before he flogs them down Greenwich Market. I assure him I'm no expert, nevertheless we inspect the works on the side of the road as if we are critics in a gallery. Out of the corner of my eye, I see a flutter of feathers.

I assume another pigeon has come to pose for my picture, but when I take a closer look, I realise it is in fact a large grey parrot that sits in the window of the tech repair shop beside me. When the traffic inevitably blocks my view again, I run inside to meet him. The parrot is called Charlie and he's sixth months old. I return to continue my sketch on the hectic street, adding the foliage and the street sign as my final flourishes, before heading inside to the required calm of the pub.

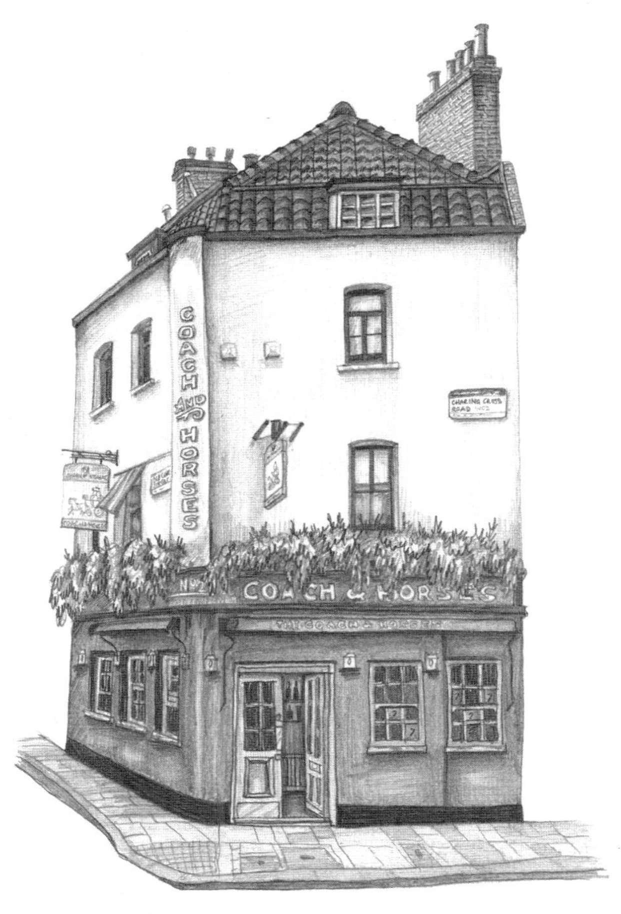

Coach and Horses, Great Marlborough Street, Soho

On a warm weekday morning, I arrive in town once more to draw another pub for my project. It's time for the third Coach and Horses pub in Soho, I walk across the busy street and face it straight on. There are large roadworks to my left, and their relentless drilling is my soundtrack for the day. I look up at the pub across the street, and the sun is so bright I can't see the roof. I pull my cap from my bag and put it on, looking up again, squinting my eyes behind my sunglasses, just making out the clean white lip at the top of the building. I retrieve my pencil from my bag, ready my hand and begin to carefully draw the straight lines of the pub.

I sketch the brickwork of the neighbouring building, which holds up the boozer's narrow frame. There's been a tavern here since the 1700s, although the architecture I draw today is younger, built in 1897. I illustrate the pleasing bricks that line each edge of the building, and the windows, opened to let the air in on this warm day. The beeps and revs that swirl around the road don't distract me from my drawing; I am absorbed in sketching the woman sitting alone inside and the tables that ready themselves for customers out front. Suddenly, a young woman appears by my side, smiles and introduces herself: her name is Saaranya, and she works at the pub. We talk around my easel, she points excitedly at the different details she sees at the pub every day, but somehow, she says, they feel special rendered in pencil on my page. I continue my sketch, the pub appearing more real with every mark on my page. A tourist airdrops me photos he's taken of me drawing, a bloke stumbles into the wobbly lamp post, my hair continually blows across my face and a skip appears tiny as its lifted into the sky by a towering crane. It's as if the whole of Soho stops in its tracks in that moment to look

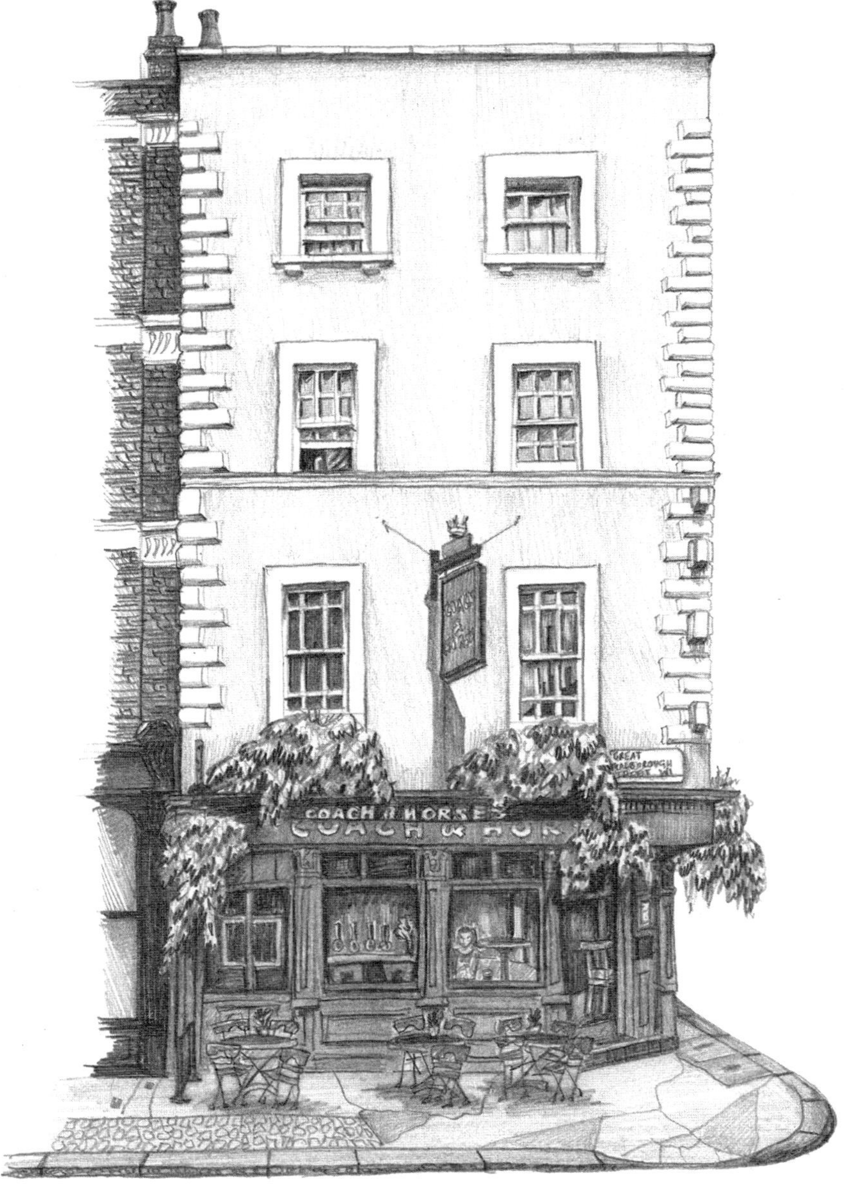
COACH & HORSES
COACH & HOR

up and watch the yellow box sway high above our heads at the very end of a string.

I step back and happily look at my finished artwork. I pack away my belongings, keep my drawing under my arm and return to the throng of Soho once more. I head inside the Coach and Horses to show Saaranya my sketch, and she hands over half a pint of lager and the freshest lime and soda I've ever tasted. I take my seat at the front of the pub with my drawing and my drinks. There's a blackboard beside me full of Polaroid photos of visiting dogs, a TV up high and Pride flags lining the bar. I look out of the window to see the chairs and tables I've just drawn begin to fill. Ahead of me is a large parked truck, covering the entirety of the pub, my sketching spot no longer in view.

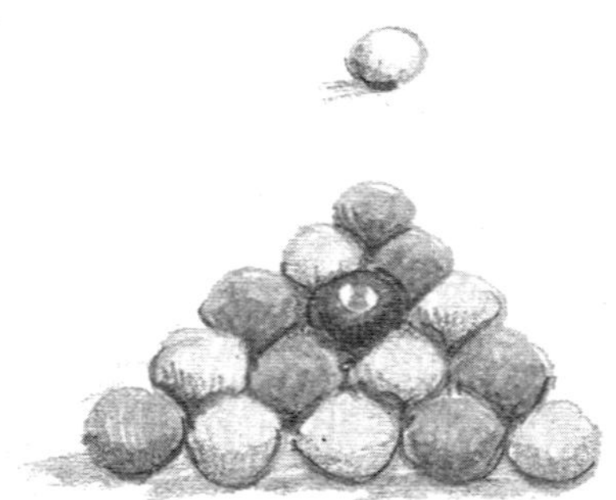

Coach and Horses, Bruton Street, Mayfair

'What a funny little pub!' a man blurts to his friend as they pass in front of my easel. From this angle, across the street, a sliver of black and white can be seen standing completely alone with only a leafy tree for company. The mock-Tudor exterior, which dates back to 1770, triumphantly stands out amongst the pale brick buildings that border it. Behind me is a shopfront of cold, smooth metal that thinly frames huge panes of glass. Sleek, modern, designer surfaces surround me in my scruffy trainers and creased dress. I fixate on the Coach and Horses opposite, almost as if the funny little pub and I are kindred spirits on this shiny street in Mayfair.

Parts of the pub disappear from view every few minutes as black cabs stop in front of me to collect tired shoppers, and delivery van drivers smile from their windows. I wave back but they don't seem to realise I'm waiting for them to move a few metres out of the way. Suddenly, a row of eyes meets mine as I look up at an open-top tour bus. Presented with a captive audience, I swivel my drawing board round to face them and show them the sketch. Their eyes then turn and look across at the pub. An eruption of applause can be heard from the top of the bus as they finally move through the green traffic light, and the pub comes back into view.

I manage to piece together the dark lines that contrast the white walls, the overlapping tiles on the roof and the tree that almost obstructs my view. I look up to see the once clear sky darken to match the grey shading on my paper. Thankfully, my drawing is finished. I take some photos of it in front of the Coach and Horses before sprinting across the road towards the pub. Weaving through the traffic, my drawing in one hand, my easel in the other, I miraculously make it to the other side, admiring the stained-glass

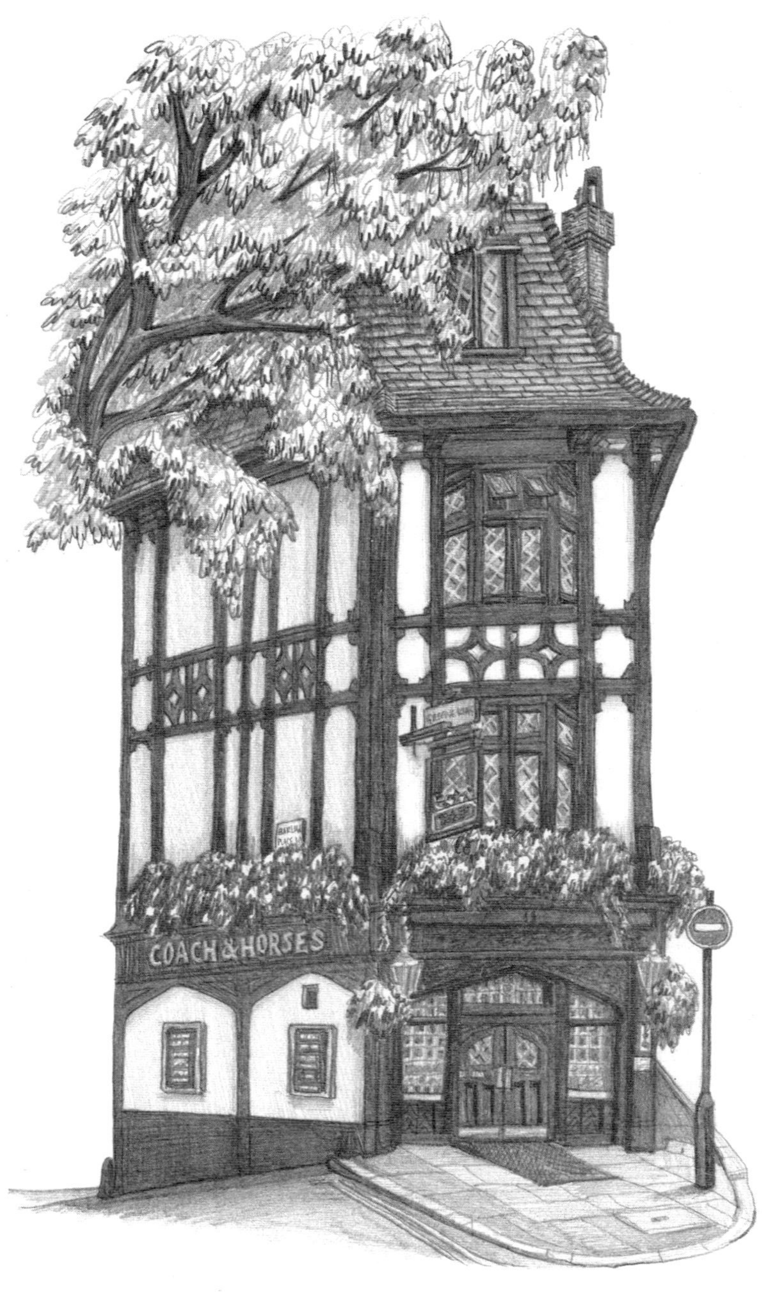

windows up close as I walk through the creaky doors. All of a sudden, other people rush into the pub, and I am herded further into the space. Their jackets are soaking wet. Turning to look out of the window, I see that the pavements are shimmering, rain hitting the stone so hard it bounces back up again. Astonished at my lucky escape, I turn to the bar, order my drink and stay here until the streets and my glass are dry.

> *'My husband proposed to me outside the Commercial Tavern at the end of a dreadful week, saying there was no one else he'd rather endure the hard days with (or celebrate the good ones with over a pint!).'*
> GEORGIA

The Coach and Horses, Hill Street, Mayfair

I walk through a different part of Mayfair, where the streets feel older than the clean glass shopfronts surrounding my last sketch. Here the buildings either side of me are made of red brick and sit grand and tall. I reach the end of Hill Street and turn up it to find Mayfair's oldest surviving tavern. Dating back to the eighteenth century, the tall, slim pub sits at the curve of two roads. Serendipitously, its address is 5 Hill Street, and it is the fifth Coach and Horses I've drawn in London, just like the Compton Street pub was number two and the second I'd drawn in Soho. Its white facade contrasts against the taller, painted neighbouring buildings. I cross the road to find the best angle and place my easel at the edge of the pavement opposite the pub, facing it head-on. I take out the clean white sheet of paper and stick it vertically to my board, looking up at the pub as I do so, deciding how to tackle it for the day.

A guy screeches his bike to a stop on the pavement, locks it to the lamp post next to me, asks me to watch it for him and heads down the road. The road is quiet, not many pedestrians about, just some construction workers in hard hats holding clipboards, people in suits heading in and out of the buildings behind me and the odd designer dog being taken for a stroll. I look up at the building's details and decide to draw the cracks in the render. I sharpen my pencil to the narrowest point and whisper the lead along the page to illustrate each individual hairline crack. The wiggly lines appear on every level, even around the newer fixtures like the security alarm and lights. For some, they might be a sign of disrepair, but to me, each beautiful fracture demonstrates The Coach and Horses' old age and gives the pub its weathered character.

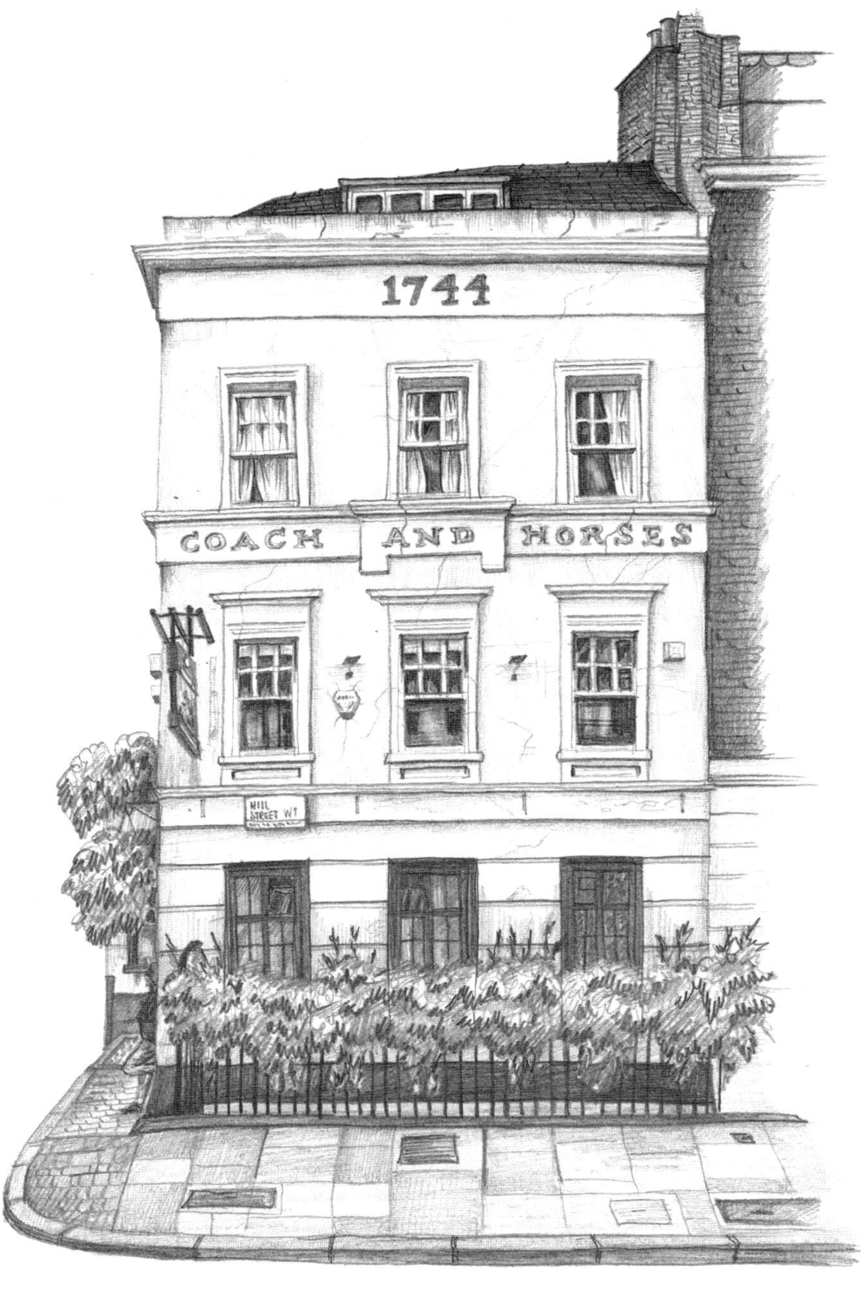
1744
COACH AND HORSES
HILL
STREET W1

I see Smart cars and black cabs race up the street. A few people stop to chat, some of them the people who work in the building behind me. They enquire after the drawing, as it's their after-work local. Another person in a suit joins the conversation; he works in a neighbouring office and is also interested in buying the artwork. Before I know it, a friendly bidding war is happening around my easel, and the drawing's not even finished. I disperse the competitors and continue to draw each aspect of the building carefully. Suddenly, as if I'm dreaming, I look up to see a fully grown tree levitating in the sky above the pub. Held by thin ropes, the tree is lifted, swinging in the breeze, across the rooftops of Mayfair before disappearing into a courtyard and out of view. Still in disbelief at the flying forest, I add the final touches to my drawing. I'm just about to pack away my things when I notice a lone punter drinking a pint while on the phone, leaning against the side of the pub. I scribble him in and carefully put my drawing in my bag.

I step over the mosaicked entranceway and into the dark, wooden interior of the pub. Inside, I see gold lanterns glistening at the top of the bar, arched mirrors reflecting behind the many bottles of spirits and a black and white photograph of a large shire horse pulling a cart in front of an old inn. The warmth of the traditional interior and the familiar features, like the pub stools, framed mirrors and curved wooden bar, entice me to order a drink, find a cosy corner and sit in the afterglow of another eventful drawing day.

Coach and Horses, Wellington Street, Covent Garden

I have my big red scarf wrapped around my neck. It's so thick it reaches my ears and covers my mouth and nose. My warm breath heats the bottom of my chin as I try to bury my head further into the soft wool. It is mid-December and I'm across the street from my final Coach and Horses, its own bright red frontage accidentally matching my scarf. I place my easel on the very edge of the pavement and stand to face it.

I look at the unfamiliar pub, wondering what treasure I might find inside after I complete my drawing. With a long way to go, I hastily begin my sketch on the empty page. Gradually, a building appears. I become completely engrossed in my work, and curious people stop to chat. Soon, the cold tips of my fingers are forgotten.

Big gift bags brush past my legs as crowds of people swarm back from Covent Garden carrying their Christmas shopping. Two brave men outside the pub perch their pints of Guinness on the window ledge. They face each other, deep in conversation. Little do they know, they've just created the perfect composition for my drawing. I jot down their stances and their beers before they're gone again. Rebecca, who works in the pub, crosses the street to introduce herself; she returns with a cheese and pickle sandwich and a packet of yellow Taytos. The warm gesture and the glee of retrieving my packed lunch from the brown paper bag gives me all the encouragement needed to continue drawing in the brisk cold air.

After adding the shiny black lamp post, the drawing finally comes together. It is complete, and I carry it inside. I squeeze through the packed room and pass it across the bar for Rebecca to look at. She very kindly hands me a Guinness on the house and I turn around to look over people's heads at the interior that surrounds us.

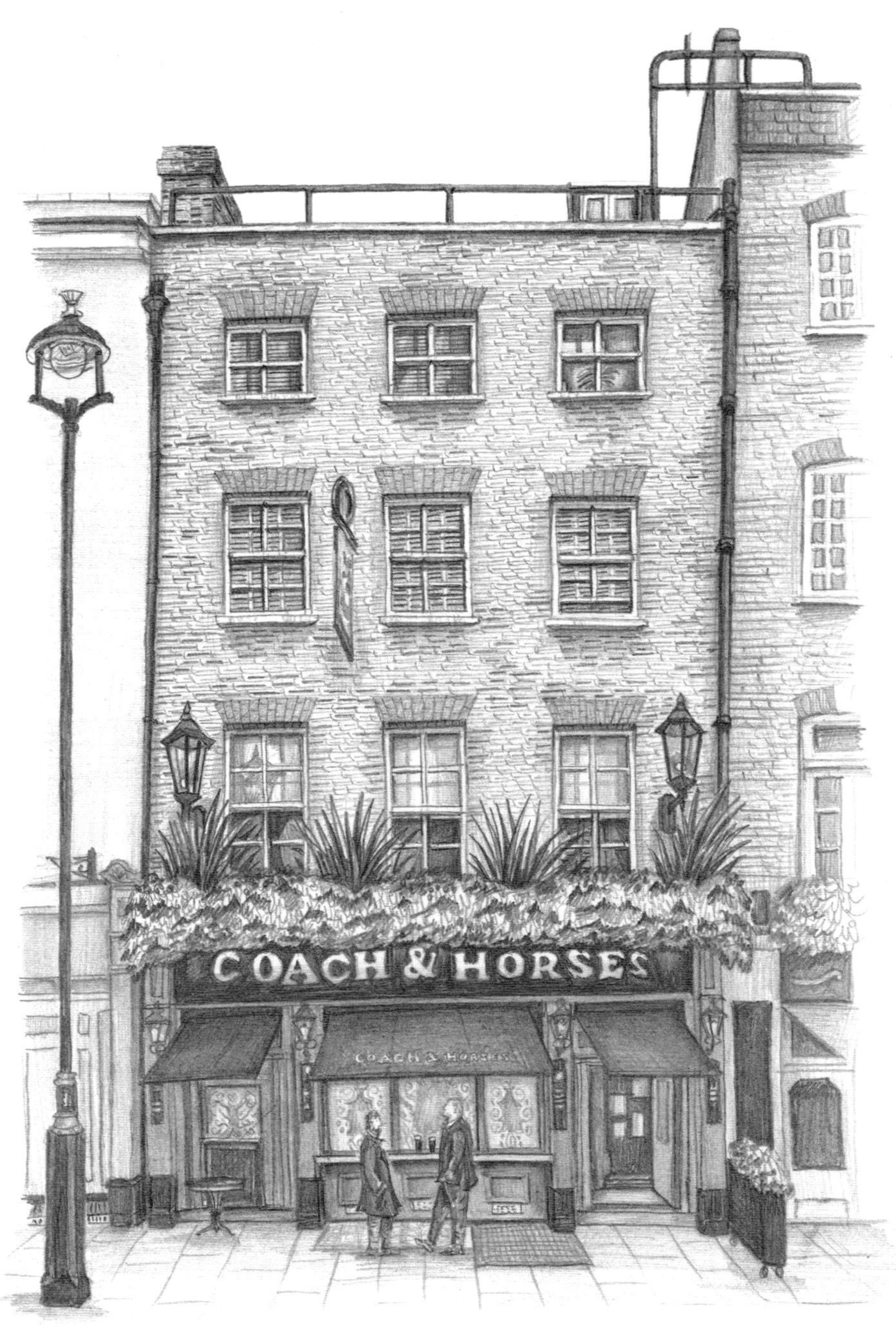
COACH & HORSES
COACH & HORSES

The green walls are covered in countless framed photographs. 'Tipperary 1989 All-Ireland senior hurling champions' is printed underneath a sports photo, the team neatly standing in a row. There are more photographs of regulars and friends pictured inside the pub itself. Alongside these are commemorative plaques, vintage posters and certificates. It's like walking into a family living room, proudly decorated with their loved ones' accomplishments for all to see.

The next time I go to the pub I am chuffed to see my drawing on the wall. I am again warmly greeted by Rebecca and take my drink to sit in the far corner of the pub. I watch a couple of old friends take a seat nearby as one exclaims, 'I can't believe the barman remembers me, after all these years … amazing, isn't it?' I look over to see a joint of beef inside the heated display cabinet which sits on top of the bar; the light from the box warming the small space and the meat inside. Some of the beef is then expertly carved into thick slices, exposing its pink inside. A bottle of hot English mustard sits next to it – on standby for their famous salt beef sandwiches. I finish my Guinness – all that's left is the bubbly foam sticking to the inside of the glass – and look around the full room, feeling completely at home and noticing for the first time that the pub carpet, with its repeating flower shapes tufted into the dark green surface, matches the one my parents have in their living room.

I look ahead to the end of this project and wonder how many pubs called 'The Coach and Horses' I will have drawn. Even after drawing just these six, I've found trying to compare them a fruitless task. Apart from name and proximity, it's clearer than ever to me that they have such distinct personalities. The people who run them, drink in them and have preserved them have given these six unique boozers their individual charm and each one continues to serve its own locals and tread its own path through London's pub history.

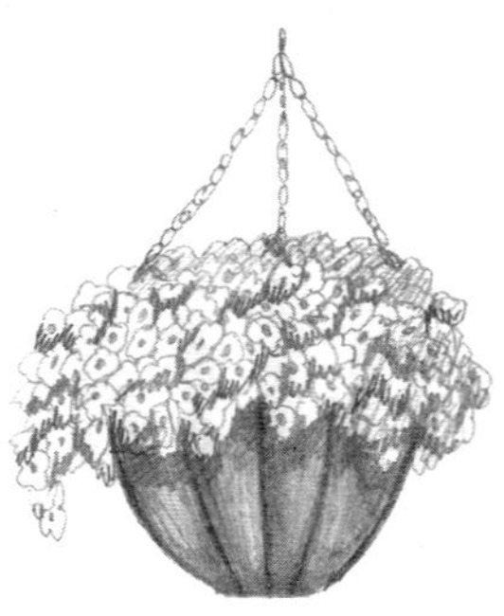

PLANTS

We might think of London pubs as sitting on streets surrounded by hard, compact layers of bricks in different hues of grey and brown, the solidity of the architecture contributing to a typical urban landscape. So when a pub provides the surface for a garden to grow – its hanging baskets overflowing with soft petals, or its walls covered in leaves and floral window boxes – it's a beautiful anomaly on the high street.

A boozer with a bush that distinguishes itself from your typical rigid facade is a challenging feat to illustrate for an artist used to drawing straight lines. I like to look at how the abundant nature both grapples with and compliments the architecture it clings on to, to ask what a tree adds to a beer garden and how I choose to draw it all.

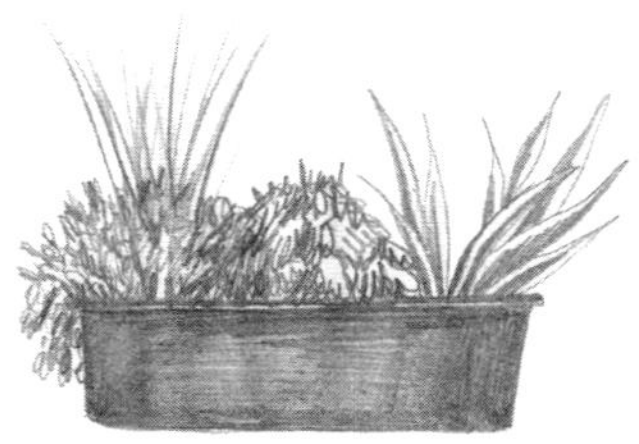

The Atlas, West Brompton

I'm drawn to the backstreets of West Brompton by The Atlas. In the spring, the pub's facade vanishes beneath a striking upright garden of ivy that engulfs the front of the building, tumbling over the doorway, just leaving space for the four windows. Travelling there, I stand on the Tube, hanging on to the handle above my head, swaying with the motion and thinking about how I will sketch the lush green pub. I walk round the corner full of anticipation for the series of scribbles and swirls I am about to create on my page. I see the pub for the first time with my sketchbook in hand, and immediately berate myself when I am confronted by an array of brown roots where the leaves should be. It's winter and the pub's greenery is dormant.

Slightly disappointed, I assess the frontage and decide to leave the tangle of trunks till last. Tentatively sketching in the outline of the pub I draw anything but the branches. I draw the windows, portraying the reflected buildings opposite in the glass, copying the brickwork and the edges of buildings behind me without turning around. I outline the little lamps that curve over the pub's name and illuminate it at night. I hold my pencil steady on the paper to illustrate the gate to the right, with its straight iron lines and curved decorative contours.

I then decide to draw The Atlas's plants from imagination, layering scribbles over the blank top half of the pub, determined to reimagine the pub before me in the summer months. The drawing is suddenly complete, and I stand back to admire it. I can see it looks quite different to the pub standing on the other side of my easel.

I take my sketchbook inside, received by a beautiful 1930s interior, refit after bomb damage in the Second World War. The pub boasts a wood and glass panel dividing the large space into two rooms.

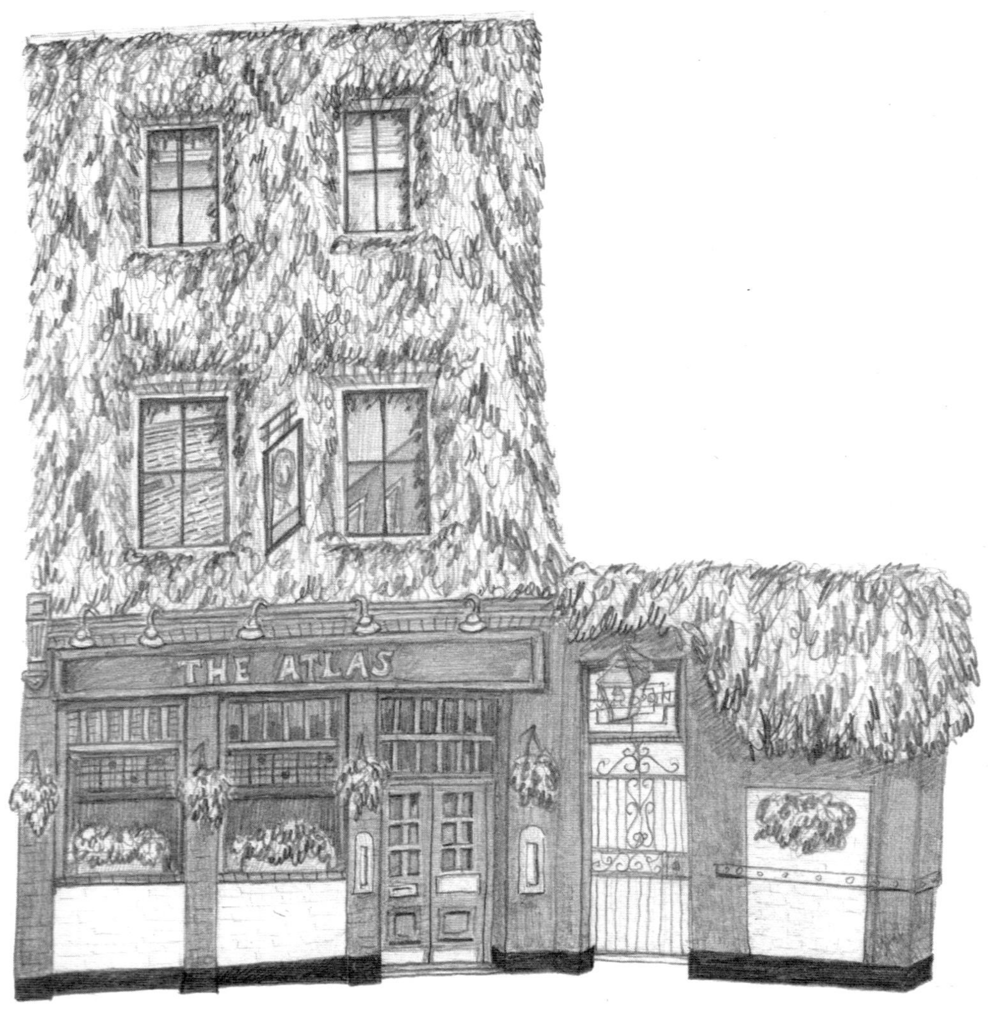
THE ATLAS

The brick fireplace and surround sports original Truman Brewery signage and an open fire beckons me to its side. I take my place at the round table next to the warming flames, open my sketchbook and look down at my drawing. I assess the luscious layers I've sketched in, imagining the pub in warmer months. But I realise the wintry pub I am greeted by today holds its own kind of beauty: the tangled tunnel of roots, the wilting leaves and the small bursts of summer foliage holding on.

My drawing of The Atlas is now proudly owned by the pub and hangs in a frame on the wall inside. I no longer try to adapt what I see before me to appease my own expectations, instead I look to find the beauty in the pub at that moment, whatever the weather and condition of its foliage.

The Hemingford Arms, Islington

The Hemingford Arms in Islington wears a full skirt made of plants. The top half of the pub is square and painted white. It is adorned with window boxes bursting with greenery, flowers and spiky leaves. I walk through the verdant archway and into the pub. A busy patterned carpet greets my steps over the threshold, a wonderful mosaic of threads in different hues of red, pink, green and navy that complement the eclectic array of shapes around the space. On the ceiling, a large number of objects and artefacts hang around the bar, from puppets and tricycles to copper jugs and musical instruments. Upstairs, I peer through the door to find a somewhat calmer room, less decorative and reserved for private bookings.

In the 1980s, the 'Hemi' was home to a hugely popular Friday night disco, run by the Icebreakers, a community-led support group for gay men and lesbians, established in 1973. The pub still plays host to a range of music nights. Today, I squeeze past punters who eagerly watch the women's rugby world cup on the screens. Each outside table is full of families awaiting their lunch, and all around they are surrounded by the foliage.

I sketch The Hemingford Arms' greenery in a series of condensed scribblings. Wider swirls create the foundation of lighter-coloured plants and show off the bouncing daylight. The denser the mark-making, the darker the plants appear, and this effect is saved for the shadowy bottoms of hanging baskets and underneath window boxes. I swap my pencil for my rubber, erasing the marks in specific spots and drenching those removed leaves in a harsher sunlight. This technique is intuitive and far from accurate; to me, it's the antidote to the rigid lines of architecture and it's how I like to draw plants.

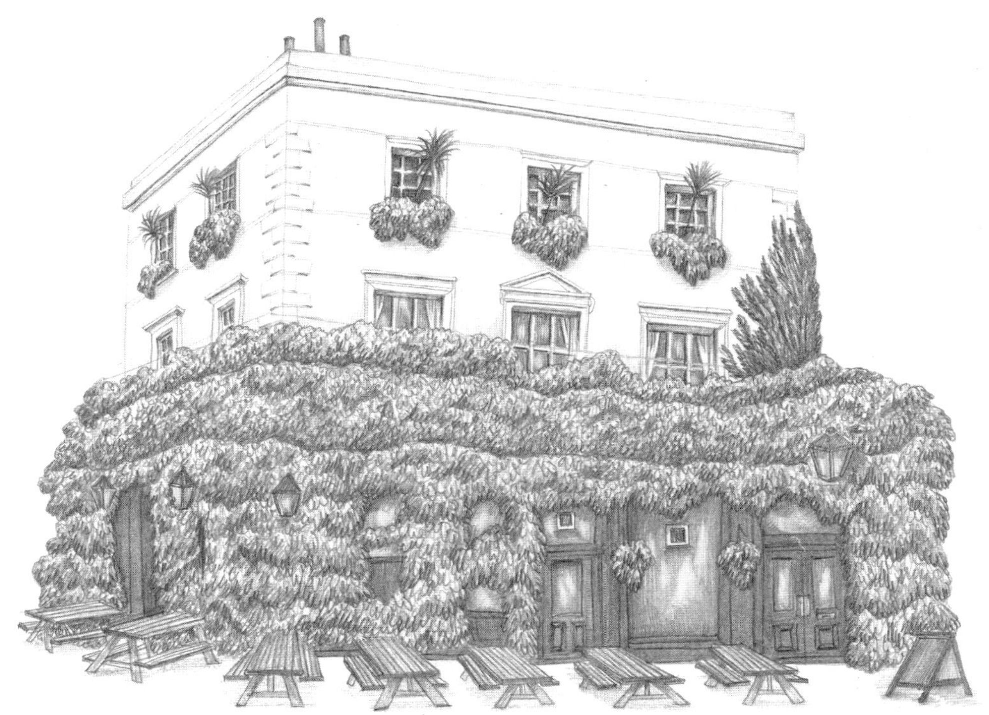

Faltering Fullback, Finsbury Park

I walk from Finsbury Park Tube station, pass under the bridge and turn off the main road for some residential respite. In the distance, I see a glut of greenery emerge from the row of houses on Ennis Road. As I get closer and turn, I am met with a prominent pub at the intersection of two streets. Practically in the middle of the road, the Faltering Fullback is hard to ignore, standing front and centre, all the neighbouring houses an appreciative audience to its frontage. A bulbous bush engulfs the building, dotted with flashes of colour amongst the green, spring flowers peering over the top of the ivy.

I place my easel on the pavement directly opposite the tavern. It's March but the weather feels almost autumnal. There are grey clouds and a cold wind; the leaves ripple in its gusts, their vivid colour contrasting perfectly with the brown brickwork behind them. I am excited to draw it all.

My drawing continues with a small pause for rain and a few in-depth chats with pleasant passersby. Without warning, a bell rings and to my amusement a stampede of school children runs into the playground behind me. The next hour or so consists of little voices trying to make conversation with me through the fence, desperately reaching on tiptoes to see my artwork over my shoulder. I swivel my drawing board round for them to have a look. An excited chorus – 'Woooow', 'That's amazing', 'Did you do that!?' – screeches from the other side of the fence. The nearby teacher smiles, thanks me and disperses my new fan club. I turn my attention back to the sea of greenery I'm about to sketch. It's the final part of my drawing and a chance for my rigid wrist to settle into some scribbles.

Walking through the archway of ivy into the pub with my finished drawing, I am immediately greeted by a small circular bar,

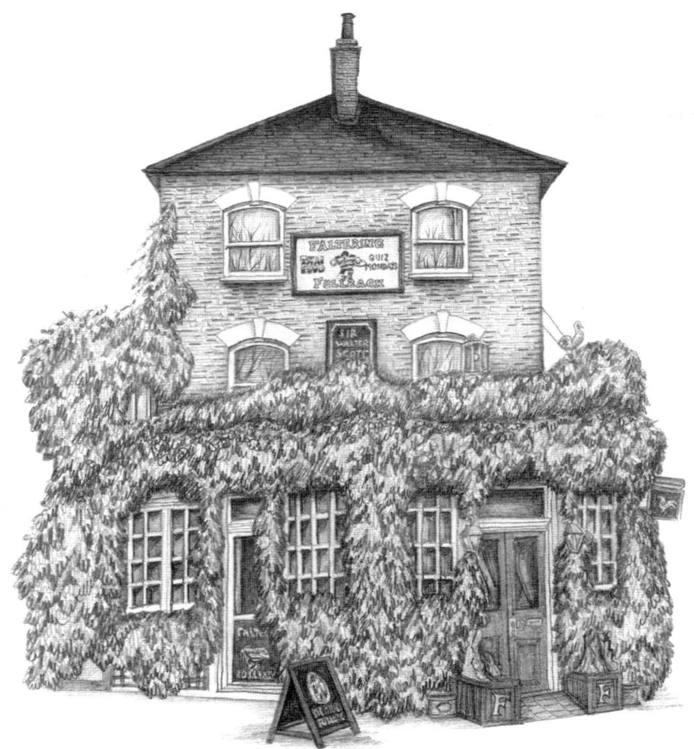

which is occupied by regulars enjoying drinks as they watch sport on the TV above their heads. It's quiet because I'm early, so I take my time to drink in the character of each room, which seem to grow as I wander through them. The back room stretches the width of the pub, with picnic benches in rows, framed jerseys and TV screens on every wall. This is the 'Sin Bin' and it's a room for the rugby fans – which makes perfect sense given the pub's name.

I continue my tour, appreciating how each room is lined with trophies, vintage signage and sporting memorabilia, with instruments and even bikes hanging from the ceilings. I eventually stumble across the beer garden, a peaceful maze made up of decking, benches and, of course, verdant plants. I settle here, buried by the leaves, for a quiet lager before heading home.

Plaquemine Lock, Angel

Approaching Plaquemine Lock, I spy Regent's Canal through the trees. Narrowboats sleepily sail down the still, brown waterway, cyclists pedal close to its edge, and I stop to look up at the tall rectangular building I am to draw today. I opt to sit in the road rather than obstruct the narrow pavement. I hide next to a big green bike storage locker, which protects me from cars driving past. The pub towers over the road, casting a shadow in my direction. The bright sunlight shining directly behind it makes it difficult to observe each individual detail of the pub's exterior.

Originally called The Prince of Wales, the Plaquemine Lock takes its newer name from a lock built by Jacob Hortenstein in Plaquemine, Louisiana in 1909. It enabled important trade and cargo to travel from the Bayou on to the Mississippi River. The connection to this English pub runs down the owner's family tree, as the great-grandson of Hortenstein and his wife Carrie B. Schwing, opened the Plaquemine Lock in Islington in 2017, serving Creole and Cajun cuisine. Even the striking murals that decorate the walls inside are painted by founder Jacob Kennedy's mother, Haidee Becker.

The herringbone brickwork requires my undivided attention. I have to make sure I lead my pencil in the right direction to create the interlocking pattern. The turquoise tiles, each one a different shade, almost mimic the reflections of the water. Finally, I approach the garden that can be seen emerging from the top of the building. A forest of different trees and plants shoot up over the ledge as if replacing the roof. Cylindrical flower baskets, overgrown and overflowing, are evenly arranged across the facade. And wooden barrels on either side of the door, holding two large palm trees, frame my entry into the pub and further add to the garden that grows around it.

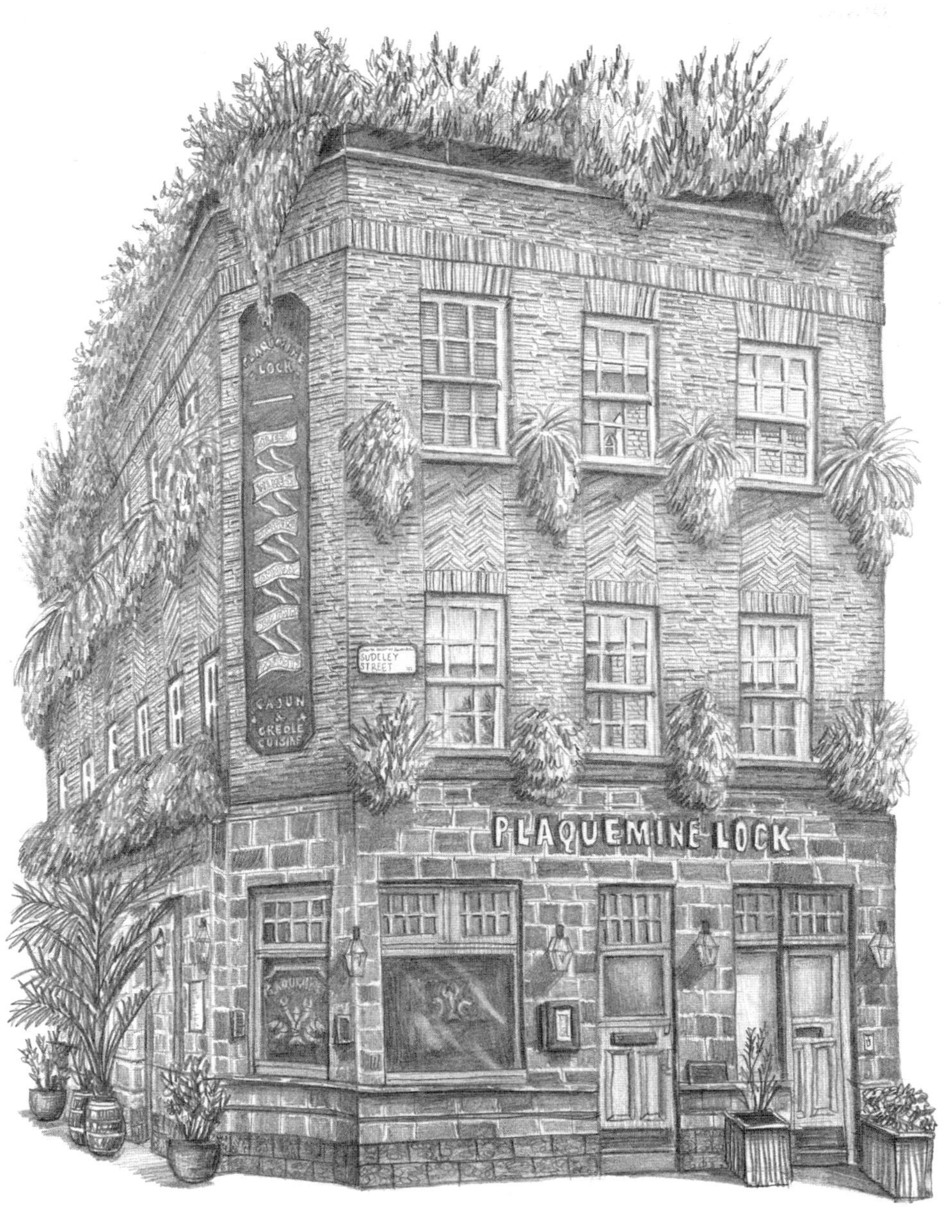
PLAQUEMINE
LOCK
CAJUN
&
CREOLE
CUISINE
SUDELEY
STREET
PLAQUEMINE LOCK

The Pear Tree, Fulham

The angled front of The Pear Tree is set back from the pavement and when I arrive to draw it, a delivery van covers its bottom half. I cross the road and wedge myself between two parked cars, patiently watching and waiting for the beer deliveries to finish. As I ready my pencil to start drawing, Hope, the manager, comes out to greet me, hearing of my project for the first time. I learn from her that this West London establishment opened in 1824 and – at the time of sketching – is due to celebrate its 200th birthday.

I focus on shading in the brickwork, white and terracotta, the two colours creating patterns around the windows. I use the very tip of my sharp pencil to sketch in the overlapping folds of the curtains that are shut behind the glass. As I draw the upstairs windows, I notice two women cross the street and approach me at my drawing board. They happily chat to me about my project; they live above the pub and very kindly bring me a mug of hot herbal tea. Thankful for their thoughtful gesture, I show them the windows I've just drawn, which belong to their flat. The grey clouds above me begin to darken and the remaining tea goes cold. I notice droplets on my paper and run for shelter.

Although situated next to a large tree and fronted by full planters, The Pear Tree itself doesn't showcase much more plant power than any other traditional London pub. Its inclusion in this chapter is due to its namesake. Many pubs across the country take their names from bushes, holly trees and the Royal Oak. The connection between plants and pubs may be traced back to Roman times, with vines perhaps signalling that a tavern sold wine. Now more frequently used as a decorative detail, plants can still give deeper meaning to their pubs. A living fruit tree can be found in the beer garden at the back of this boozer, and the pear tree is at the centre of the leafy sanctuary where the pub's locals gather and where celebratory events are held, like the pub's forthcoming birthday party.

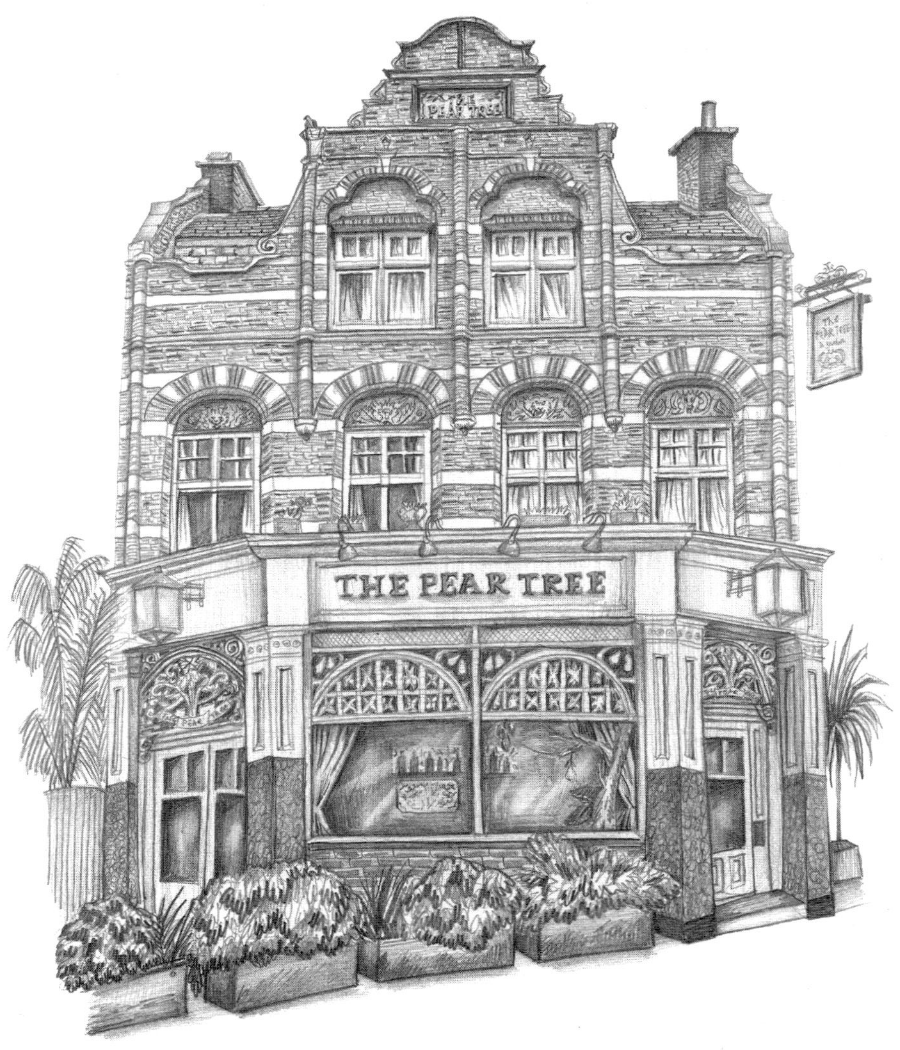

The Churchill Arms, Notting Hill

A mountain of layered and overlapping foliage engulfs this pub
in a swathe of textures, from soft vibrant petals to leafy mounds.
The Churchill Arms, built in 1750, draws people from all over
London and the world to admire its prize-winning display – it's the
only pub to have received an award from the Chelsea Flower Show.
Drawing it, I am careful to carve through the plants and let the pub's
other details sing in the small gaps. I pay particular attention to the
flags, their irregular curved edges flapping in the wind, the windows
that emit a warm glow from within the pub and the sign, with
Winston Churchill's prominent portrait, a stern expression amongst
the surrounding soft greenery. The pub is thought to have been the
local of Winston Churchill's grandparents back in the 1800s.

To differentiate between the variety of plants with only one colour I use
the end of my grey pencils and controlled pressure from my right hand,
creating the darker and softer shades of the hundreds of flowers. Small
round shapes with little to no colour are designated as petals, while
stronger overlapping lines form leaves spilling over one another under
the vibrant blooms. I add dark shadows beneath these sections to give
the feeling of layers of delicate plants curving over the hard building.

The foliage doesn't stop at the pub's entrance. As I sip my crisp
glass of wine, I admire the ceiling above my head, which is filled with
cascading indoor plants of many varieties. The different hues of green
complement the deep red patterned carpet and bring vibrancy to
the classic and cosy interior. The windowsills hold houseplants that
almost merge through the glass with the abundant flora outside. The
Churchill Arms confidently chooses to stand out, accenting this busy
road in Notting Hill with its bold, unapologetic garden and providing
a passerby or punter with a moment of wonder in the busy city.

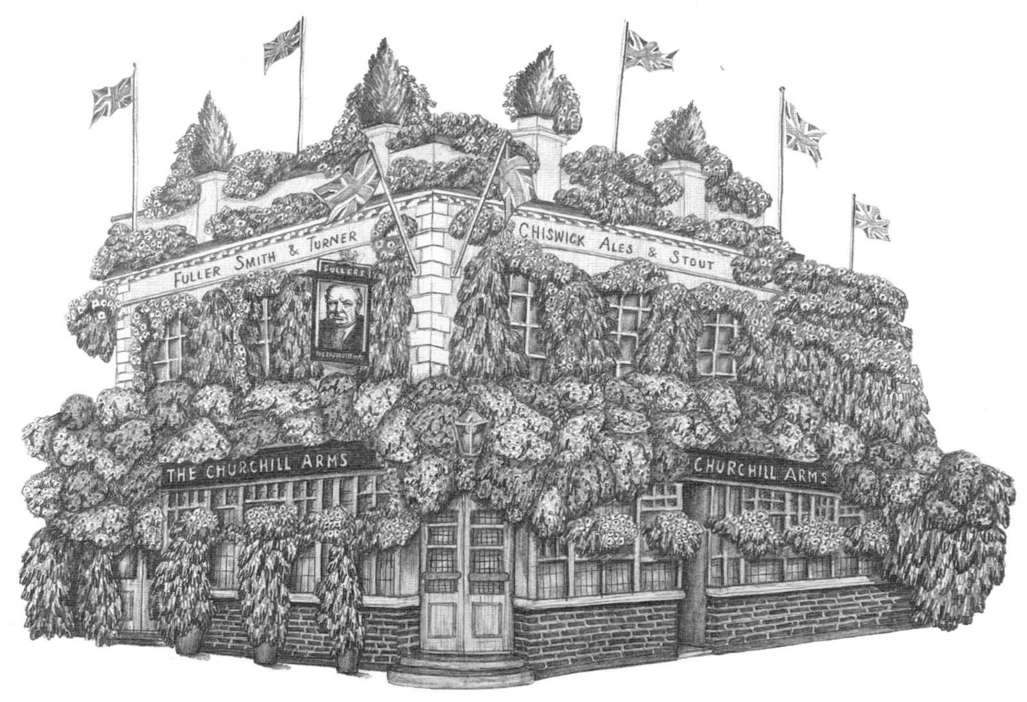

'In 2004, I met my wife at a small table near the front door of The Churchill Arms – a mutual friend introduced us and accompanied her that evening. This strange girl walked in wearing a leather skirt, asked me what I wanted to drink (nothing, as I still had more than half a lager in front of me) and proceeded to buy a bottle of red wine at the counter which we promptly finished together. To this day, she keeps reminding me that she bought us our first drink!'

DEON

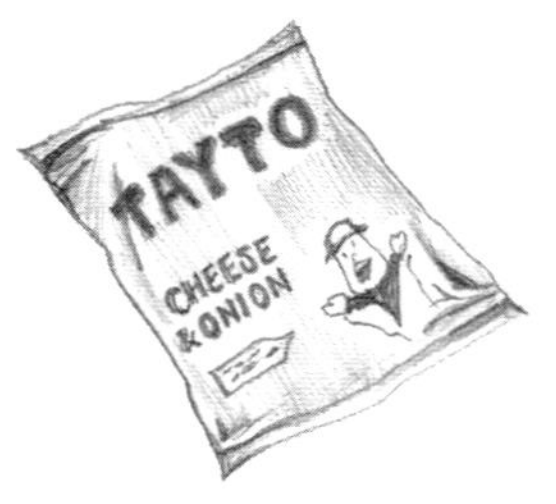

WATER

The rivers, ponds and canals of London play host to many different watering holes. From wellie-wearing bar staff and fluctuating tides to scenic views and flooded beer gardens, the taverns on the Thames are full of surprises.

The history of pubs on the water runs deep: sailors and boatbuilders made use of such taverns during their time off, artists were inspired by the scenic views to create their paintings and poems, and even pirates could be seen sailing past to make a lucky escape.

Today, the beauty of a riverside boozer is just as exciting. As I travel to these pubs with my sketchbook, I often wrestle with the wet conditions and rising waters. I take time in between pencil strokes to appreciate the stunning surroundings of these particular pubs and find calm in their unique soggy settings.

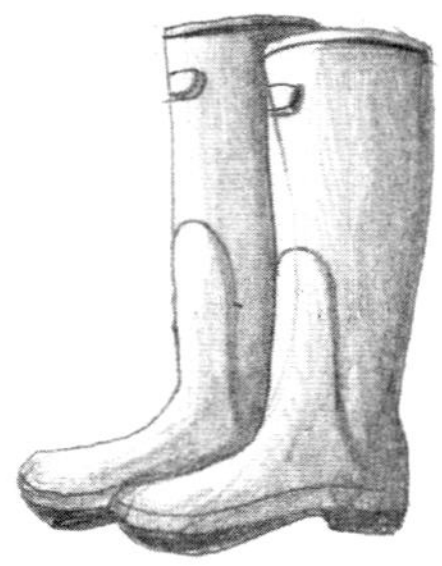

The White Swan, Twickenham

**Strolling along a rough track, dotted with puddles of water, I stop
to find the driest patch for my chair and easel before looking up at
today's pub. It looks different to the pictures I have seen. After a
few minutes of assessing the building for my drawing, I realise I'm
at the wrong place. I discover that another White Swan resides in
a neighbouring postcode, and that one was my intended subject for
the day. After a quick look at the journey time on my phone, I decide
to stay put. This is still a London pub after all, another one added
to the pub project, even if it's not the pub I first intended.**

I turn away from the building to appreciate my own backdrop:
the River Thames. I look out over the water reflecting the blue sky
stippled with clouds, the river lapping very gently at the bank of mud
a few metres behind me. White swans glide along the river's surface,
their elegant necks upright and poised. I turn back to see another
swan, illustrated on the pub's sign, and get my pencil out to draw it.

The weather is warm and the track is busy with walkers. Friendly
people stop to tell me about the pub; one girl suggests it's the best
first date spot, another raves about the beer garden on the river and
the views from it at sunset. Dogs of all sizes come and sniff the legs
of my easel, some get close enough for a gentle chin scratch, others
so close I'm sure their muddy, damp coats will splatter my paper.
Dajana, who works at the pub, brings me a cup of tea and a biscuit.
I have no choice but to place it on the floor while I sketch, its milky
brown surface replicating that of the murky puddle next to my feet.

I draw the branches reflected in the windows, the shadow under
the canopy and the proud painted swan with its curved neck.
I continue to shade in the details around the white building when
I spot a notice illustrating today's tides. This prompts me to turn

back around and look at the tranquil scenes behind me, only to realise the water that once lapped a few metres away is now only a few feet behind my chair. With that, I begin to notice that the road is deserted. I see the bar staff come out sporting wellies, heading towards the flooded beer garden across the path. I quickly pick up my chair and move it a few steps forwards towards the pub, before sitting back down and continuing to sketch. A few minutes later, I am required to move again as the water chases me. I repeat the process until the river is halfway across the path and tickling the bottom of my travel stool. I finish my drawing just in time and with the Thames on my tail, I snap a photo before running up the steep stairs into the pub. I laugh with the other punters who also made a lucky escape, we look out to see the river where the path once was and the empty beer garden with its tables and benches submerged.

I enjoy a swift half and pack my miraculously dry drawing into my backpack. I find a sliver of pathway and walk along it up the hill on to dry ground. As I exit the flooded walkway, I overhear a group of young friends giggling at the tourists taking photos of the flooded space outside the pub; they can't believe the enthusiasm for this natural tideway. For these young locals, it's a daily way of life, but for visitors like me it's a phenomenon.

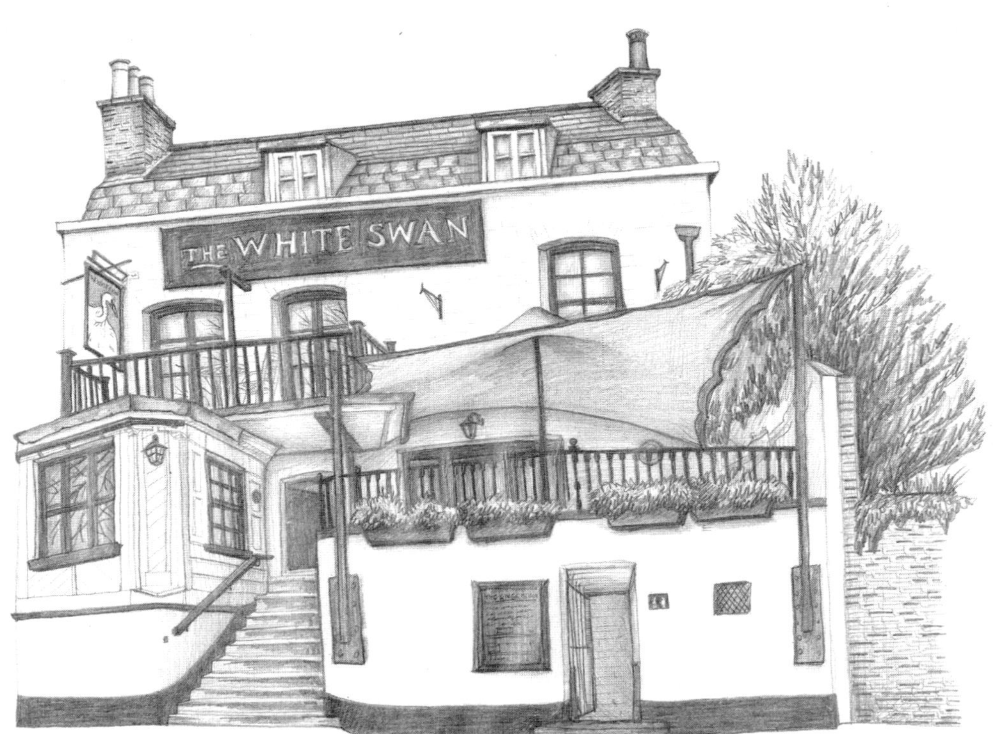
THE WHITE SWAN

The White Swan, Richmond

I walk with purpose across the green from Richmond station and through the remnants of Richmond Palace. Once an impressive Tudor royal residence, it was demolished by grief-stricken Richard II after the death of his wife and was rebuilt multiple times since, including by Henry VII after a devastating fire. Today, all that remains is the gatehouse. Its beautiful large archways and red-brick turrets surround me as I find the small passageway to Old Palace Lane. The first thing I am struck by as I turn down it is the fragrant smell of wisteria. The tiny purple flowers drape over the white house ahead of me, perfuming the path I travel down and introducing me to the quiet countryside scene. I meet The White Swan, the pub I was meant to draw the previous week; the elegant bird illustrated on its tall sign guides me to the front of the building.

The pavement across from the pub is especially narrow so I park my easel in between two cars. I unpack my drawing board and balance my sketchbook on it. I extend my easel, so the paper is at my eyeline, and pull apart my chair to take a seat between the two car bonnets. I am here just before the pub opens, but I see shadows move across the windows from within, and suddenly I hear the doors unlock. A group of friends who have been on a morning walk head straight inside, followed by two colleagues in messy workwear. I am brought a cold glass of coke, the ice rattling against the glass as it's carried carefully across the street to my sketching corner.

I take a break for lunch and sit on the bench outside the pub, looking at the parts of the building I've already drawn on my paper: the pitched roof with overlapping tiles, the closed window shutters on the first floor and the plants that droop over the flower boxes. Feeling the wind pick up and whistle down the quiet street, I rush

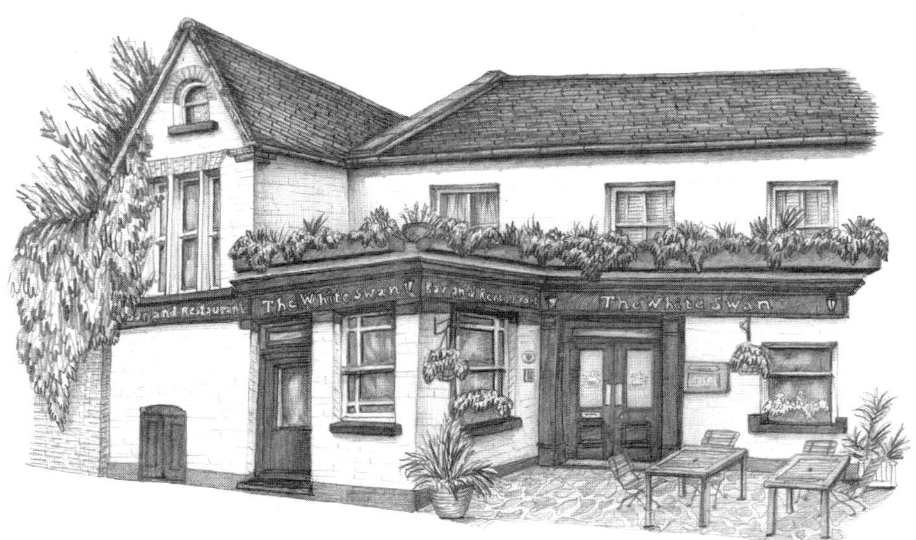

back to my easel as the weather turns. I finish off the final part of my drawing with the paving stones out front, each stone a different shade and shape, grounding the plants, tables and the pub itself. As I pick up my sketchbook and hold it in front of me to take a photo, a light spray of rain blows across the page and the droplets sink into the surface. I put on my jacket, grab my belongings and run inside to shelter myself and my drawing.

The rain has now settled on the road, turning its colour from light grey to dark graphite. I walk out feeling content after a bowl of chips and a lager. My drawing is safely stowed in my bag, and, on a whim, I decide to walk the opposite way down the street. The smell of wisteria is even stronger now in the damp air. Trees hang over the road, droplets sliding off their glistening leaves and hitting the pavement, and the sun peeks through the clouds just as I near the end of the lane. Suddenly the road opens up, and the River Thames comes into view, its drab brown colour reflecting the arched bridge to my right. I take a seat on a bench and look out over the expansive water, watching slow boats glide under the arc of a newly formed rainbow.

White Cross, Richmond

I arrive in Richmond early; the shops are just opening as I walk down the busy road. The smart streets are clean and glossy, and single-decker buses pootle past as I dash through the traffic. People are on their way to work, and I am on my way to the pub. I turn down Water Lane and catch a glimmer of the river peeking between two buildings. I eventually arrive at the water's edge and the pub. I take my seat underneath a tree, its wide branches casting a handy shadow on a hot day like today. There is an empty bench behind me and a ramp between the pub and me. Cars are parked at the top of its steep, pebbled incline, and the bottom disappears into the Thames. I pull apart my red travel stool and set up the rest of my drawing equipment as usual. Beside me is a convenient square bollard; its surface is flat enough for me to set my pencil case and water bottle down on it, acting as a little side table by my easel. The pub is shut and the paths are quiet. I look ahead and press my pencil against the blank page.

I draw the White Cross's symmetrical facade, first jotting my outline on the page, next illustrating the tiny details that decorate it. There are plant pots and books propping windows open upstairs; the warm morning breeze blows the thin curtains across the glass. The leaves of the climbing wisteria are reflected in the window, and some bricks are darker with weathering and age. The staircase to the right twists in a tangle on my paper, I've made the steps so uneven no one could walk on them, but I like them that way.

While I'm absorbed by the details in front of me, the bench behind me plays host to an array of different sitters. The first are two friends who share a bottle of wine early in the morning: they are drunk and cheerfully chat to each other while they watch the boats skim across

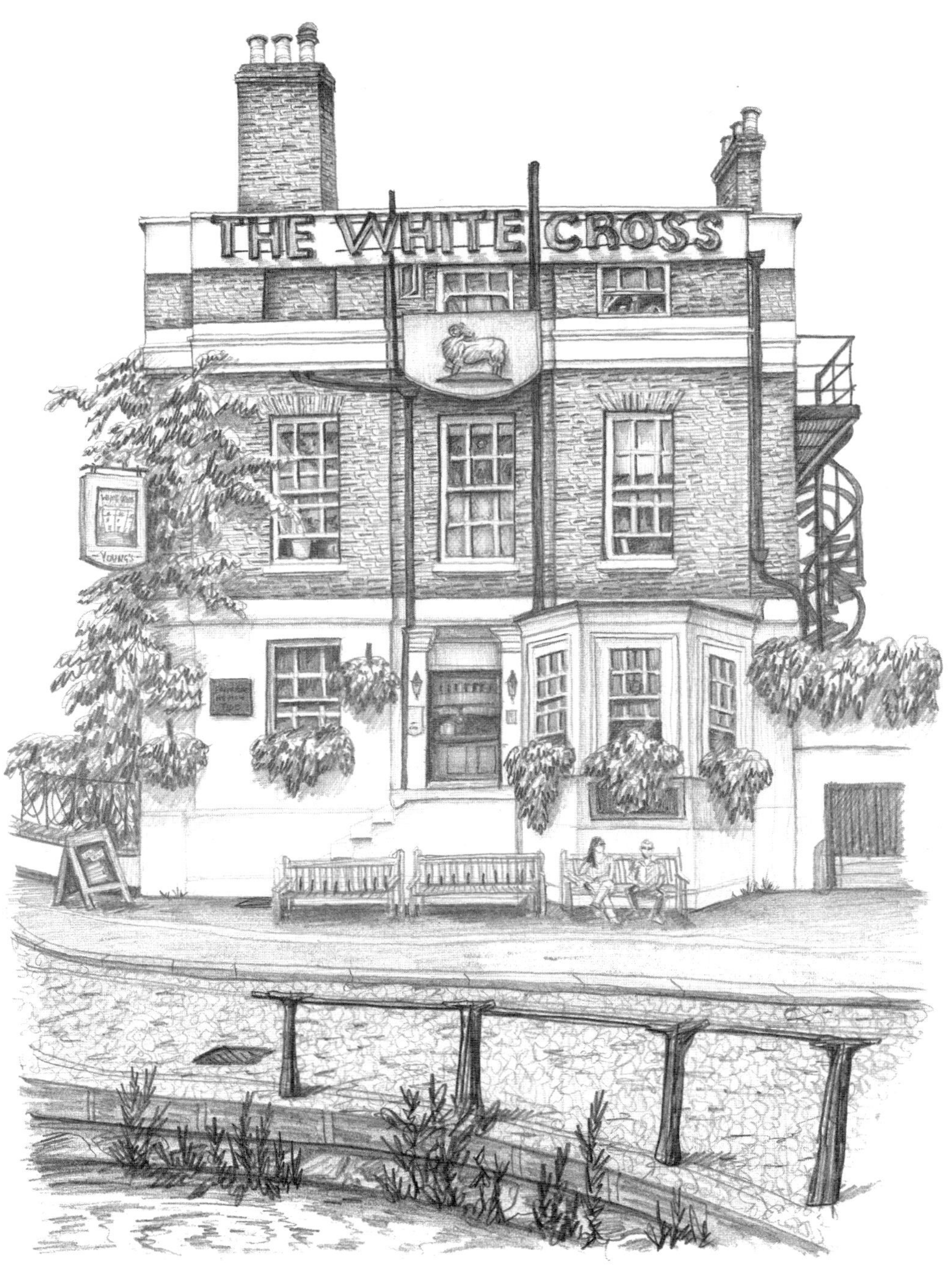

THE WHITE CROSS
YOUNG'S

the water in front of them. They stay a few hours before leaving
to find more drinks. Next, a family from Spain: they are visiting on
holiday and have come to see 'the pub that floods'. Before they head
inside for lunch, the couple sit on the bench while their two young
children run around the tree trying to catch the pigeons. Then, two
white-haired women take their place on the bench: they sit together
so quietly I barely notice they are there. After a while they come over
to see my work, and I can see they have been drawing too. They show
me their progress in their large sketchbooks – bright pastels and bold
marks fill their pages, depicting different sections of the water next to
us. One artist's drawing shows a man gliding on his paddle board,
accompanied by his dog standing on the board behind him, both
kept steady by the slow pushes of the oar. Another closer look at
the river's surface and all its wondrous colours.

Soon, my friend Margo arrives. She buys a coconut from a stall
nearby and offers me a sip. The drink is a refreshing break from the
hot sun that's found its way through the tree's shadows. We suddenly
notice that the water, once at the bottom of the steep ramp, is now
brushing the back of the car's tyres at the top. The river's surface seems
to have risen in a flash, and my pencil begins to move a little quicker
across the page. The water comes into view on my drawing as it rises
closer to my feet at the edge of the ramp. A local urgently moves their
car further up the hill and we pack away before the tide reaches the
wall separating us and the water. We race to sit on the bench in front
of the pub, letting out a sigh of relief and laughing about our lucky
escape. I walk towards the ice cream van and grab us two 99s. I look
over expecting to see my sketching spot submerged but find that the
water never rose past the wall and the tide has already gone back out
again. Feeling I may have slightly overreacted, we sit outside the pub
and finish our ice creams, looking out over the Thames that tricked us.

The Angel, Bermondsey

I exit London Bridge station and start my journey to Rotherhithe.
I reach the Thames Path which leads me along backstreets, curving
round cobbled roads, peeking at the river through residential
buildings. I finally come to an opening, a chance to stand at the
river's edge and look out over the choppy waters. To my right is
a beautiful Bermondsey boozer dating back to the 1830s.

As I draw The Angel, studying its red, brown and brick facade,
I notice a set of steps next to the pub, leading to more steps down
into the water below. I tentatively climb a few, hearing the powerful
splash of the water before I see it. I look over the edge to see that the
space between the steps and the pub frames a swirl of river which
violently crashes against the sides in its bid to escape the small gap.
As I descend the steps, a woman who works at the pub brings out
tables and chairs, curating them around the open space. She invites
me over to see the collection of shells on top of the wall. A blanket of
small rocks, shells and broken glass covers the surface. She explains
that children collect them and leave them here to dry, resulting in a
beautiful assortment of treasures for all to see. I draw the steps on my
paper, still able to hear the crashing water even from a few metres away.

I head inside through the Lounge Bar door and am greeted by the
bar lady, who hands me a Coke and a packet of crisps that I take to the
back of the pub. I sit by the large window and look out over the water.
The tide is so high that people in boats are at eye level when they pass
and water sprays against the windows, leaving a dried-up residue on the
glass. I look across the lapping brown river and spy Tower Bridge,
The Gherkin and The Walkie-Talkie. People brave the balcony outside,
walking along the narrow decking with their plastic cups, sitting and
standing shoulder to shoulder with strangers observing the mighty

Thames and the London landscape beyond it. They look out over the same waterway that once carried smugglers, river pirates and thieves.

Behind me the room is laid with terrazzo flooring, and differently shaped tankards line the walls which are made of rich wooden panels. These panels are dotted with portraits of naval officers, photos of boats and drawings of the Thames Tunnel. The quiet murmur of conversation can be heard in the neighbouring room; familiar South London accents resound across the bar. A couple brings their drinks and sits at the table in front of me, one of them saying, 'This is where we had our first date, all those years ago.' They sit closer together, wistfully looking out over the water surging behind the pub.

'My favourite pub memory? Begging my parents
for money for the sweet machine and beating my older
sister in a game of pool aged five.'
IMOGEN

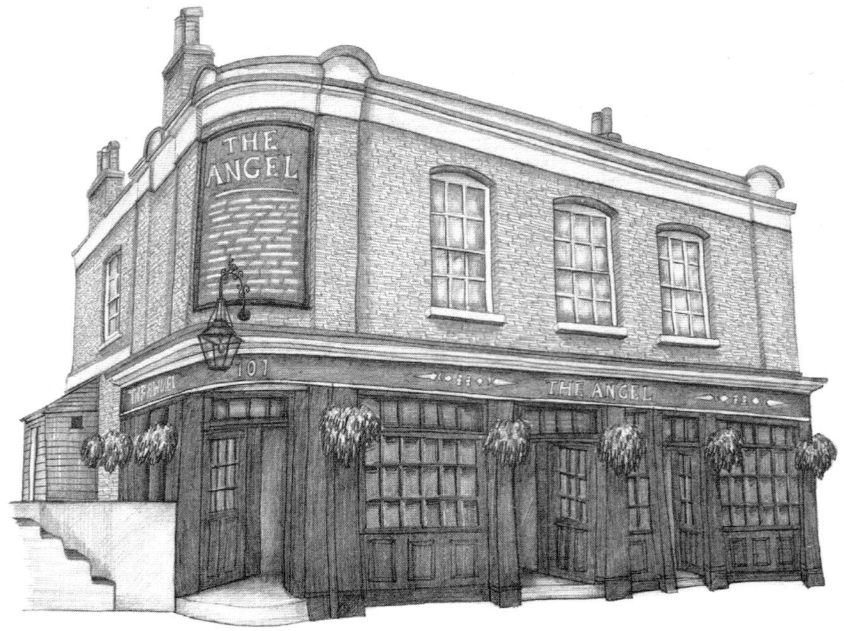

The Dove, Hammersmith

I walk down a sweet little alleyway which curves round to reveal
a pub made of bricks, with a swinging sign and two old-fashioned
lanterns. This picturesque lane has been home to a public house
here since the seventeenth century, its doors welcoming famous
faces such as King Charles II, actress Nell Gwynne and poet James
Thomson. As I duck my head through the doorway, the light is low,
dark wooden beams line the ceiling, and a bar greets me on the right.
I walk through a small entrance which leads to the other side of the
bar, amused to see a tiny snug with only two stools and a window.
On the wall is a certificate from *The Guinness Book of Records*
certifying that this miniature space has been awarded the record
for smallest public bar room in Britain.

I continue my journey through The Dove, its walls decorated with
plaques and photographs, its floors scattered with round tables and
small cushioned stools. The interior is comforting and old, and the
space is quiet and dark. I follow the light at the other end of the
restaurant room, the bright sunshine from the window beckoning me
to the back of the pub. I exit through the door and stand on the deck.
Looking out over the awesome view, which is framed by the plants
surrounding the beer garden, I observe how the other side of the river
is lined with green bushy trees. I notice a blue walkway to my left,
a bridge that leads to private boathouses. I study its gates and see
it is open – I've just found my drawing spot for the day.

I leave the pub in pursuit of the bridge. I step on to it; there's a
gap between each slat of wood and I can clearly see the water lapping
the bank beneath me. I feel a weird wobble shiver through my body.
My legs stiffen and my gaze lifts away from the drop below. I try to
suppress my fear of heights and eventually reach the middle of the

walkway to look over at The Dove. The building is submerged amongst the greenery that grows around it – the angle is perfect. I take a deep breath, open my bag and begin to take out my drawing tools. Too scared of losing a pencil through a gap, I keep them in my pocket. My legs shake as I bend down to retrieve the paper from the depths of my bag. My chin is constantly raised and my eyes look straight ahead, so as not to remind myself of the water that moves beneath me. I tentatively start my drawing, the wispy lines less straight than usual, the tremors from my ankles having made their way through my legs and up to my hand which moves shakily across my page.

I slowly turn my head to take in the views across the water. I see streamlined rowers glide, their bodies moving back and forth in sync, the boat seeming almost weightless as if just skimming the surface of the water. I look behind me at tiny cars driving over another bridge in the distance. I see people walking along the banks of the river, looking between the rocks, hoping to find historic treasures. I peer beneath me at last and see all types of birds: geese with long black necks and wide flat feet that grip the rocks they step on; seagulls bobbing in the water, their white wings tucked neatly away and their bright beady eyes staring right back at me. Even the pigeons swoop in to join the flock, their grey smattering of feathers camouflaged amongst the stones as they weave and hop around them.

After finally relaxing into my position on the walkway, I begin to embrace the gaps beneath my feet, using them to spy on birds and insects floating along the river. I now draw The Dove with conviction, sketching a pair of geese inquisitively inspecting the riverbank, shading the shadows of individual rocks and scribbling the different textures of plants around the pub. I finish my drawing, holding it high in front of me for a photo. I triumphantly exit the bridge and find myself back in the pub's beer garden, clasping my drawing and a glass of wine and looking proudly back at the bridge I conquered for my sketch.

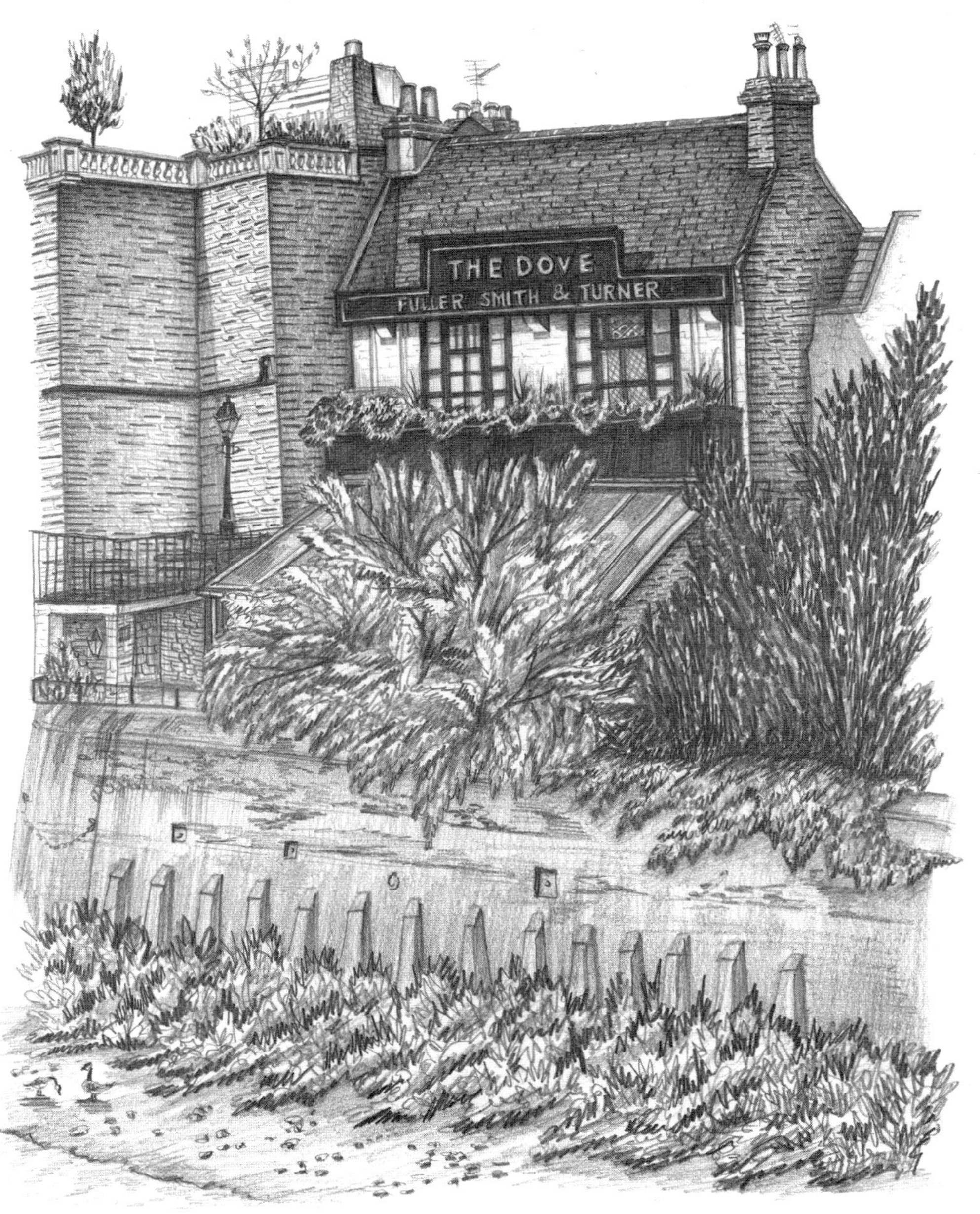
THE DOVE
FULLER SMITH & TURNER

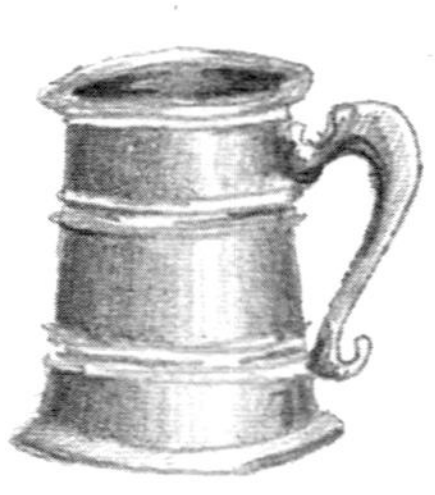

ANCIENT

Londoners have been infatuated with pubs for centuries, from painting and drawing them to writing in and about them, as well as drinking in them: pubs have long been a way of life in the city. The walls of these ancient taverns have hosted authors, celebrities, artists and royals, they've watched London's landscape burn, rebuild and change, and they've preserved and passed down the stories we still tell today.

As I wind through alleyways, hike the waterways and duck under doorways, I stumble into some of the city's oldest boozers, sketching those taverns that have sat in the same spot for hundreds of years, slowly sinking into the pavement, held up by history.

From the preserved exteriors to the haunted corners, these infamous inns not only take me back in time but also show me just how integral these pubs are to the city today, as they have been for centuries. I learn their stories from informational plaques, eavesdrop on historical pub tours and listen to the bar staff share their knowledge with all who have entered these ancient London pubs.

The George, London Bridge

I exit London Bridge station, pass the huge shiny bottom of The Shard and weave between the throngs of people charging up and down Borough High Street. A hovering lantern and iron letters that read 'The George' lead me through a pair of large open gates into the courtyard outside the pub. The timber-framed gallery lining the front of the building is the first thing I notice. This is a unique feature of the last surviving London coaching inn – each wonky spindle of the balustrade boxes in the balcony and each window behind it slopes in a different direction. The building I see before me today was rebuilt after a devastating fire in 1676 which destroyed many buildings across Southwark, including the original inn. The plaque above the door commemorates the original sixteenth-century tavern and reveals that the current Grade I listed pub is owned by the National Trust.

I move back to assess the whole building, its wide shape stretches across the space, and its galleried frontage is unlike any pub I've drawn before. I reverse until the pub is in full view and I can't step back any further. I feel cold, hard metal against the back of my leg and turn to see that it's a keg, one of a mountain of them. I decide to nestle myself in the pile, using one to sit on and another to lean my sketchbook on. Hidden amongst the silver barrels, I take out my pencil, sharpener and rubber, turn my sketchbook on its side and flip over the cover to reveal a clean, blank canvas.

The quiet cobbled space between me and The George lies still. The only movement is a few bar staff carrying supplies and greeting me while I draw. I silently sketch the outline of the building and then colour in each murky window with the tip of my pencil. I push the graphite into the paper to shade underneath the balconies and scribble the mounds of flowers that hang over the balustrade.

As I illustrate, I imagine the horse-drawn coaches arriving in the yard 350 years ago, the sound of their wheels and the horses' hooves gently echoing off the walls, the low-lit lanterns guiding in patrons and the smog of London hovering over the black and white facade.

Today, the rumble of cars and buses reverberates around the courtyard, the never-ending noise of drilling from a faraway construction site fills the air and the large bin lorry reversing through the gates beeps incessantly. Two bin men come over to have a look at my drawing before attaching the large tub full of bottles from the night before to the back of the truck. The bin upturns, and the glass violently crashes into the rear of the vehicle. They eventually jump back in the truck, and I wave to them and smile, as the lorry leaves a sour stink in its wake. A tour group enter the gates; they don't notice me burrowed beneath the beer and I eavesdrop on their history lesson. I overhear the guide talk of The George's association with Charles Dickens, his time spent here and his inclusion of it in his novel *Little Dorrit*. I eventually emerge from the pile of kegs, stretch out my legs and photograph my drawing in front of the pub. The group of Americans on the tour surround me and take photos of the artwork too. We chat briefly about the pub's ancient architecture before we go our separate ways, they on to their next historical conquest, and I into the comfort of The George.

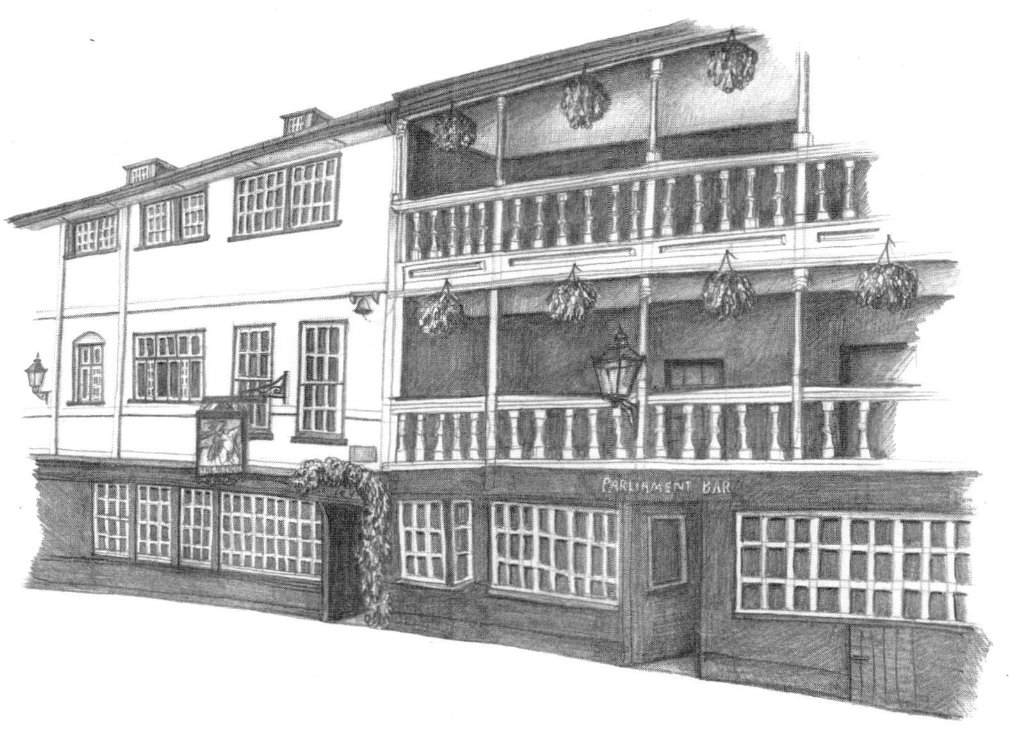
PARLIAMENT BAR

The Mayflower, Rotherhithe

The old warehouses that line my walk, their brown and black bricks weathered, create a repetitive montage of textures along the cobbled brick streets of Rotherhithe. I eventually reach St Mary's Church, with its tall steeple, stained-glass windows and red-brick arches – a standout building on the now-residential street. Across from the eighteenth-century church is another anomaly amongst the converted shipyards and warehouses. The Mayflower has a gently sloped roof with overlapping tiles and black crosshatch windows that contrast against the white painted facade of the pub. The only vibrant colour comes from the overflowing hanging baskets of flowers, the blue plaque and the pub's swinging sign.

Drawing the sign, I shade in the crashing waves and the miniature Mayflower ship with its wide sails blowing in the wind. The pub's sign tells the story of the ship's first stage of its turbulent voyage in 1620 from its homeport of Rotherhithe to Southampton, captained by Christopher Jones of Rotherhithe, who is buried at St Mary's church close to the mooring point of the ship and across the road from the pub. The dark windows that mask the pub's interior reflect a gentle light off their unusual pastel-coloured glass. I mimic the window's shine, swapping between my two pencils and turning to the softer lead for the darker panes and the harder pencil for a lighter touch. I delve deeper into the pub's history through both drawing and encounters with passersby. One particularly knowledgeable onlooker informs me that apparently there's been a pub on this site since around 1550. She goes on to reveal that the original tavern was named the Shippe Inn, and that, after a fire, it was replaced by The Spread Eagle and Crown, until it was rebuilt a third time in 1957 after war damage, finally rising as The Mayflower I see in front of me today.

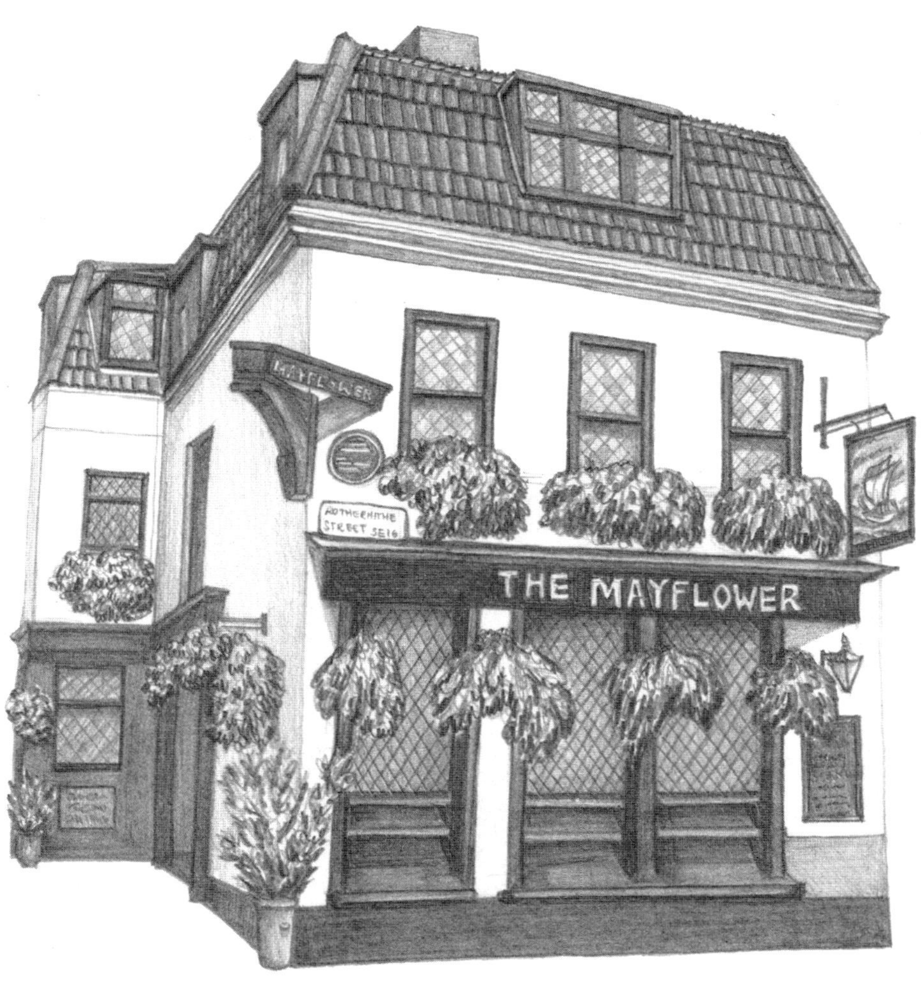
MAYFLOWER
ROTHERHITHE
STREET SE16
THE MAYFLOWER

I leave my spot outside the pub to duck into the gloomy doorway and grab a pint of lager. I look around to see that the ode to the pub's namesake doesn't stop with the sign I just drew. The walls are busy with framed artworks of ships, and nautical-themed artefacts – such as old-fashioned fish cages, lanterns and a wooden helm – hang from the dark beams above my head. As I wait for my turn at the bar, the room fills up around me with early evening bookings. Bizarrely, I see a visitor excitedly purchase a stamp with their pint. Confused by this unfamiliar exchange, I inquire and find out that The Mayflower is the only licensed pub to offer this service and US and UK stamps are available at request behind the bar. A stamp along with their pint helped seafarers short on time buy their postage to write to loved ones without leaving the pub. A convenient novelty back then, as it still is today.

I find a seat on a low wooden bench, sitting with my back to a fish tank and facing a stag's head that hangs above the fireplace. The highly adorned walls, the hanging heirlooms and the atmospheric aura of the confined interior make me feel like I'm drinking inside a wondrous maritime capsule.

The Old Bell Tavern, Fleet Street

It's a drizzly day in London; the pale, grey sky seems to inform the mood of the city around me. Londoners hurry out of Blackfriars station, heads down, brollies up, faces skewed. The moist air is unrelenting, not quite wet enough to run for cover, but too wet to relax outside. I have earmarked a dry spot for the day, an unconventional sketching location and a first for me: a coffee shop. I step inside the quiet cafe and join a small queue of people ordering their takeaway hot drinks. I order mine to stay in: a cup of English breakfast tea and a butter croissant. I take my drink and pastry over to the large window that looks on to Fleet Street. On tiptoes, I pull myself up on to the high bar chair, lean against the narrow shelf that spans the window and look up to meet The Old Bell Tavern that faces me squarely across the street.

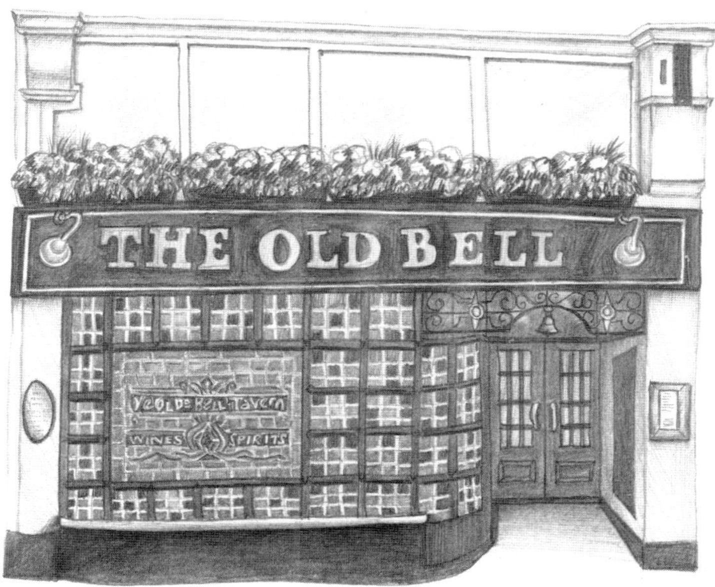

Built by Sir Christopher Wren, principal architect and part of the committee in charge of rebuilding London following the Great Fire, The Old Bell Tavern dates back to around 1678. Looking straight ahead and sipping my tea, I focus in on the exquisite window that makes up a large part of the pub's facade. I decide to highlight this feature and sketch out only the bottom half of the building on my page. I meticulously shade around the small lettering in the centre of the window, colouring each pane of glass in a different shade of grey.

Between my gaze and the pub's frontage is the restless hustle of Fleet Street. Red buses stop directly in front of my subject, prompting me to twiddle my pencil between my fingers, impatiently waiting for the traffic to shift. The ceaseless pedestrians that travel along the pavement in front of me distract me from my endeavour and entice me to watch the different people passing by instead. Fleet Street, famously known for its connection to journalism and the historic home of many iconic newspaper publications, played host to the first printing press in the 1500s. The Old Bell Tavern has not only served journalists for centuries, but the building is thought to have originally been used as accommodation for the stonemasons who worked on rebuilding nearby St Bride's Church after the Great Fire.

The small bit of tea at the bottom of my cup has gone completely cold, only crumbs are left from my pastry and my drawing is finished. I look outside to see a brighter sky. I leave the coffee shop, thanking them for their hospitality, and bring my sketchbook with me across the road. I dart through a pause in the traffic and, on the other side, I walk underneath the small golden bell and through the door. A dimly lit room sits immediately to my left, the emerging sun outside seeping through the colourful glass, refracting beams of green, orange and red into the dusky space. I continue forwards towards the bar, its large, curved wooden shape taking up the centre of the room. There are people sitting at tables all around

the moody space, enjoying food, drink and quiet conversation.
I walk up to the bar and order a lemonade and some sweet chilli crisps.

As my fizzy drink is poured, I stuff the packet of crisps into my
coat pocket and pay. Suddenly, a raucous rabble of voices behind me
signals the entrance of a never-ending crowd of people, who quickly
surround me. They are all sporting the same blue cap, some shouting,
'It's your round now, isn't it?' and 'What's the next pub after this?'
I grab my drink, sympathetically nod to the barman who seems to
be working alone today and make a beeline for a table at the back
of the room. I look around the space, catching glimpses of written
history on the walls, notable newspaper cuttings in frames and
a huge golden bell that hangs behind the bar. I finish my crisps in
seconds and take one last look at my drawing before exiting through
the back door and into the alleyway.

A pigeon skips in front of my feet as I follow it down to the
gates of St Bride's Church. I look up at the tall steeple, also designed
by Sir Christopher Wren. I recall a romantic story told about this
very steeple during a historic pub crawl I once attended myself, a
bit like the crowd of jolly pub crawlers I've just left behind. A local
apprentice baker, William Rich, wished to create a spectacular cake
for his bride-to-be, Susannah. Taking inspiration from the steeple
of St Bride's Church, he went on to create an impressive layered
cake for her, thereby setting a trend and starting the tradition of
the tiered wedding cakes we know and love today. I smile up at
the steeple and across at The Old Bell Tavern one last time, before
I turn the corner and return to Fleet Street. I join the wave of people
marching down the historic pavements. looking up at the ancient
buildings, rebuilt and preserved for us alongside the ever-growing
contemporary landscape.

The Grenadier, Belgravia

It's a pleasantly warm September day as I pass through the streets of Belgravia, their smooth cream buildings mirrored down the elegant road. The house numbers are painted so meticulously, each window box so well maintained, that I start to feel a little underdressed in comparison. Walking on to Wilton Row, the street begins to bend, the surface beneath my feet becomes uneven and the buildings that line the road change. Old wooden garage doors, brick homes and white rendered walls all mix and match along the path: still a very clean promenade, just one with a little more variety. As I approach the end of the street, a taller building stands alone, with white render and blue window surrounds, a red door and an old guard box. A historic gem at the end of the mews: The Grenadier.

The swinging pub sign gives a clear indication of the pub's history and namesake. The painting depicts the Grenadier Guards, with an officer standing in front of his regiment, leaning on his rifle. The building was originally built in 1720 as an officers' mess – a venue where military personnel could come to live, eat and socialise. As I sketch in the guard's fluffy bearskin, pushing my pencil down hard to achieve a dark grey shade, I watch people enter the pub. A couple excitedly takes photos outside, swapping the phone between them and posing one at a time inside the red guard's box. A man in a suit strides up the stairs into the pub with a laptop under his arm. A painter with white emulsion on his boots sits on the bench with a pint and chats loudly on the phone. Lunchtime hits and the pub begins to fill. I continue my drawing, leaving much of the paper unshaded to mimic the white render.

Soon it's time to go inside and relax after four solid hours of drawing. I step through the thickly painted doors and am

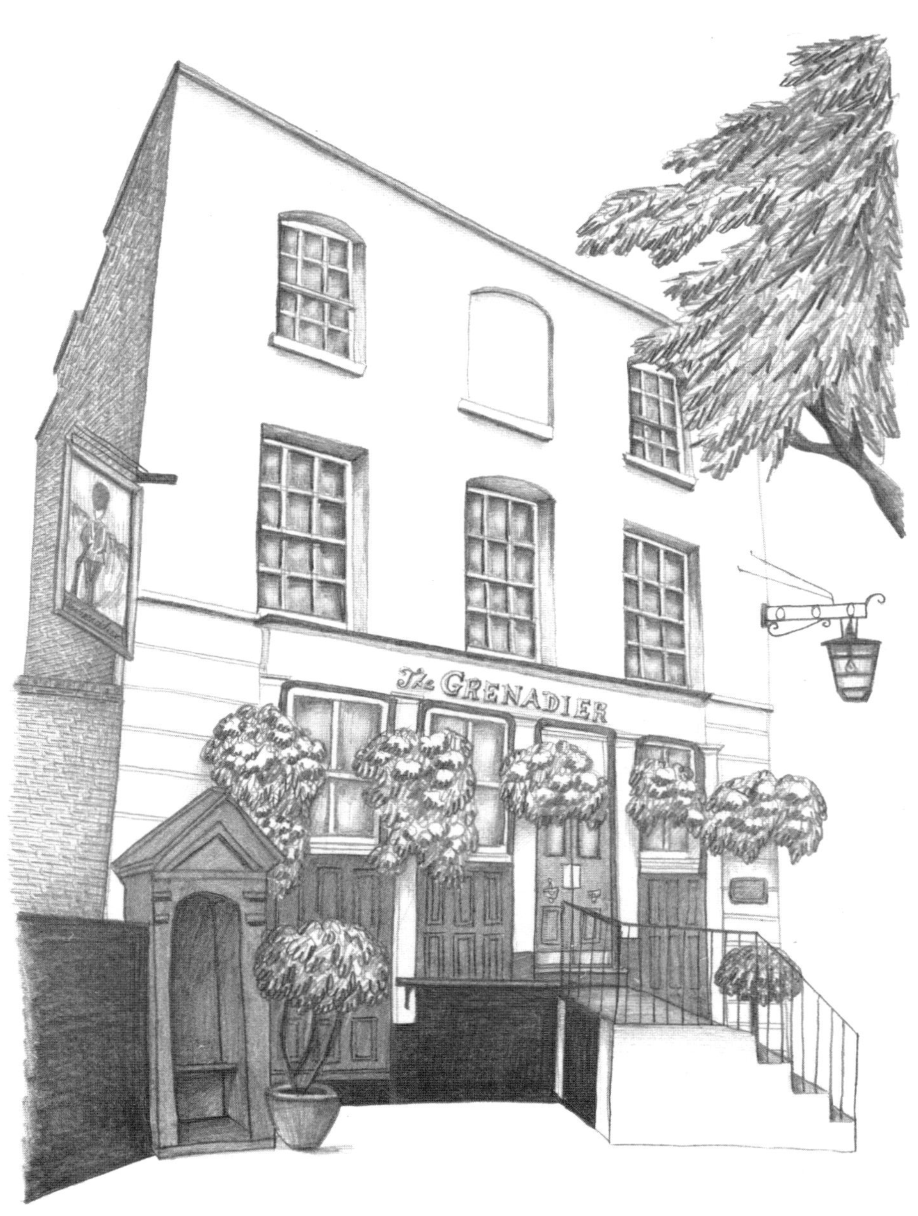

The GRENADIER

immediately met by the bar only a few steps in front of the entrance. The front room is modest in size, with only a few tables and stools. The suited man works on his laptop in a corner, and the couple eat scampi on a higher table. The barman greets me politely and quietly; I match his low volume and order a ginger ale, craving a cold fizzy drink to refresh myself after working away in the sun all morning. I take my drink and sit around a small square table next to the unlit fireplace.

The walls are covered in military memorabilia; there's a leaning mannequin dressed in the same guard's uniform as the pub sign and another uniform encased in a glass cabinet. There are paintings of battles, photos of battalions and portraits of military leaders. I place my drawing on the table, a surface barely big enough to fit both my drink and my artwork. I look up at the ceiling, which is plastered with banknotes of different currencies from all over the world, some even scrawled with writing. Supposedly, the notes are offerings made by visitors who want to help pay off Cedric's debt. Legend has it that a young soldier, Cedric, was beaten to death here after cheating at a game of cards. Exactly when this happened is unclear, perhaps in the 1800s during the month of September, which is when the resident ghost is meant to be most restless. While I don't witness any paranormal activity on this particular visit, I definitely sense The Grenadier's connection to its past: proudly displaying its military relics and preserving its antiquity for visitors to come.

'The Grenadier … where my then-girlfriend (now wife)
and I celebrated after I proposed in Hyde Park.
That pub will always hold a special place in our hearts
as the place where our family story began. Today,
we await the arrival of our first child.'
TOMAS

The Lamb and Flag, Covent Garden

As I walk around the outside of Covent Garden Market, a man in a waistcoat balances an object on his nose and counts down loudly through his microphone. Just around the corner, loud bass comes from a speaker and a group are doing a dance routine and encouraging the crowd to clap along. I pass people drinking outside pubs, sitting in restaurants, discussing the theatre show they just saw and others racing through the streets from work. A black cab screeches to a stop beside me and drops off a couple of friends, who pay the driver and walk ahead. I follow behind them, turning up the same cobbled hill to The Lamb and Flag. Situated in what was once a violent area, the pub was known in the early nineteenth century for hosting bare-knuckle prize fights, earning it the nickname 'The Bucket of Blood'. Nowadays, visitors flock from around the world to see Covent Garden and many make their way to this iconic – and thankfully less bloody – historic London pub.

Approaching the pub, I see my friends amongst the crowd. It's a pleasantly warm evening in the city, and the space outside The Lamb and Flag is full. The windows at the front of the building are open and two blokes sit in silent company at the windowsill facing the horde of jovial after-work drinkers. I head inside to order a pint, stepping over the uneven threshold and noticing the paint that's worn away on the open door from years of use. The tables I weave between are also scuffed at the edges from the many elbows that rest there each day. I look up to see a black and white photograph framed on the wall: an image of the same building in 1948, sporting large lettering that reads 'Barclay, Perkins & Co. Ltd'. The name of this major London brewing company was clearly given more importance than the pub's own, which was typical at that time. I order my pint

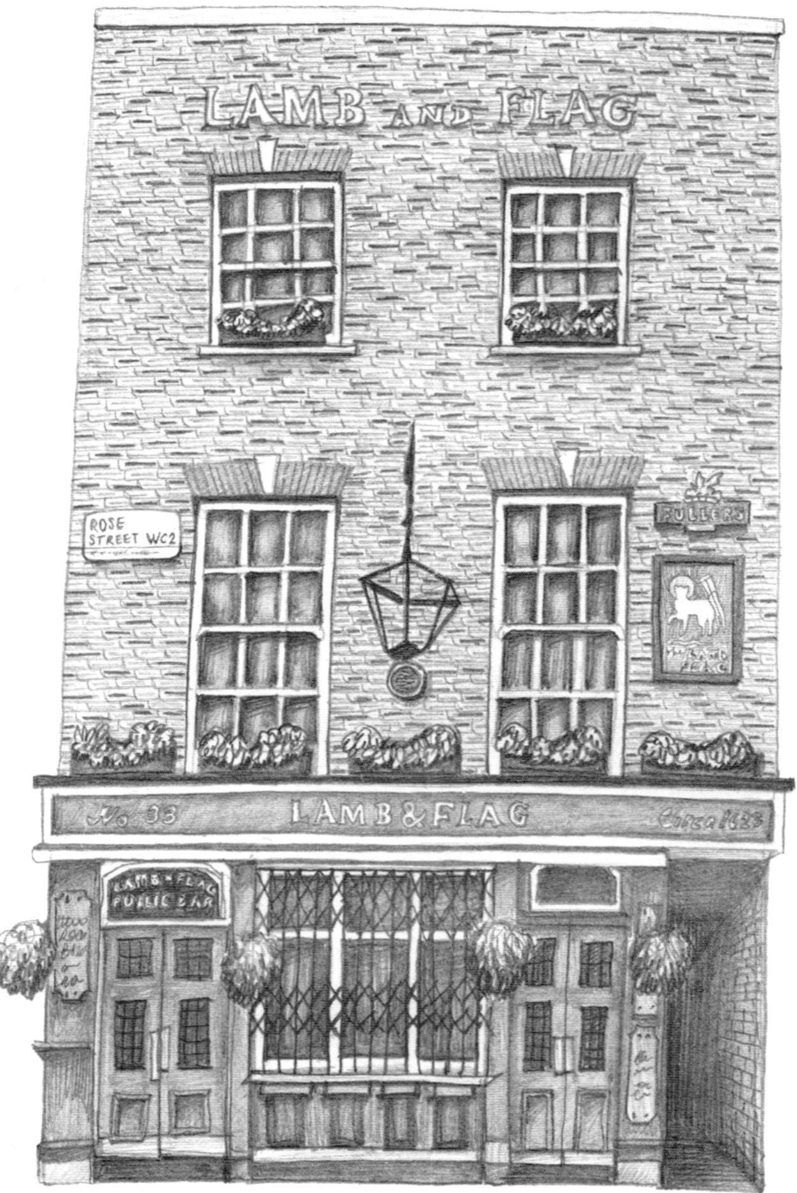
LAMB AND FLAG
ROSE
STREET WC2
FULLERS
No. 33
LAMB & FLAG
LAMB & FLAG
PUBLIC BAR

at the bar, surrounded by others who patiently wait their turns, before returning to my friends.

When I draw The Lamb and Flag, I pay special attention to the 1950s brickwork, which conceals an inner framework, thought to be an eighteenth-century house. Each brick is neatly laid in a repeating pattern according to shade. I lightly colour around the lamb which holds a flag with its front leg, originally a carved image at the top of the building, now only painted on the sign. The building is closed up when I draw it in mid-winter but on my return windows and doors are flung open.

The gathering outside is managed by a lone security guard, who notices my drawing of the pub as I show it to my friends. He excitedly whisks me and my artwork around the building, upstairs to the restaurant, down to the back of the bar and through the alleyway to the side entrance to show all his colleagues who work there. I thank him and settle back into my pint. We stay at The Lamb and Flag until the only light that remains is the warm glow from the lantern on the wall and the candlelight on each table.

The Spaniards Inn, Hampstead

There's dense forest either side of Spaniards Road, where branches overlap beneath swathes of delicate leaves. Horse chestnuts frame my walk towards the pub, their fallen conkers clogging the path ahead of me. The woodland is impenetrable; no sky can be seen through the tangle of trees, only green. I take off my jacket as I near the toll house and read the plaque on its wall as I catch my breath. The eighteenth-century building was erected to collect tolls from passing travellers. No longer in use, it still stands across the road from the much older Spaniards Inn. I wait as the traffic files through the narrow gap between the two buildings, eventually managing to hop across the road between cars and reach the other side. I look up at the spooky exterior, its dark windows and the large looming lantern over the creaky door look like an illustration from a Gothic novel. I push against the front door, but it's locked, so I creep around to the side entrance and tentatively step inside.

A warm wooden interior welcomes me; the sixteenth-century pub has thick beams which hang a few inches above my head, period fireplaces and different paintings of the pub on the wall. The room has a charming and cosy atmosphere. I have brought a print of my drawing to the pub as a gift for them. I shyly take the artwork out of my bag and check it. I see the dark lines, the shading that contrasts with the cream page it lies upon and the tree's branches that peer into the drawing, hugging the pub. The two people waiting to seat visitors at the door greet me and are kind and enthusiastic about my artwork, taking it to show their colleagues. I continue towards the bar and order myself a tea and some brunch.

While I wait, I explore each room of the pub. I walk up the worn wooden stairs, following the footsteps of many historic figures who

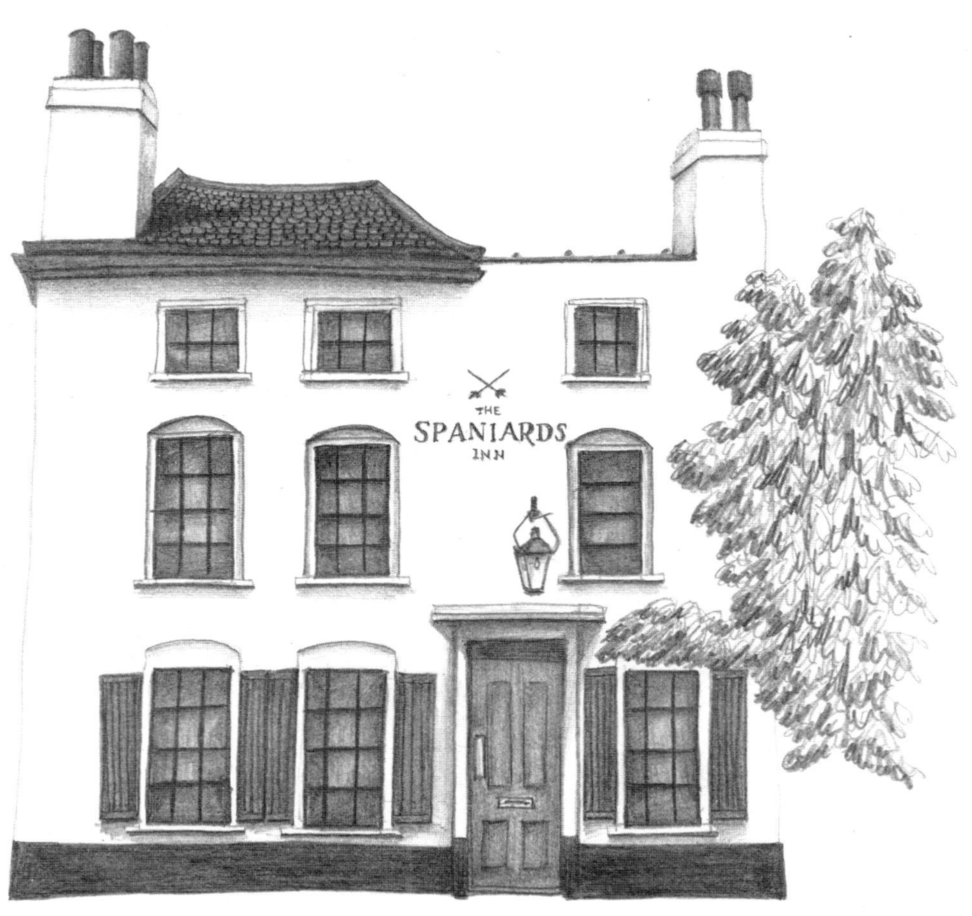
THE
SPANIARDS
INN

have also visited this ancient tavern. Said to be a writer's paradise, it has served as inspiration to novelists such as Charles Dickens and poets like John Keats and Lord Byron. Two dining rooms upstairs, with their lopsided windows and leaning rooms, are named after Keats and Dickens, their names painted on the doors. It's even thought that resident ghosts influenced some of the plot in Bram Stoker's *Dracula*. Learning this, I hastily wind back down the creepy hallways, rushing towards the bar to bring myself back to the present day.

I choose a solitary seat in a side room and wait for my food. I blow on my tea and watch the walkers come in with muddy boots, order at the bar and go to find a seat in the large beer garden. I look out of the window to see more trees surrounding the seats outside: it's an overgrown haven for the weary walkers coming from Hampstead Heath. Suddenly, a voice behind me engages me in conversation. A remarkably well-dressed gentleman in a suit, with a napkin tucked into his collar and a large brandy at his hand, sits at the table in the corner. 'A wonderful pub, isn't it?' he says, and I agree. 'I've been to Kenwood House down the road, and I've been past the toll house before, but never this pub. I don't know what took me so long.' I smile and we both remark on the 'wonky' architecture and the 'rickety' floors, agreeing it's these characteristics of pubs we both admire.

I turn back to enjoy my meal and read my book. Upon leaving the pub I wish the gentleman a nice day, before I head towards the door. The pub is fuller now, with a group eagerly waiting at the bar and the beer garden beginning to fill. I take one last look at the room; with its aged interior and ancient atmosphere, it's a place I hope will be here for another 440 years.

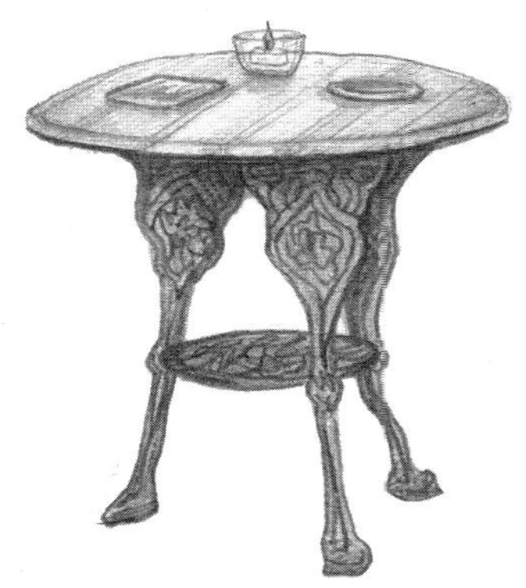

*'The pub is The Grove Tavern, at the corner of Adie Road and
Hammersmith Grove. It's actually not such a pretty place …
it holds sentimental and childhood memories for me! I remember
there being a Ladies' Bar and suppose there must have been a
Gentlemen's Bar too. These are wartime memories or just post-war.
They were happy days … I remember the intense London fogs due to
coal-fire pollution: staring out the window and not seeing more
than a few feet ahead, neither garden nor street being visible.'*

PENELOPE

LANDLORDS

From landlords and landladies to managers and staff, the people who own, license and run these establishments are at the helm of the pub. Their particular insight into their communities, their generous hospitality and the way they choose to run their pubs form the very backbone of these London boozers.

I am in awe of the hospitality I receive across the city, the kindness I am shown and the enthusiasm for the project. Whether it's a pint on the house after a drawing day or a message to ask me to come sketch their pub, I always look forward to visiting these beloved places – often run by big characters.

As I draw my way through the city, I meet the passionate people looking after these watering holes and see how they work tirelessly to preserve them for generations to come but still take the time to stop for a chat, pour your drink, introduce you to the pub dog and welcome you inside their pub.

King Charles I, Kings Cross

I leave home with only a sketchbook, a pencil, a sharpener and a rubber. I have been recommended a pub near Kings Cross, so I head in that direction. I exit the train and am immediately consumed by the chaos; fast-moving Londoners internally growl as they weave through people and traffic. I pace behind them, taking advantage of their slipstream and head in the direction of Northdown Street. I turn right down the quiet backstreet and approach the front of the King Charles I pub; its bright green and yellow sign sits above a yellow doorframe. I spy a tall, chunky tree stump and decide its exposed flat surface will be my makeshift drawing table for the day. I open my sketchbook at the first blank page and begin to draw.

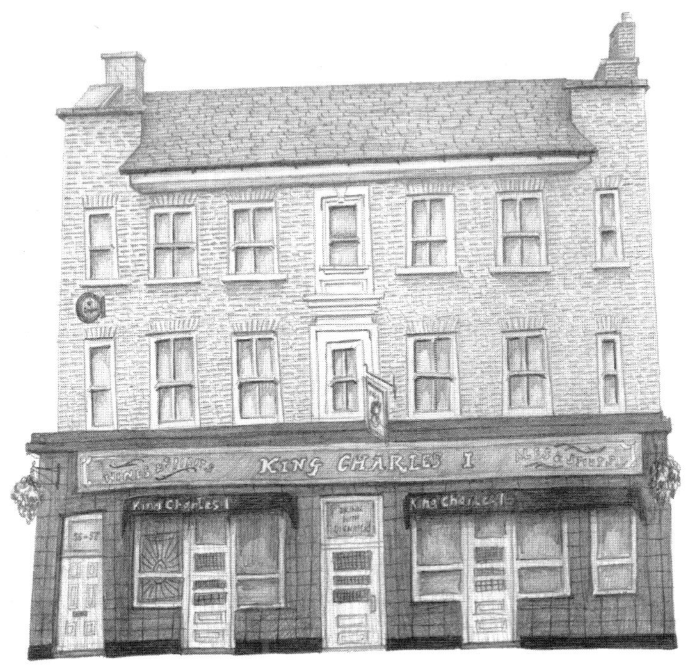

Only an hour into my work, someone emerges from the pub holding a large glass of red wine. He makes his way towards me and the tree, introduces himself as Simon and hands over the glass of red – it's on the house. I learn that the pub was saved in 2015 by supportive and loyal locals and is now a community-owned backstreet boozer. Simon works at the King Charles I, a familiar face to regulars, and he's delighted I've come to draw it. He walks back across the road, leaving me to continue my drawing. Before my pencil touches the paper again, a regular exits the yellow doorway sporting a smart tweed suit, walks over to chat and tells me this has been his beloved local for many years. He goes back into the pub only to pass by another punter who is striding across the street to meet me. The regular lunchtime drinkers take it in turns to come out and watch my progress, stuffing cash in my hand for prints before the drawing is even finished and offering me more glasses of red wine. I finally finish my drawing, my back sore from bowing over the tree stump, my heart warm from the welcome.

I walk into the pub and sit myself and my drawing opposite the bar. The inside is cosy, just the one room, with a sweet, small bar at the centre. A couple of friends surround the jukebox and line up another song. Around the room are animal heads, their beady eyes staring ahead, a gilded gold mirror, various music posters and a piano tucked in the corner. I merrily chat to the others on neighbouring tables as I finish my final glass of red wine. I promise Simon a print and thank him for his hospitality before taking my drawing home.

Today, three years later, when I walk into the King Charles I, I smile as I pass my framed drawing by the door and head towards the bar where Simon still greets me with the same warmth he did that first day. I order a red wine, take it outside and sit on the bench with friends, looking out across the road where the tree stump once was.

Duke of Wellington, Belgravia

I can see the Duke of Wellington pub, also known as the 'Duke of Boots', as I walk down a quaint street in Belgravia. Each house is immaculately painted, each front garden in full bloom. It's mid-morning and the street is quiet. I take out my phone to photograph different angles of the pub before settling on a position to sketch from. As I'm doing this, a man jumps out of a parked car with his dog on a lead. He asks if I'm drawing the pub today. I nod, and he smiles with excitement. His little dog wags its tail vigorously; his floppy ears lay over his cheeks, and I stroke his curly coat of black and white. This is Digby, the pub dog. And his owner is Michael, the landlord.

They leave me to it, and I continue to set up on the corner of the pavement. The square pub faces me at an angle, and I draw its contrasting shadows in the windows, the tiny ashtrays and the different textures of the pavement outside. On one side of the building, the brickwork is two-toned. A passerby tells me that the pub was hit during the Blitz and that the lighter bricks were used to patch the damage. Looking at them now, I see the pub's endurance.

My friends Hannah and Kat bump into me absorbed in my sketch. We can't believe our luck, and I take a break for lunch while we catch up over a beer. The warmth hits the outside tables, and we relax in the glow of the afternoon sun. I cross the road and get back to work, and they continue on their way. Suddenly, another dog greets me: a little, rotund pug snuffling around the bottom of my easel. Its owner proudly exclaims that his dog, Billy the pug, has been a regular much longer than resident pub dog Digby and that I should draw him instead.

I meet Michael again as he returns to the pub later in the day. He brings Digby back over and voluntarily refrains from seeing the drawing until it's finished, holding in his excitement at the pending artwork. I jot down a little portrait of Digby next to the pub before I declare the artwork complete. As I pack away my belongings, my friend Clemmie screeches her bike to a halt and surprises me on the pavement, having noticed me on the street on her way back from work. I am tickled by another chance encounter, reminding me that London really does feel quite small sometimes, like a village of locals rather than a city of strangers.

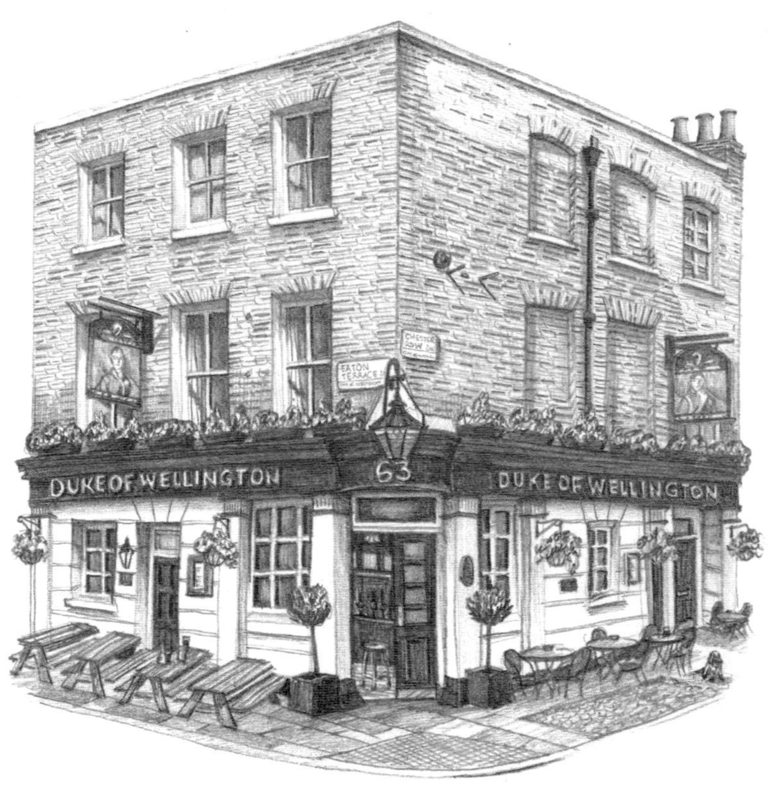

Turner's Old Star, Wapping

I find a grassy patch opposite Turner's Old Star. A block of flats lines the street behind me and there's an open green to the right of the pub. The unusually shaped boozer I'm about to sketch looks like a flat wall with a building attached behind it. It intrigued me from the moment I first saw a photograph of it. I start my drawing with its angular outline. I hear a voice and lift my head up from my easel. The landlord, Paul, calls over and casually asks me to come show him the drawing when I've finished, then he disappears into the pub.

The sun heats the top of my head. My hair feels hot, and I put my sunglasses on to stop me from squinting at my subject. My friend Mariana emerges from the pub with an ice-cold bottle of beer; I press the icy glass against my forehead for relief before taking a sip. We stay outside the pub for a few more hours while I sketch; she sits on the low brick wall, I'm on my stool. I carefully compose the windows with my pencil tip, sketching the small stained-glass panes and adding marks for the etched glass. The tiny pub sign depicts the famous painter J. M. W. Turner donning a black top hat and coat. Turner became involved with Sophia Booth, a Margate landlady, who was later made landlady at the Wapping tavern, which was then known as 'The Old Star'. Paul proudly tells me the current sign was painted by a local artist and friend of the pub, Ed Bucknall. I sketch in Turner's little top hat before my drawing is complete, and I take it inside. As I pass by the entrance, I notice another piece of the pub's history. I read the London Dungeon plaque attached to the exterior. Lydia Rogers was found guilty and confessed her crimes of evil pacts and witchcraft here in 1658.

Mariana and I sit opposite the bar, order a couple more bottles of beer and enjoy the traditional interior of the room: the beautifully carved bar, even more etched glass and dark wooden floorboards. We play a game of pool with my drawing propped up against the wall next to our drinks. The familiar sounds of the ball rolling over the green felt, satisfyingly knocking against the wood and dropping into the pocket fill the quiet space. There are only a few other occupied tables during the quiet weekday lunchtime. On one is a lone local, who asks to see the drawing and is very kind about my work. This is his nearest pub and he's been coming here for years. Paul and his wife Bernice have run this local for over two decades, their longevity is clear to see as they chat to visitors, old and new, welcoming them inside the Turner's Old Star like family. As I leave, Paul thanks me and requests prints of the drawing so he can gift them to his regulars.

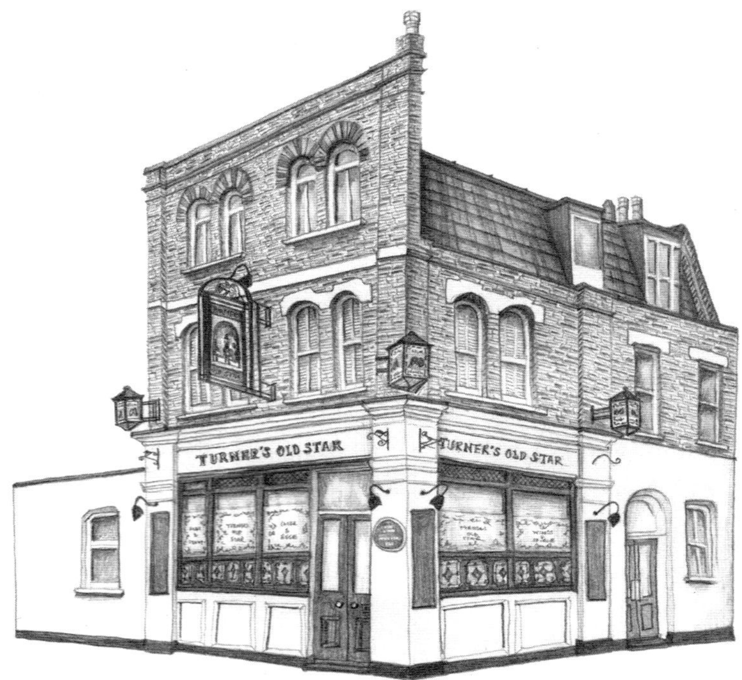

The General Napier, Honor Oak Park

It's starting to rain strongly now on our way home, so my friends and I sprint down the dark residential street and dip into The General Napier to catch our breath and shake the droplets off our coats. The pub is busy; it's karaoke night and the next person is revving up to take their place behind the mic. We walk to the bar and order a round of drinks and a few packets of crisps to share. We choose the table by the front door and open the crisps, laying the packets flat so the crispy morsels sit on a makeshift plate. We share our snacks and talk loudly over a punter passionately singing 'Wonderwall'.

I peer over at the darts board and suggest a game. I am standing behind the imaginary line, the dart between my fingers, ready to make my throw, when to my surprise I notice my own drawing next to me. The smoothly shaded building, its blue walls coloured grey. The looping fairy lights in front of the pub, my pencil stroke strongly lining the black wire. The same lights I can see glinting through the steamed-up windows beside me. My framed rendition of the pub is hung on the wall next to the front door. I realise the person who originally commissioned me to draw it has gifted the pub a print, a present for his local. Excited and proud, I take a photo of my framed drawing, before taking my throw at the board.

One of the landlords, Michael, comes over to meet us, noticing we aren't regulars, and welcomes us to the pub. He introduces us to the other proprietors of The General Napier, Becks and Mart. We chat about my drawing, and he thanks me for creating it. After hearing that I'm looking for a studio, he suggests that I could take residence in their outbuilding. He introduces us to the pub dog, Blu, who totters slowly between the tables, and flops down in front of the bar, looking up at each punter passing by with sweet doting eyes.

This warm welcome off a wet street in South East London compels us to settle in for another round of drinks and darts and cheer on the karaoke, before reluctantly heading home after last orders.

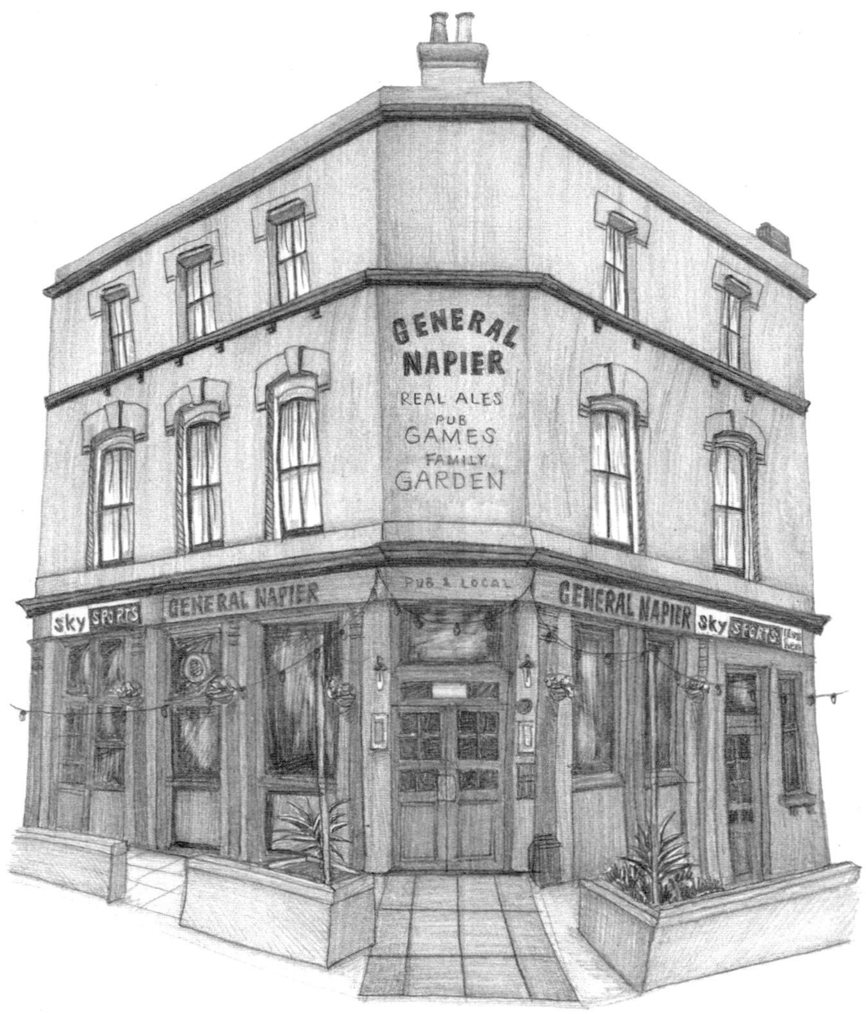

The Globe Tavern, Borough

I stand in the belly of Borough Market; the sounds and smells of food saturate the air around me. Dense crowds move in sluggish waves between the market stalls, peering at the offerings around them. I tuck myself next to the market shutters opposite the rounded front of The Globe. A security guard comes to ask what I'm up to. I explain, and he points up to the ceiling to warn me about the pigeons perching directly above my head. I notice the splatters on the floor next to me, but I decide to risk it and stay put – anything for the perfect angle. The large railway bridge that cuts through the market's roof also covers the top of the pub. I decide to move its steel tracks to the corner of my page with my pencil, bending reality, so the full pub outline comes into view.

An enthusiastic individual bounds around the market, chatting to traders at length, laughing with the stern security guards and buzzing about the space, spreading smiles wherever he goes. All of a sudden, he heads in my direction and greets me as if we're old friends, even though I've never seen him before in my life. His name is Archie, and he is one of the landlords of the pub, which he runs with co-landlord and partner Chris. He welcomes me to the market, excitedly peers over my shoulder at the drawing and insists I come in for a drink when I'm ready. Someone from a nearby stall offers me some delicious gelato to keep me going. I am stopped by countless tourists who are excited to learn about the project and experience a piece of pub culture. A waiter waves at me from the restaurant window above the pub. I see eagle-eyed visitors take photos by the pub's side door, which was the setting for Bridget Jones's flat in the films. The chaos of the market continues to rattle around my still, solitary stance.

Once I'm finished, I pack down my easel, my drawing board and my pencil case into my bag, leaving only my drawing out so I can show Archie. I head inside the busy pub, where some people stand around the long bar and others are tucked into corners on high stools. I approach the bar and show the landlord the drawing and he generously offers me a drink on the house. Seeing I am unsure what I fancy, he suggests a gingerbread stout as the weather is turning autumnal. It's not usually my sort of thing, but I trust his judgement. I take my drink to a corner of the pub and sit watching the people happily drinking and chatting in groups around the barrels outside.

Archie calls me over and introduces me to the pub dog, Jasmine. A small brown and white Jack Russell with a pink collar, she is skipping around the other side of the bar, holding a champagne cork in her mouth. I watch as she drops it on the floor, placing her two little paws in front of her and stretching her torso in an arch. She wags her tail, looks up and picks up her cork again. I scramble to grab my pencil from my bag and add little Jasmine in the corner of my drawing, along with her emotional support champagne cork. Before I leave, Archie asks how I found the beer. I can be honest: it tasted great and was the perfect end to an autumnal day outside this iconic boozer in the heart of Borough Market.

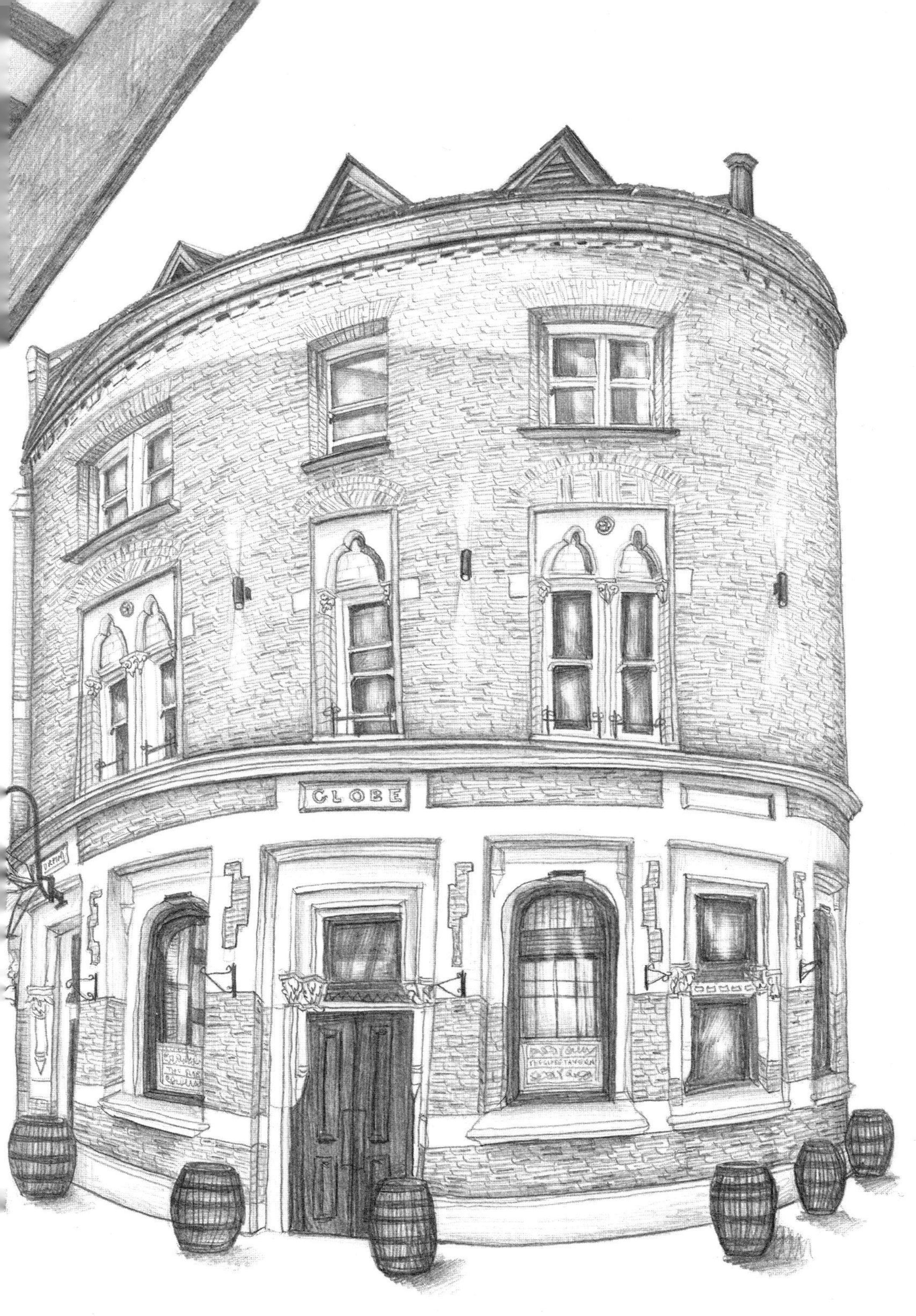
GLOBE

The Keys, Tower of London

It's five degrees in London and I exit London Bridge station pulling
the collar of my long wool coat tightly around my neck. I stride
in the direction of Tower Bridge, picking up the pace to get some
warmth back into my bones. I walk over the bridge looking out
at the Thames. A red double-decker bus crosses under the iconic
archways of the bridge; the bright blue, wintry sky behind it. I continue
my march towards another London landmark and soon find myself
walking around the grounds of the Tower of London. I stand in front
of two identical fish and chip kiosks and a souvenir shop. I take out
my phone and drop Andy a message to say I'm here. He gives me
a call and tells me which gate to go to. I walk towards the meeting
place to be let in by two security guards, and there he stands before
me. Andy's black hat mushrooms out towards the top and tapers
down to the brim. He wears a long black coat with wide red stripes
which make a linear pattern and curve round his cuffs and collar.
In the middle of the belted jacket, on his chest, is a stitched red crown
and the King's initials 'C R III'. He greets me warmly and chats to
me as we walk round the Tower. I've never met a Beefeater before.

On our journey, I am introduced to the chief Yeoman Warder, who's
not in uniform today, before continuing over the moat and through
a large brick archway. I see a stone building and a swinging pub sign,
beneath which are parked two white vans. Andy is shocked and very
apologetic that the pub frontage is completely covered by the vehicles.
I laugh, because although it's a common occurrence during my usual
on-the-street sketching, I didn't expect to run into this problem
inside the Tower of London. We decide to check out the inside of
the closed pub and wait for the vans to move. Andy unlocks the large
wooden door, and I'm relieved to step into the warmth of The Keys.

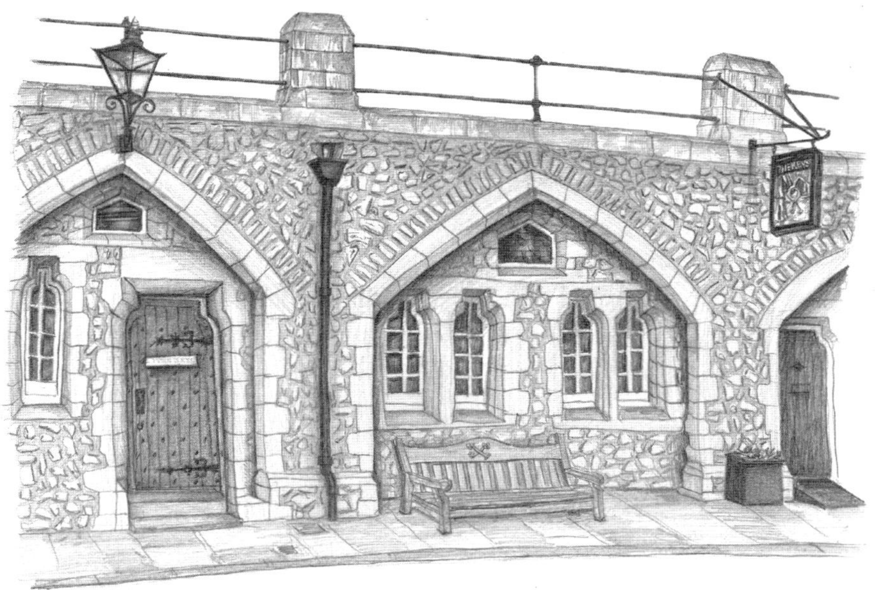

I look down at my boots to see a pinkish carpet with a distinct tufted pattern of thistles, roses and clover surrounding intricately jewelled crowns. I look up to see two rooms. The larger space is long, with a parquet floor, round high tables and red leather benches lining the wall, each emblemed with a pair of crossed keys. Andy leads me around the space. His in-depth knowledge and passion for the history of the pub and the ancient traditions of the Yeoman Warders are a delight to witness.

This solo tour leads us to cabinets displaying the different attire: one with bright red jackets, shoes with ribbons and white collars, the other featuring the same outfit Andy wears today. There are engraved cups along a wall and a large pewter bowl which the Yeoman Warders use to ceremonially toast and welcome new members. The room is covered in commemorative artworks, portraits, photographs and, at the very end, a large axe crossed with an ornate pole hung behind glass.

There's a small disco ball which hangs from the centre of the ceiling, slightly out of place. Andy smiles as he recalls it being left there after a New Year's Eve party (I suspect it was a raucous one from the look on his face). A raven head adorns the bar, where the special beers on tap include 'Beefeater bitter', 'Treason' and 'Yeoman'. Andy tells me it's £3 a pint and I gasp at the bargain. Photographs of celebrities who've visited the pub line the smaller room: Tom Hardy, Ben Stiller, Barack Obama and even the Muppets. This room is reserved for off-duty Yeoman Warders looking for a more relaxed bar environment. There's a TV in the corner and a large group photo of the Beefeaters at the top of the space. It's been over an hour, and I feel overwhelmed with excitement at the space I've had a chance to encounter in such detail. We head outside and are thankful to see the vans have gone. Andy leaves me to draw, and now the real work begins.

I take a few steps back to look at the old armoury turned pub. The Keys' exterior is comprised of one stone wall, a door, a swinging sign and arched windows. I look to my right to see a huge grey tree, its leafless branches occupying the sky above the pub, and I sit a few metres from it to begin my drawing. I work steadily, moving my hands in my fingerless gloves, sketching in the architectural details of this unique London pub. Behind me walk Henry VIII and Anne Boleyn, who smile at me, and the actors are let through the rope which cordons off this space from the public.

I pull my hat over my ears, let out a cold breath and begin to draw each individual stone on the wall of the pub. Andy pops back and introduces me to two more Yeoman Warders, one is the official landlord of The Keys, the other a newly joined member, not yet in uniform. I congratulate him before continuing with my sketch. I am brought a cup of tea which saves my fingers from freezing, and I scoff a cheese sandwich beside what is supposedly the most haunted tower.

I continue to draw The Keys with care, shading the shadows beneath the arches, engraving the keys on the bench and colouring the wall behind the misshapen stones. The Beefeaters' private pub is finished, just in time to see Andy walk up the hill to meet me.

We walk through the deserted grounds as the early evening sky turns dark. We make a quick detour into the Yeoman Warder's office, a tall, pitched room in the round. He shows me the keys for the Ceremony of the Keys, a 700-year-old ritual performed every night at the Tower and the namesake of the pub I've just drawn. He hands over the weighty set of large keys and a gold lantern, before snapping a picture of me on my phone holding the ancient artefacts. My fingers defrost as I warm up in the office, learning more about the Yeoman Warders. Before I go, Andy invites me and friends to join him at The Keys at a later date as his guest. I agree and excitedly leave the historic tower with my drawing, looking back on a momentous day for my project and ahead to the £3 pints I'll be back for soon.

'Just after Covid, I remember when we came out of lockdown, I was just about to put my necktie on, just about to start working, I looked out the window and there was such a big crowd of people, such a huge crowd of people waiting outside. I looked out, and it was every generation possible, from about twenty to about ninety, all standing in a queue and they were anxiously waiting for the pub to open. I could see their smiling faces, everyone was talking and interacting and joking. I just looked at all their faces and it was really emotional. For the first time in a long time I just thought, the world is right again.'

TERRY, MANAGER AT BLYTHE HILL TAVERN

LOCALS

When I first began this project, the architectural intricacies of city taverns absorbed my attention. I was determined to do these buildings justice and capture their beauty through my art. As I began drawing from life, these details were accentuated by the moments of the day: the weather, the animals and the moveable parts of the pub that brought these drawings alive. But what I didn't anticipate were the human connections I would also make over my easel.

From the curious people who stopped to pay my drawing a compliment to those enthusiastic punters who offered their particular insight into the pub and its area, each encounter, however small, impacted my experience of drawing and my perspective of that pub. Suddenly, the project became much more than architectural documentation, it became layered with storytelling, emotion and connection.

The locals I have met throughout my journey so far have greatly enhanced the project and this book. They are the ones who lead me to new pubs in the city, offer kindness when perhaps my energy wavers, share knowledge which I then impart through these pages and they are the ones who keep their pubs and communities alive. These locals are the souls of their pubs and are at the heart of every drawing I do.

After all, what is a pub without its people?

The Wenlock Arms, Hoxton

It's mid-morning and Wenlock Road is deserted. I peek through windows as I walk, seeing people at desks working on computers. The large glass windows of offices reflect the winter sun across the street and smooth grey buildings line the road that leads me towards the pub. I see the red pub sign hanging over the grey pavement, a flurry of foliage beneath it, and I approach the end of the road to find The Wenlock Arms.

The last time I entered these double doors on the corner, I was joined by friends on a sunny Saturday afternoon. After enjoying a meal together around the corner, we stopped for a pint before heading home. A few more pints and many hours later we were still at the pub, playing a game of round-the-world darts, sampling different ales recommended by the bar staff and sitting on the bench outside watching the sun set on a warm midsummer evening. It was the kind of evening where nothing significant happened, but it was so perfect that it is cemented in my mind forever.

Today, I'm back to sketch the pub and there's no midsummer sun to keep me warm, just the comforting memories from my last visit.

I take my drawing board out from my bag and extend my easel to standing height. The back of the board slides on to the easel, and I place my paper on top, sticking it into place with my masking tape. I exhale a cold cloud in front of my face, pull my scarf a little tighter round my neck and put my gloves on before getting started. The street is quiet, with only my pencil and me moving on the corner of the pavement. I look up to the roof tiles, shading each one, changing the pressure of my hand as I move between the squares. Then, I look into the closed pub's windows, adding the tiny glasses that line the bar and the hanging lights which will illuminate the space later.

I turn slightly to my left and decide to include the front door of the flat which is connected to the pub and part of the same building. I see a man walk out of the same door and head in my direction. He asks if I'm drawing the pub, and I invite him to see my paper and show him my progress so far. He introduces himself as Matt and tells me he lives above The Wenlock Arms. He explains he's seen me drawing from his window while he's been working from home and offers to grab me a coffee before heading off briskly down the street.

Suddenly, a cyclist zips past the pub, performs a speedy U-turn and shouts, 'Finally!' before stopping in front of my easel. I recognise him: he works at The Wenlock Arms and is happy I've come to draw their pub for my project. We chat briefly, and he offers me a drink and heads inside to open up. It's now lunchtime and the still road begins to soften with the sounds of co-workers chatting as they head out for food, neighbours strolling home from their morning errands and the machinery of the tile factory rumbling behind the large shutters beside me. A man in overalls appears from the door of the tile factory and stands to look at my drawing for a while before imparting his local knowledge. His name is Willis, and he tells me the pub was saved from demolition due to a campaign led by the local community in 2010. Also, David Beckham learnt to play football on the green opposite, apparently, because his grandparents lived down the road and used to drink here. Willis tells me this pub is his and his colleagues' frequent after-work haunt. He comes in and out of the factory to chat to me for the remainder of the day until I finish my drawing. He gathers his co-workers and friends from inside the factory and, before I know it, a group of them have their phones out to pap the finished piece. During this phone frenzy, Matt returns from his flat to have a look at the finished artwork, too.

I head inside the pub just as it opens at 4 p.m. to find only one other bloke in there, practising his darts with a pint of hazy ale.

I leave my drawing on the table and collect my own beer from the bar. I sit between the window and the warmth of a newly-lit fire, looking at the pub's cosy interior, its traditional decor and the focal bar in the middle of the room, remembering the first time I came to visit. Glancing at my phone, I see an email from Matt upstairs. He wants to buy the drawing I've just taken off my easel and a print for the pub, too. Next time I'm here my print is hanging proudly on the wall, the original just upstairs in the flat above, and I bring another print for Willis too.

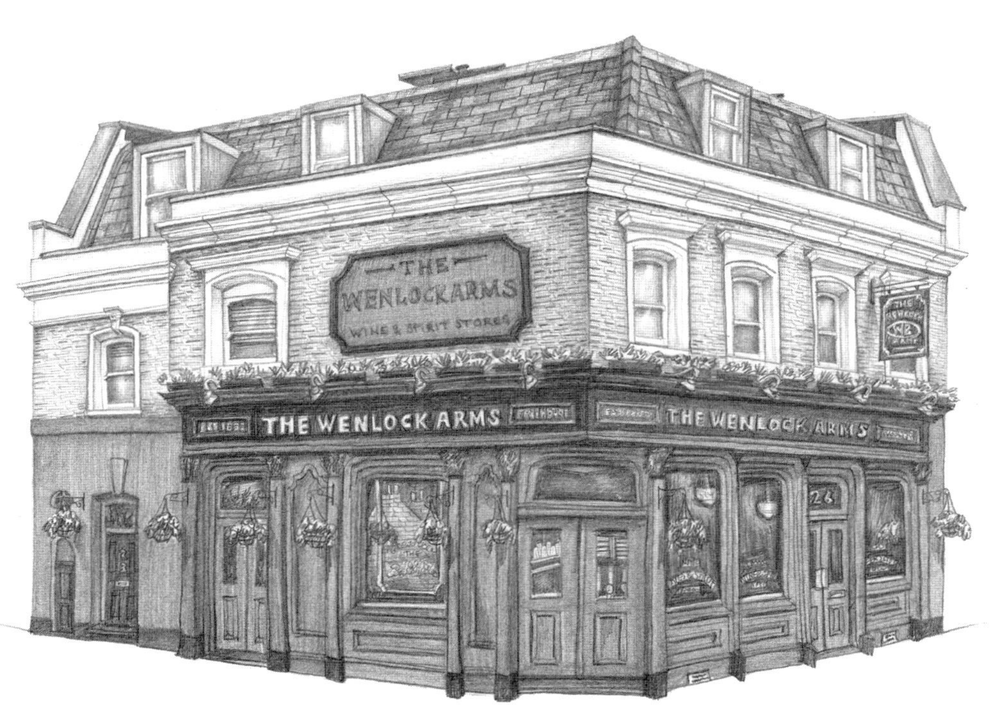

Town of Ramsgate, Wapping

I place my stool down on the pavement across the street from the Town of Ramsgate pub, watching cars and single-decker buses bump over the cobbled road between us. The small rectangular building pokes out between an alleyway and a taller neighbouring wall. The foundations of the pub are said to be as old as 1545, although it's thought a pub has probably existed here since the 1460s but the current building dates from around 1758. I get my tools out to start sketching the sweet sandwiched facade, and the repetitive process of outlining and shading in the brickwork takes up most of my morning.

A van slows down a few feet in front of me, and I see a familiar face. It's Paul from Turner's Old Star just down the road. He shouts hello from the driver's seat and reminds me I owe him a print of his pub drawing. We laugh it off, I promise to drop one in soon, and his van continues to rumble down the street.

A group of old friends circle around my easel and chat about the pub before heading inside to continue their East End pub crawl, ticking off their next stop. A white-haired, elderly gentleman stops by my side and says he saw me drawing while he went past on the bus. His name is John, and he lives on this street. We stay chatting for a while before he heads home with his shopping.

I continue to illustrate the different squares and rectangles that make up my picture. I softly shade the paving stones that lead down the alleyway to Wapping Old Stairs, a staircase down into the Thames.

An hour or so after our first encounter, John re-emerges holding a large book, *London's Lost Riverscape*. He hands it over for me to flick through. It's filled with old photographs and drawings of riverside factories. John is knowledgeable on the subject, and we talk about the ever-changing landscape of the city. He recommends I find

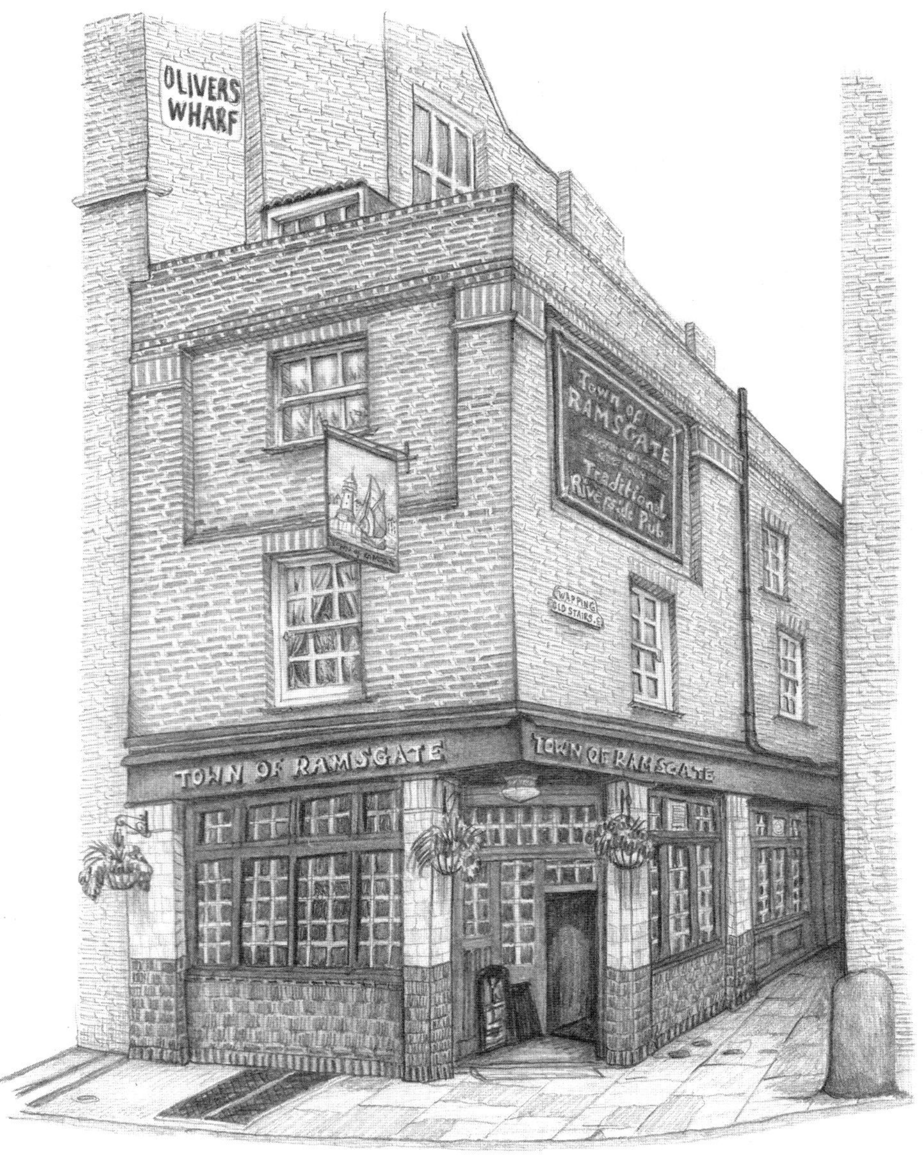

OLIVERS
WHARF

Town of
RAMSGATE

Traditional
Riverside Pub

WAPPING
OLD STAIRS

TOWN OF RAMSGATE

TOWN OF RAMSGATE

a copy of the book for myself, perhaps in an antique shop, and explains he'd give me his copy if it weren't so rare. We remark on our shared interests, before he slowly makes his way back home again.

I make the final touches to my drawing, my wrist sore from the repeated and considered motion of drawing bricks. I shade in the building that hugs the side of the Town of Ramsgate and the historical signage that remains on the side of the Grade II listed pub. I learn that local residents Janet and Peter took over the pub in 2005, and their daughter and her husband, following in their footsteps, have been running it since 2022. Just before I finish my artwork, John appears one final time, to see my finished piece. We chat some more and part ways as new friends.

The Rifleman, Twickenham

I first heard about The Rifleman at a Christmas market in South East London. As I used to travel around the area to sell my prints at various markets, I had the chance to tell people about my project in person and hear their pub suggestions first-hand. There was one faraway boozer that stuck in my mind after a stranger named Rob talked about it very passionately. After Christmas, as I plan my new pub drawings for January, The Rifleman is at the forefront of my mind. I choose a day and embark on my long journey to Twickenham. I walk from the station over a quaint bridge, looking down at the gentle stream; the sky above is a beautiful icy blue and the January air feels cold and crisp. I walk down the residential street

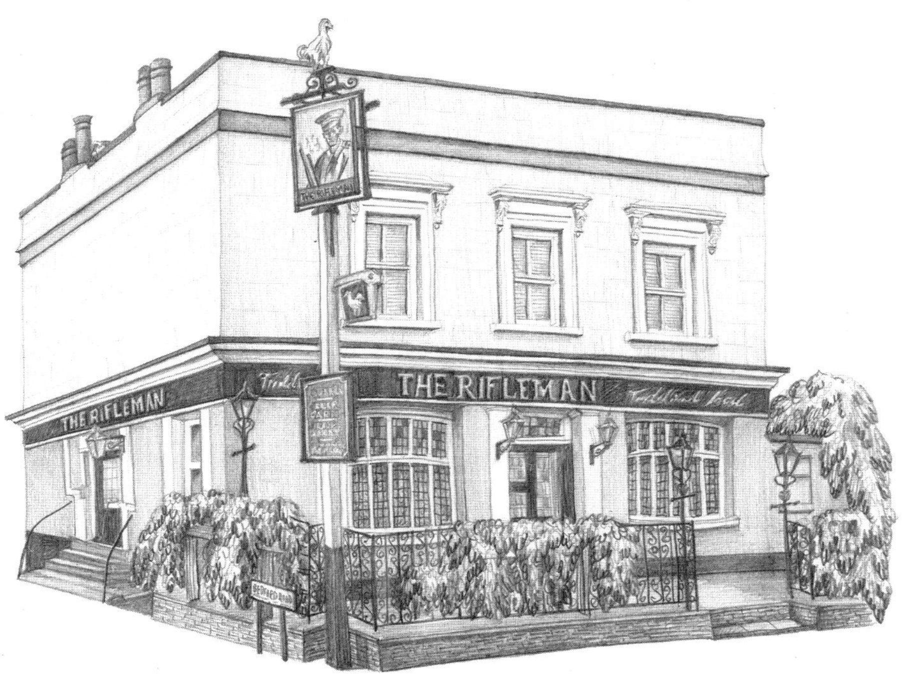

towards the pub and park myself on the very corner of the pavement, one leg of my easel in the road to make space for passersby behind me. I take out my pencils, placing them upright in my pocket for easy access, but one tumbles out and hits the edge of the pavement, bounces, twisting in the air again before falling, as if in slow motion, between the gaps of a cast-iron drain cover. I pause in shock and say my goodbyes, then reach into my bag for a replacement.

As I look up to begin my sketch, I hear a woman gleefully approaching – 'Ooh it's like a vision from the streets of Paris' – so excited to see someone sketching her street *en plein air*. The landlord, Steve, pops out to introduce himself, telling me that Rob has already explained my task for the day. He kindly asks me to let him know if I need anything, before heading back in to set up the pub for opening time. I see a figure on the flat roof of the pub, a hand moving side to side holding a paintbrush, and I quickly scribble the roof painter's hand into my sketch. The road is sleepy and quiet on this weekday afternoon, but every passerby who does come along stops to chat.

Soon, Rob joins me on the pavement and chats to me at length about his local. He talks about the pub's namesake, a local resident called Frank Edwards, who was said to have dribbled the football across No Man's Land and towards German trenches during the First World War. He is animated when he talks, fondly looking across the road at the pub. He explains that he meets the same group of friends here every Friday afternoon and calls it their 'early doors drinking den'. He describes the other locals in great detail. Another group of friends also meet here every Friday; they practically have assigned seats and share a bottle of wine like clockwork. He leaves me to my work, and I suddenly see the once-blue sky turning murky. I can feel the air shifting, so I sketch down my final details before protecting my sketchbook from the droplets that ensue.

Rushing through the door, the immediate hit of warmth is a welcome relief from the grey drizzle that's just started outside. I am thankful to Rob for telling me the seating arrangements for locals – I find a vacant table by the bar. I order a pint of local ale called Naked Ladies and enjoy it whilst refining my drawing in the warmth of the open fire. It's just me, one other silent regular and Steve, the landlord. I am near to finishing my drink when two of Rob's drinking buddies arrive and come over to introduce themselves. They have heard I'm drawing their local and offer to buy me another beer to say thank you. I show them the sketch, and we talk about the pub and their fondness of it. I notice the other crowd of Friday afternoon regulars arriving; the group of women order their wine and find their usual seats. I am introduced to Kev the painter whose hand is in my drawing, Steve passes me another ale and suddenly I find myself happily in the middle of the 'early doors drinking den', accepted as one of them.

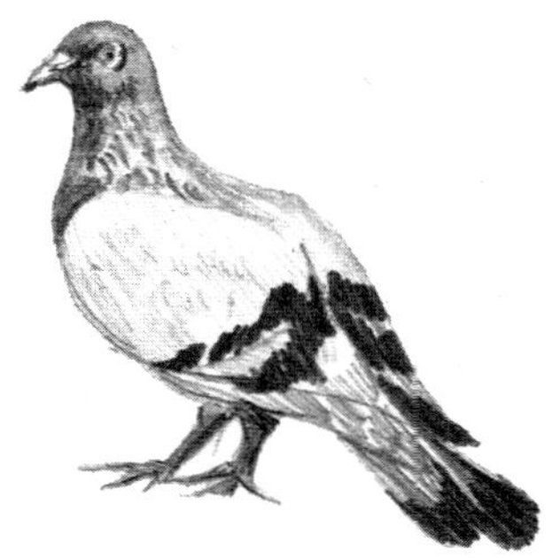

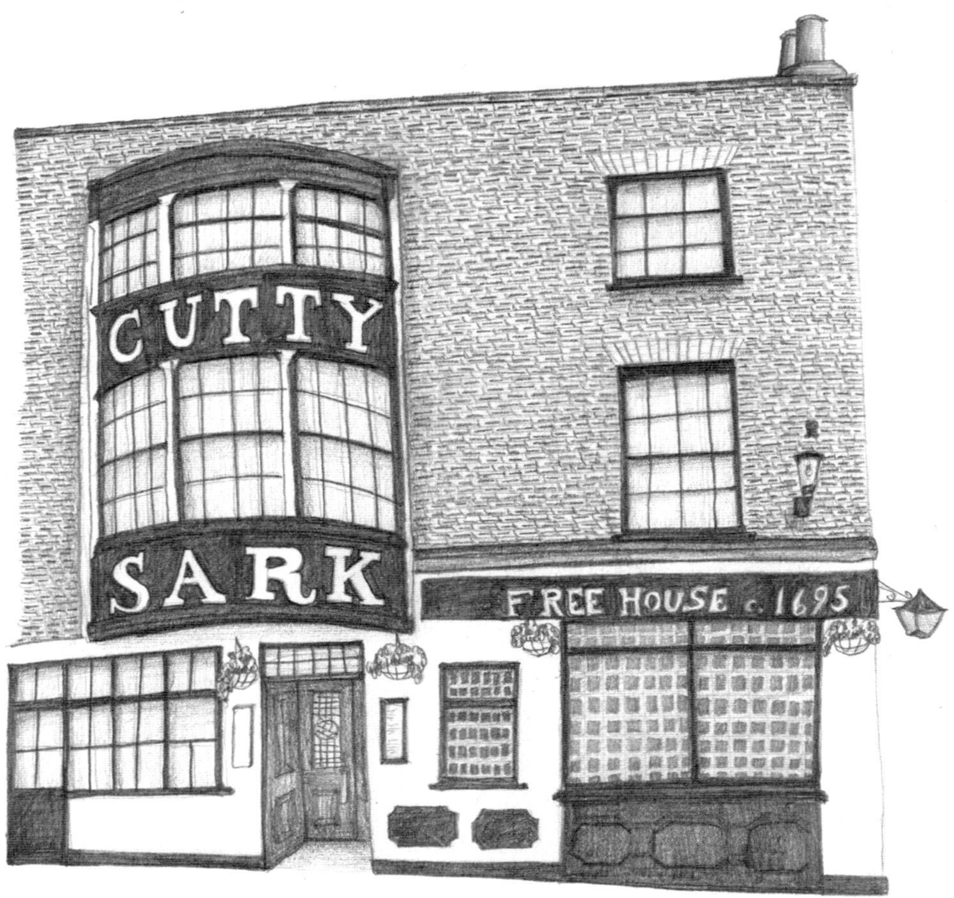

CUTTY
SARK
FREE HOUSE c. 1695

The Cutty Sark, Greenwich

My handlebars rattle over the cobbled alleyway behind the Trafalgar Tavern, chattering my teeth together as the front tyre hits each bump on the path. I turn round the corner and the River Thames comes into view, its expansive choppy surface suddenly opening the space ahead of me. I come to a halt with the Thames at my back and my next pub, The Cutty Sark, in front of me. I take my sketchbook out of my bag, lay my bike on the ground and take off my helmet. There's a small ledge that surrounds a huge black sculpture of an anchor, and I sit on the wall beside the solid installation as I begin my sketch.

The Georgian building is sweet and simple in design, with one large curved window, a brickwork facade and big white writing. The Grade II listed pub's namesake is situated a short cycle towards the centre of Greenwich: the *Cutty Sark*, a 150-year-old tea clipper turned museum, sits overlooking the water by the entrance to the Greenwich foot tunnel. I illustrate the pub's window frames, individual squares of glass and the year 1795 on the pub's painted sign. I hold my sketchbook close and lean over the page, covertly bringing the pub to life on my lap, barely anyone noticing that I'm drawing. I think I have gone unseen but later that day I receive a message enquiring about the drawing from a local called Matt, who coincidentally had been with his partner and had spotted me sketching their local but had been too shy to come say hello. Matt secretly buys the drawing as a gift for his partner – to remind them of this serendipitous moment and as a treasured keepsake of their favourite London local.

The Sekforde, Clerkenwell

The tree is in full bloom, its pale pink blossoms contrast against the brown brick walls of Sekforde Street, petals blanketing the ground in a blush carpet. I admire the tree before turning towards The Sekforde, its curved Georgian frontage a daunting shape and a change from the straight lines I'm used to sketching. Nevertheless, I am here, armed with my pencil and ready for the challenge.

The day begins with careful marks; an outline slowly appears on my page as I intuitively follow the architectural lines I see over the top of my drawing board. I begin to notice a flow of students pass by me mid-morning, on their way to lectures at the nearby university. Most rush past, some covertly peer back to glance at the largely bare page. Margaret skips over excitedly to say hello; she is mother to the landlord, Harry, and working at the pub today as he is away, expecting the imminent arrival of his baby. She is happy I am drawing it, and heads inside before coming out again with a cup of tea and a brownie to keep me going. I am overcome by her welcome, and the drawing has barely begun.

I fixate on the frontage ahead of me. I draw the sign's portrait of Thomas Seckford, the MP and lawyer who once owned the land on which the pub sits. I delicately sketch his tiny pointed hat, his ruff and his Elizabethan attire with its heavy folds and pleats. The buildings and the large tree beside me are reflected in the first-floor windows. The afternoon approaches and the still spring day warms. The sun pokes out from behind the pub and harshly hits my face. I take a seat on my stool as I feel my legs begin to tire after four hours of sketching.

I pop inside for a breather and Margaret offers me a tour. We head upstairs to a tranquil, bright room. On the wall is a painted portrait of the current owner's grandmother, and round the corner

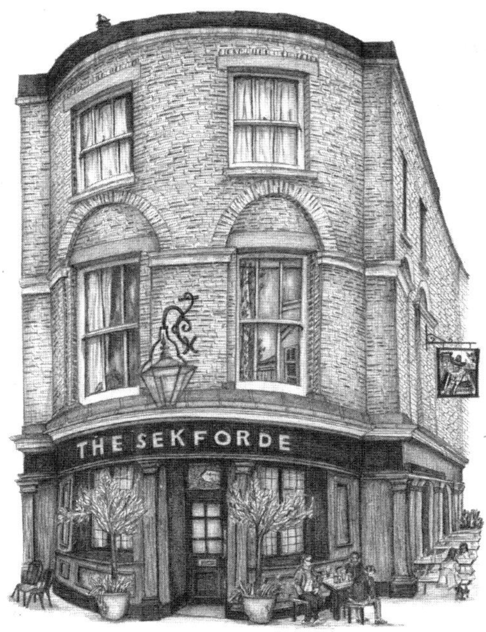

a striking blue painting that stretches the length of the renovated annexe. I'm told that Pink Floyd used to frequent the pub when they owned a recording studio along the same street. Downstairs, the main bar space is cosy and thoughtfully curated. Even further down is the basement, an atmospheric room with an impressive mural spanning the back wall, painted by artist Ian Harper.

I head back outside to my easel, and the sleepy street begins to awaken as I continue my sketch. I meet a few friendly neighbours of the pub, and they chat over my easel about the pub's recent difficulty battling a licence review from Islington council. The conversation is not news to me. I have been following the stories surrounding The Sekforde and its heartbreaking predicament, with noise complaints from a select few neighbours. Unfortunately, this is not the first time I've encountered a London pub that has struggled with similar complaints. We share our experiences of the hearing we attended in support of the pub last month. I recall how the community passionately rallied around The Sekforde, showing up in large numbers as supporters of the pub, old and new, made speeches to defend their local and keep it safe. It was a real example of solidarity and, thankfully, The Sekforde was saved. The council decided not to impose the restrictive and potentially catastrophic licence conditions.

The flurry of students I saw this morning are returning after a day of classes. Many who passed by earlier are now seeing the evolution of the pub on my page as they head home. This time, they stop to have a closer look, and their enthusiastic reactions give me the encouragement I need to continue. More and more groups of local students stop and soon crowds around my easel appear every few minutes. My day outside The Sekforde turns into my longest drawing day so far, spanning eight hours in total. This is somewhat due to the complexities of the building's shape, but mostly down to the in-depth encounters that punctuate my day. I'm totally exhausted by the time I finish, mustering the last of my energy to draw the pigeon on the roof.

A couple of regulars buy me a glass of wine to say thank you for drawing their local. Delighted, I take it inside with my drawing and soak in the social surroundings of The Sekforde. The seats around me begin to fill, locals order their after-work drinks, others come for dinner before heading home and some visit for the first time. I sit in a cosy corner, wood panelling behind me, my drink resting on a small round table alongside my eight-hour sketch. I silently celebrate my successful drawing day and watch the regulars greet Margaret and the others working behind the bar. Thinking about the pub's recent struggles, I'm relieved that The Sekforde will continue to benefit the community that fought so hard to save it.

The Kings Arms, Kennington

I jump off the train at Elephant and Castle, exit the station and head towards Kennington Lane. I walk along a wide road lined with houses, shops, trees and a torrent of traffic. I continue towards a red-brick beacon that curves down a side street, The Kings Arms sign swaying gently over the path, beckoning me towards the pub. The lights are off inside, the black door shut and the pub dormant for the time being. I step back to find the best angle and decide it has to be the edge of the pavement, with my back to the oncoming traffic. Feeling somewhat exposed, I concentrate on unpacking my bag.

With my easel in position and my little red stool holding my pencil case and a bottle of water, I make the first marks on my fresh blank page. The sweeping shape of The Kings Arms proves difficult to capture at first, but once an outline appears I get stuck into the details. First, the sloping roof with its slats and half-open windows. The bright sun casts distinctive shadows on the exterior and I quickly capture their shapes before the sun moves behind a cloud or the shadows change direction. I work my way down the page, absorbed by each tiny brick, the writing on the blackboard and the shadow each detail casts behind it.

A postie in a blue shirt and cap appears and asks to see the drawing. He says, 'Ten out of ten', gives it a thumbs up and continues towards his van. The traffic moves slowly beside me, and the drawing transforms with each mark on the page. Passersby begin to stop and stare. One of them is an elderly gentleman: he's quiet and doesn't speak much English but has a beaming smile across his face as he nods to the drawing. He hands me a pistachio chocolate bar then turns around, hands behind his back, and continues his leisurely stroll. Another is a cyclist on a large electric bike: he mounts the pavement, comes to an abrupt halt by my easel and we chat at length before he takes a photo, wishes me well and calls, 'Continue!', and cycles away. Then the shouts from cars begin. 'That looks really good', from a topless bloke in a white van sunning his arm out of the passenger window. Another kind driver passes me a bottle of coke from his delivery van window, hoping it will keep me cool while I sketch in the harsh sun. A 'Cheers!' can be heard from a high lorry as it edges past. Even the bus drivers take their time to smile and wave.

Feeling overwhelmed by the enthusiastic reception on this busy South London street, I reluctantly come to the end of my drawing and snap a photo before heading into The Kings Arms to meet some friends. Happily, another warm welcome is waiting for me inside. I enter the large carpeted room which is bright and airy; regulars sit on high stools and attentively watch the horse racing above the bar. I head over to order a round and meet Anne and Jackie who work there. I show them the sketch, along with the other regulars, and choose from the wide selection of Taytos on offer – cheese and onion, spring onion, roast chicken, beef and onion, the list goes on. I grasp the three pints of cold lager and hold on to the packet of pickled onion crisps with my teeth. I head out to the beer garden and pass the drinks around our table. Martin, the landlord, comes out to greet us, excited about the new artwork of his family pub. He makes an order there and then for the original, and some prints for his mum and his sister Cathy. My friends and I sit in the warm beer garden for hours, sharing crisps, beers and pizza. There's football on in the background, a little dog weaving between tables and a young musician playing the guitar and singing inside. Martin transports pizzas to tables and chats to other punters old and new. It's clear we aren't the only ones here made to feel right at home in The Kings Arms.

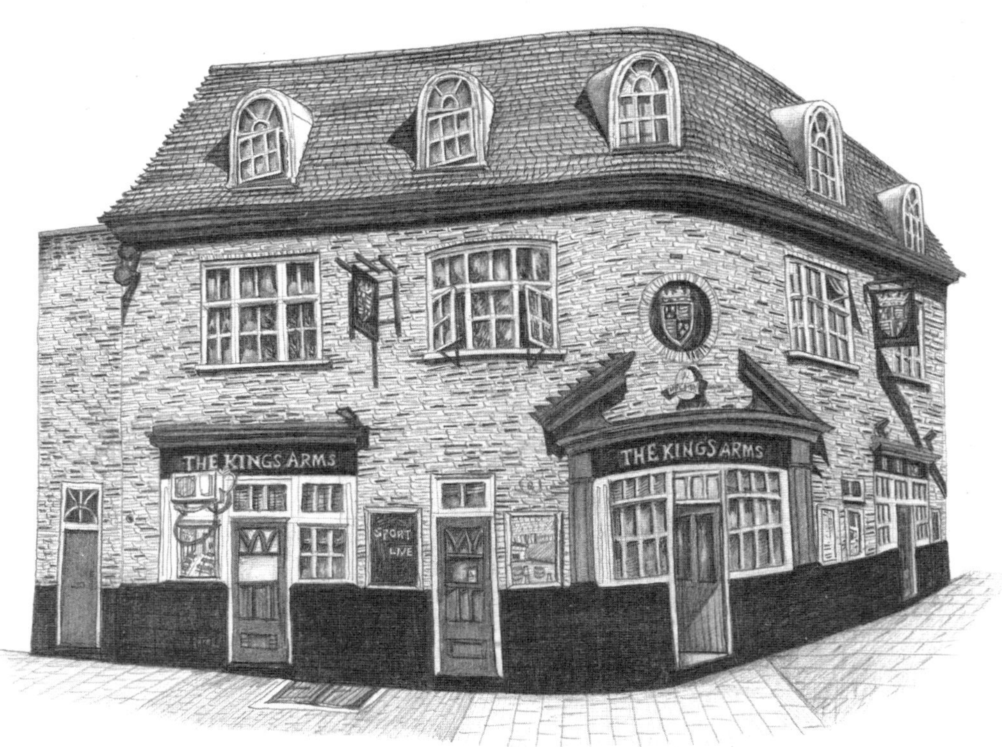

THE KINGS ARMS
SPORT LIVE
THE KINGS ARMS

CHEERS

For as long as I can remember I have always loved to draw. I vividly recall begging my family to give me a subject to sketch, a six-year-old artist with my legs dangling underneath my chair and my chin resting on the kitchen table in anticipation as I poised my pencil for action. I would ignore their fanciful suggestions of mermaids and dragons and would ask them to try again, until eventually I gave up and opted for the vase of flowers that decorated the end of the table. Regardless of whether I had drawn that same vase from the same angle the day before, I turned to face it with fresh eyes. I zoned in on the delicate petals, shading each one as I saw appropriate. My favourite part of the drawing was often the shadow the vase cast across the wooden table: this was where the object suddenly came to life on my paper. I sat for hours at that table, drawing the same vase of flowers, craving those familiar subjects for my drawings. In fact, I was so passionate about art I would practice on any surface within my vicinity that seemed fit for purpose. The headrests inside my Dad's Vauxhall Zafira, the wallpaper behind the sofa and, to everyone's dismay, my older sister's GCSE coursework (which I clearly felt needed embellishment). As I got older, I would draw portraits of my mum sitting on the sofa as we watched a film together after school. I carefully illustrated the folds in her clothes, each book on the shelf behind her and even the steam rising from her mug of tea, and with each mark I made, I delighted in the details of the mundane. Looking back at those early years the signs were clear: my dedication to repeatedly dissecting one subject matter, my appetite for detail and the pleasure I found in drawing; these impulses still ring true today and form the backbone of this project.

The life in pubs is what draws me to them. The live music nights where the musicians huddle in a corner and their sounds fill the room, altering the atmosphere in the best way possible. The characterful landlord who darts between tables, collecting glasses, striking up a conversation with anyone who walks in. The roars flooding in from outside whenever the beer garden door swings open in the summer. The clinking of glasses and soft mutterings from the few punters at the bar in the afternoon. The comfort, solace and familiarity, like the familiarity of those subjects from my childhood, are what bring me back to pubs, both to enjoy them and to draw them.

Since you've caught me at a relatively early stage of my London pub endeavour and you've read here about drawings that were created at the very beginning of the project, you and I realise there is a long way to go. Even over my first four years of this work, I have seen that change is inevitable, but pubs are not. Instead of this filling me with fear, regret or a building pressure, I am truly excited for the years ahead, and only more determined to capture as many of these cultural institutions as possible. I will continue to honour them and do my part in preserving them, even if that's simply their memory. As I discover more kinds of pubs, in far-reaching corners of the city, I am eager to illustrate more life than ever before. That might mean capturing more fleeting details with my pencil, like the people drinking in windows and pigeons, who will inevitably be there.

It also means I will continue to record the life of pubs through words, collecting the stories of those who know their local best, recording the kindness shown to me by landlords, landladies, managers and communities. I will always share those moments when I am taught something new about a pub's history or when I meet a living legend at the bar or when I am simply welcomed inside and adopted as a local for the day. I can't wait to share more of the life of locals; they are at the soul of this project and at the centre of every drawing I do.

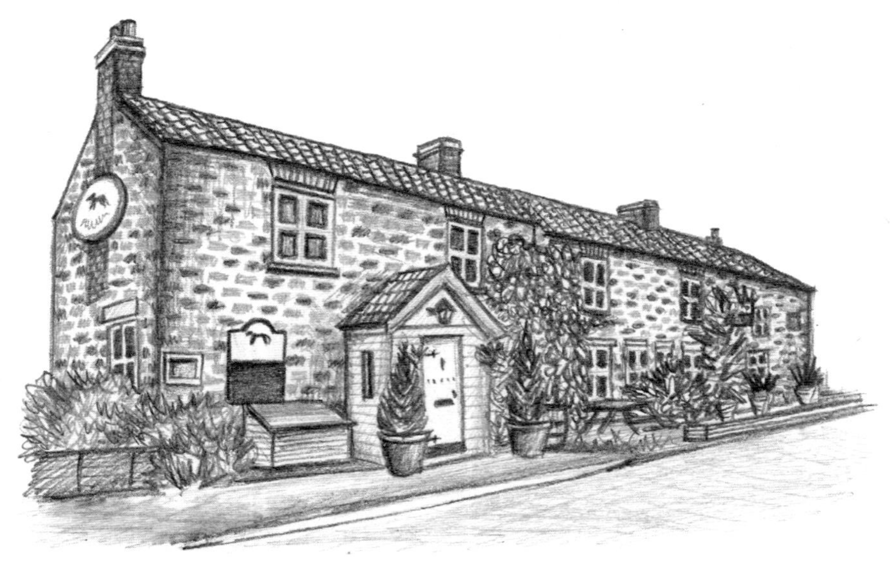

The Black Horse Inn, drawn when I was sixteen

THANKS

To my agents, Alice Hoskyns and Sophie Lambert, for believing in me and the book before I did.

To Charlotte Humphery, for your expert editing and for gently guiding me as a first-time author.

To my parents, for encouraging and celebrating creativity at every stage of my life and for all those trips to The Black Horse Inn – a truly formative pub education.

To my sisters, growing up surrounded by three exceptional artists has fuelled my ambition and hope every step of the way.

To every single friend who has ever responded to my 'pub?' texts, however last minute.

To every champion of this project, from words of encouragement and pub suggestions to those who've bought prints, calendars and original drawings. This book wouldn't have been possible without you.

To my art teacher Timothy Walsh, for teaching me how to draw.

To the pubs and your locals, for your hospitality and your trust.

To London, for your people, your pubs and my home.

And finally, to Jack, for your unwavering optimism and support for this project, this book and the future. This book is for you.

Locals: Pubs, A–Z

Locals: Pubs, by borough

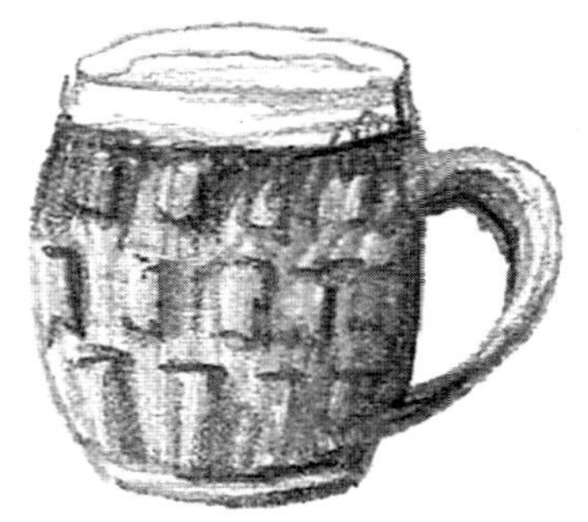

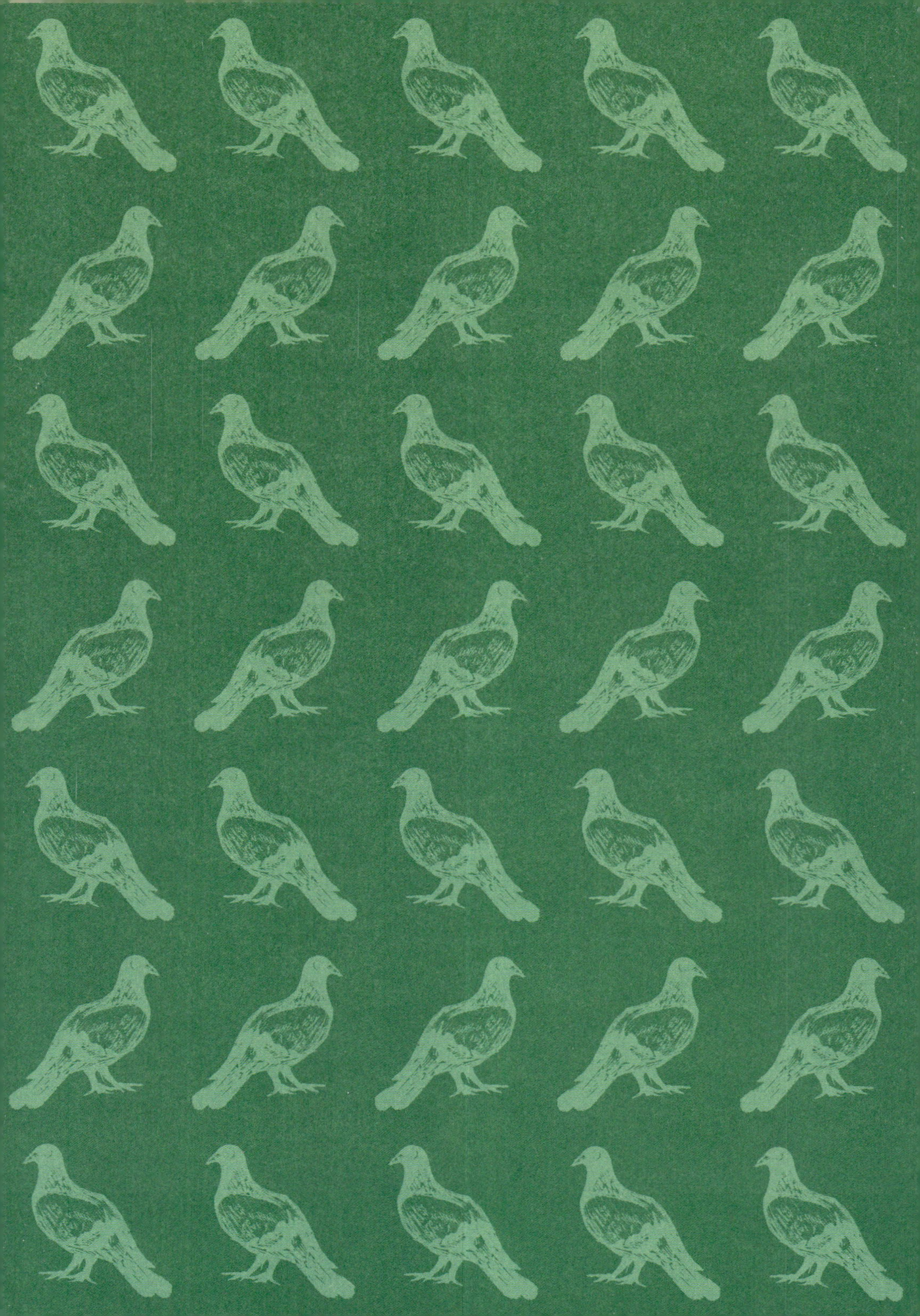